Utopian Moments

Textual Moments in the History of Political Thought

SERIES EDITORS

J. C. Davis, Emeritus Professor of History,
University of East Anglia, UK

John Morrow, Professor of Political Studies,
University of Auckland, New Zealand

Textual Moments provides accessible, fresh, short readings of key texts in selected fields of political thought, encouraging close reading informed by cutting-edge scholarship. The unique short essay format of the series ensures that volumes cover a range of texts in roughly chronological order. The essays in each volume aim to open up a reading of the text and its significance in the political discourse in question and in the history of political thought more widely. Key moments in the textual history of a particular genre of political discourse are made accessible, appealing and instructive to students, scholars and general readers.

Utopian Moments is the first title in the series. Future volumes will cover republican, federalist, cosmopolitan and feminist thought, sovereignty, human rights and more.

Utopian Moments

Reading Utopian Texts

Edited by
Miguel A. Ramiro Avilés and J. C. Davis

BLOOMSBURY ACADEMIC

First published in 2012 by

Bloomsbury Academic
an imprint of Bloomsbury Publishing Plc
50 Bedford Square, London WC1B 3DP, UK
and
175 Fifth Avenue, New York, NY 10010, USA

Copyright © 2012 Miguel A. Ramiro Avilés and J. C. Davis;
individual chapters © the contributors.

CIP records for this book are available from the British Library and the
Library of Congress

ISBN 978-1-84966-682-4 (hardback)
ISBN 978-1-84966-821-7 (paperback)
ISBN 978-1-84966-685-5 (ebook)

This book is produced using paper that is made from wood grown in managed,
sustainable forests. It is natural, renewable and recyclable. The logging and
manufacturing processes conform to the environmental regulations of
the country of origin.

Printed and bound in Great Britain by the MPG Books Group, Bodmin, Cornwall

Cover designer: Burge Agency

www.bloomsburyacademic.com

Contents

Contributors

Matthew Beaumont Senior Lecturer in the Department of English at the University College London (UCL); author of the books *Utopia Ltd.: Ideologies of Social Dreaming in England 1870–1900* and *The Spectre of Utopia: Utopian and Science Fictions at the Fin de Siècle*; editor of Edward Bellamy's *Looking Backward* for Oxford World Classics.

Jonathan Beecher Professor of History at the University of California, Santa Cruz; author of the books *Charles Fourier: The Visionary and his World* and *Victor Considerant and the Rise and Fall of French Romantic Socialism*.

Susan Bruce Professor of English and Head of the School of Humanities at Keele University; editor, *Three Early Modern Utopias: Thomas More: Utopia/Francis Bacon: New Atlantis/Henry Neville: The Isle of Pines* and *William Shakespeare: King Lear*; and, with Valerie Wagner, *Fiction and Economy*.

Maurizio Cambi Professor of the History of Philosophy at the University of Salerno; author of the books *Il prezzo della perfezione: Diritto reati e pene nelle utopie dal 1516 al 1630* and *I tempi delle città ideali: Saggi su storia e utopia nella modernità*; editor of the book *L'isola degli ermafroditi*.

Gregory Claeys Professor of the History of Political Thought at the Department of History, Royal Holloway, University of London; author of the books *Machinery, Money and the Millennium: From Moral Economy to Socialism, Citizens and Saints: Politics and Anti-Politics in Early British Socialism, Thomas Paine: Social and Political Thought* and *Searching for Utopia: The History of an Idea*; editor of *The Cambridge Companion to Utopian Thought*.

J. C. Davis Emeritus Professor of History at the University of East Anglia; author of the book *Utopia and the Ideal Society* and the chapter on More's *Utopia* for *The Cambridge Companion to Utopian Thought*.

Laurence Davis Lecturer in Politics at the National University of Ireland, Maynooth; editor, with Ruth Kinna, of the book *Anarchism and Utopianism*, and, with Peter Stillman, of *The New Utopian Politics of Ursula K. Le Guin's The Dispossessed*.

Claudio De Boni Professor of the History of Political Thought at the University of Florence (Italy); author of *Uguali e felici: Utopie francesi del secondo Settecento*.

John Gurney Visiting Fellow, School of Historical Studies, Newcastle University; author of *Brave Community: the Digger Movement in the English Revolution*.

John Christian Laursen Professor of Political Science at the University of California, Riverside; editor, with Cyrus Masroori, of a new edition of Denis Veiras's *History of the Sevarambians*.

David Leopold University Lecturer in Political Theory, University of Oxford, and Tutorial Fellow, Mansfield College, Oxford; editor of William Morris's *News From Nowhere*; author of *The Young Karl Marx: German Philosophy, Modern Politics, and Human Flourishing*.

George M. Logan James Cappon Professor of English (Emeritus) at Queen's University, Canada, and a Senior Fellow of Massey College in the University of Toronto; author of *The Meaning of More's 'Utopia'*; principal editor of the Cambridge edition of *Utopia*, and editor of More's *History of King Richard the Third*, the third edition of the Norton Critical Edition of *Utopia* and *The Cambridge Companion to Thomas More*; senior editor of the sixteenth-century section of *The Norton Anthology of English Literature*.

Gaby Mahlberg Lecturer in Early Modern British History at Northumbria University; author of *Henry Neville and English Republican Culture in the Seventeenth Century: Dreaming of Another Game*; editor, with Peter G. Stillman and Nat Hardy, of a special issue of *Utopian Studies* (vol. 17, part 1, 2006) on Henry Neville's *Isle of Pines*.

Cyrus Masroori Associate Professor of Political Science at California State University, San Marcos; editor, with John Christian Laursen, of a new edition of Denis Veiras's *History of the Sevarambians*.

Neil McWilliam Walter H. Annemberg Professor of Art & Art History at Duke University; author of *Dreams of Happiness: Social Art and the French Left 1830–1850*.

Nadia Minerva Professor of French at the University of Catania (Italy); author of *Utopia e... Amici e Nemici del Genere Utopico nella Letteratura Francese* and *Jules Verne aux Confins de l'Utopie*; editor of *Per una Definizione dell'Utopia: Metodologie e Discipline a Confronto*; with R. Baccolini and V. Fortunati, *Viaggi in Utopia*; and, with C. Imbroscio, *Jules Verne: Mondes Utopiques, Mondes Fantastiques, Francofonia*.

Richard Nate Chair of English Literature and Coordinator of European Studies at the Catholic University of Eichstaett-Ingolstadt; author of *Wissenschaft und*

Literatur im England der frühen Neuzeit, Amerikanische Träume: Die Kultur der Vereinigten Staaten in der Zeit des New Deal and *Herbert G. Wells und die Krise der modernen Utopie.*

Bronwen Price Principal Lecturer in English at Portsmouth University; editor of *Francis Bacon's New Atlantis: New Interdisciplinary Essays.*

Miguel A. Ramiro Avilés Associate Professor of Legal Philosophy at Alcalá University and member of the 'Bartolomé de las Casas' Human Rights Institute at Carlos III University; author of *Utopía y Derecho: El Sistema Jurídico en las Sociedades Ideales*; and editor of *Anatomía de la Utopía, Las Palabras y el Poder*; and, with Patricia Cuenca, *Los Derechos Humanos: La Utopía de los Excluidos.*

Lyman Tower Sargent Professor Emeritus of Political Science at the University of Missouri-St. Louis; founding editor of *Utopian Studies* (1990–2004); author of *British and American Utopian Literature, 1516–1985* and *Utopianism: A Very Short Introduction* (2010); author, with Lucy Sargisson, of *Living in Utopia* (2004).

Peter G. Stillman Professor of Political Science at Vassar College; editor, with Laurence Davis, of *The New Utopian Politics of Ursula K. Le Guin's The Dispossessed*; and, with Gaby Mahlberg and Nat Hardy, of a special issue of *Utopian Studies* (vol. 17, part 1, 2006) on Henry Neville's *Isle of Pines.*

Edward H. Thompson Formerly Senior Research Fellow in Economics, and Director of the School of American Studies, University of Dundee; editor of J. V. Andreae: *Christianopolis.*

K. Steven Vincent Professor of Modern European History at North Carolina State University; author of the books *Pierre-Joseph Proudhon and the Rise of French Republican Socialism; Between Marxism and Anarchism: Benoît Malon and French Reformist Socialism*, and *Benjamin Constant and the Birth of French Liberalism.*

Acknowledgements

The editors would like to acknowledge the generous financial support of the project Consolider-Ingenio 2010 "El Tiempo de los Derechos" (CSD2008-00007) and the support of the 'Bartolomé de las Casas' Human Rights Institute and its President, Gregorio Peces-Barba.

Our contributors and the editorial team at Bloomsbury Academic in their responsiveness, good humour and expertise have made this volume a pleasure to edit. Our thanks to them all.

Introduction

J.C. Davis and Miguel A. Ramiro Avilés

Thomas More inaugurated the modern tradition of utopian writing in 1516. Since then we can find in Western literature a vigorous expression of ideas about the nature, content and forms of utopian literature. How might this exceptionality be explained, and what does it tell us about those societies which produced this flowering of what is simultaneously a literary genre and a series of explorations of the limits of political and social possibility?

After some initial hesitation, Renaissance Europe (roughly fourteenth to seventeenth centuries) witnessed growing confidence in its ability to break down the barriers of distance, ignorance and, to some extent, a sense of inferiority, to acknowledge the extra-European world. That world became, and continued to be, a kind of mirror for European writers, exposing both the potential and the flaws of the societies that had shaped it. Utopian writing could turn that into a magnifying mirror in which both potential and flaws could be dramatized, highlighted as a spur to reform or used satirically to deflate complacency. Europe has examined itself by exploring the lives of others, and the liberation of fiction, offered by utopian writing, enabled a more systemic and radical self-examination.

The technological innovation that gradually equipped Europeans for global exploration, trade, colonization and empire also reinforced self-belief. Technological development rested in part on the advancement of science and the expansion of scientific knowledge. This, in turn, was a process that reshaped their sense of humanity's relationship with the environment, nature and God. Could the discovery of the laws of nature provide new, sounder or even more natural, principles upon which well-functioning societies could be built and human misery be reduced, if not eliminated?

Related to this was a confidence, slowly and painfully gained, that change itself could be mastered, taken out of the realm of fortune and providence to be purposefully shaped by human agency. Such confidence rested on a sense that it was possible to see beyond the surface of events and understand those unseen, underlying factors of history that shaped human destiny. If such factors were to be used for good, there had to be a guide to the good society towards which history should be driven. This sense that the unregulated flow of history could be brought under regulation has waxed and waned over the last few centuries but we should not underestimate its importance to utopian writers like Harrington, Condorcet and Cabet. It co-existed with what might now appear to be an alarmingly naïve belief in the possibility of limitless access to the resources which could sustain social change as well as the quest for social justice, making deliberately chosen re-orderings of society viable.

Wherever we look, in the last five centuries, partly because their understandings of the world, their environment, nature, space and time have changed, Western societies have become immensely richer, more populous, more urban and more linked in more ways to the greater world than they ever were. They have undergone demographic transformations in terms of, amongst others, population size, life expectancy, age distribution and net reproduction rates. They have participated in revolutions in mobility, communications, information transfer and data accumulation. They have witnessed the convulsions of political and social revolution as well as the technological sophistication and enormously enhanced destructive capacities of modern warfare. Latterly, the scientific and technological innovation, which underpinned many of these changes and a sense of progressive potential, has come to seem rather more threatening. Bearing the weight of so much change, Western societies have, on the whole, had to adapt by becoming gradually less (but only less) hierarchical, patriarchal and dominated by closed elites (although there are signs that the pendulum may be beginning to swing the other way). To the extent that these and other changes were progress, they were, of course, uneven progress. Nevertheless, the mere prospect of such change continuing made it possible to ask not only "What are we?" but "What do we want to be?": a questioning in which the utopian imagination has been critically active.

As we journey further into the twenty-first century, however, such confidence is apparently faltering and problems, which seem unmanageable for even the wealthiest and most powerful of Western societies, multiply. To enumerate only the most obvious of these – managing our impact on the environment; dealing with the fiscal implications of the welfare state; caring well for growing numbers of the elderly; preventing the future for the young being a bleaker prospect than that experienced by their parents' generation; fashioning more inclusive societies; overcoming social alienation and disaffection and dealing justly with the violence that may be associated with them – is immediately to confront their apparent intractability. Not so long ago, the triumph of the free market over the command economies was greeted as unqualified good news. More recently, the inability of the free market to control financial excess and the consequences of mounting debt has been exposed. In this century, powerful Western nations have been drawn into dubiously motivated wars they have found difficult to 'win' and from which they find it almost impossible to disengage without humiliation. Meanwhile, the corruption of a free press and of once trusted social institutions seems worryingly possible. Everywhere we see the democratic deficit of the apathy, indifference or principled withdrawal from participation of otherwise qualified citizens. Alongside this, we might put what we could call an 'ideological deficit'; that is to say the absence of any ideology that lays claim to being able to address the most intractable of these problems and their underlying causes. And part of this malaise might be attributed to a sense that the kind of states that we have developed and which preside over us do not have the capacity to deal with these issues.

That 'realism', which might have served us well in the past, might now confront a world so beyond its policy options, let alone its 'solutions', that it would be easy to despair. New solutions have to be imagined, and given the interconnectedness of the problems we face those solutions have to be systemic. Such systematic re-imagining of society, politics and humanity's relationship with the natural environment has been offered to us repeatedly over the last five hundred years by utopian fiction. This volume, with its invitation to look again at some of the classics of the modern utopian tradition, has, in this regard perhaps, a certain timeliness. The suggestion is not that here we might find a checklist of solutions to our present problems but rather that, in exploring and coming to understand both the possibilities and the limitations of utopian thinking, we may be better equipped to nurture the principle of hope in our own times and to discipline the imaginative capacities necessary to establishing a new, better and sustainable 'reality'.

This book then offers fresh readings of a range of those classic utopian texts extending from Thomas More's *Utopia* of 1516 to Ursula Le Guin's *The Dispossessed* of 1974. Each essay focuses on a moment in the text and uses it to engage with a closer reading of the work as a whole. We have assembled an international team of distinguished experts on the works in question and have asked them to produce a short and accessible guide to their reading of the text. We have kept the scholarly apparatus to a minimum but their responses reflect the cutting edge of current thinking about these utopian writings. Our hope is that the result will not only be stimulating in its own right, but will encourage you to turn to these utopian texts, and others, and to read them critically for yourself. The selection we have made here is necessarily arbitrary and, even with coverage of nineteen utopian works, limited. We have, nevertheless, attempted to reflect the value and diversity of utopian literature over the last half millennium and to consider those texts that either have had a significant influence on the tradition or have raised the most critical problems of the genre. We have devoted three of the essays to More's *Utopia*, both because it is in many senses the foundation work of the modern utopian tradition but also because it self-consciously embodies and reflects so many of the continuing issues faced by utopian writing. One of the most immediately striking features of assembling a collection of readings of utopian works is the diversity of the works in question. There are, nevertheless, recurrent themes with which they engage, albeit in different ways. The final part of this introduction will draw attention to some of them.

Over the last thirty to forty years, there has been considerable debate about the form and nature of the literary utopia. It is a debate that, as the works chosen here illustrate, can be traced back to the utopias themselves. Almost all their authors show a searching interest in questions of form and, above all, in the relationship between fiction, reality and an imagined alternative. It has been common amongst commentators to see the fictionality of much utopian writing as a strategy to evade censorship, but that rarely tells anything like the full story. More pressing reasons are inherent in the nature of the comprehensive transformation of social and political relationships which utopian fiction envisages. Such transformation is bound to require imaginative leaps. To make that alternative world 'real' to the reader, the author requires their imaginative participation and, as in the cases of so many utopian authors – More, Bacon, Harrington, Bellamy, Le Guin, for example – an artfully constructed fictional narrative is the chosen means. That fictional narrative has to establish and bridge the distance between what is and what might be. In the process, it exposes the folly of our 'wisdom', the self-deluding fantasy that sustains our 'normality', and the fiction that is our 'reality'.[1] Just as the communities we inhabit are imaginatively constructed by us, so the 'reality' that adheres to them is, to an extent, fictitious. Post-modern literary theory may have brought us to conclusions akin to this, but modern utopian literature's grappling with form and imagination has been informed by them from the beginning. From More to Le Guin, these essays tell us, utopian authors have been playing, teasingly, with the potentialities of literary form. Central to this has been the fundamentally aesthetic question: What can we use to help us grasp an unfamiliar 'reality' in order to use that grasp to shape better lives and societies?

Also apparent through a reading of these essays is that utopian works rarely settle for a one-dimensional form but are almost always multifaceted. They are demanding of their readers. Often they appear to defy easy interpretation, laying false trails, subverting their own claims and questioning their own premises. More's *Utopia* is, of course, a masterwork of this kind but Fourier's studied 'bizarreness', Bacon's oscillation between display and concealment, the struggle of Bellamy's Julian West caught between two socially shaped psychologies and Le Guin's protagonists' desire to escape a world of limited, linear possibilities for a more open escape from social oppression – all of these exemplify the same tendency. Inhabiting a new world – even in the imagination – should be and has to be made an unsettling experience. Thomas More's doubling as Morus in *Utopia* is echoed in Julian West's double identity in *Looking Backward*. In one case, More's utopians might use their superiority to claim rights to use the territory of others as 'necessary'. In another, the inhabitants of Henry Neville's Isle of Pines have declined so far into arcadian sloth and decay that their inferiority to their Dutch discoverers is all too painfully obvious. Utopia may only be imagined; it is the other that has to be discovered. Spatially, it means an imaginative venturing into the unknown: sailing to the New World, to *terra australis incognita*, or voyaging to the moon or the centre of the earth. But it is also instructive to note the influence of the half-known exotic. As three of the essays below illustrate, More's Utopians, Veiras's Sevarambians and the inhabitants of Sinapia all take something from Persia in the shaping of their ideal society. Utopian writing may have been largely a Western phenomenon, and it may rest in part on cultural confidence verging on a sense of superiority but, at the same time, that confidence is qualified by a critique exposing the profound failures of contemporary Western societies and a willingness to look outside of those societies, both in time and space, for better alternatives.

These utopias are inescapably political. They begin with a sense of unease or dissatisfaction with existing political, economic, social, legal and welfare arrangements and a need to imagine a political order that can maintain a radically improved society. This means that they must deal with issues of partisan advantage and conflict. They must re-order the relationships between minorities and the majority and between the weak and the strong. They must establish institutions that work with, rather than against, the new order while increasingly, from Wells to Le Guin, seeking to establish a new order capable of change.

What is also striking is the number of occasions on which these utopian writers seek to penetrate behind the superficial appearance of things to underlying causes. As George Logan argues in the case of More, their analysis of the problems is systemic and their responses are likewise systemic. The whole of the socio-political order must be recast if the causes, and not merely the symptoms, of social misery are to be addressed. For Morelly then the distorting forces of history had to be addressed, and by the later stages of the Enlightenment, as in the cases of Condorcet and Cabet, science (especially social science), reason and technocracy could be envisaged as taming history and bringing it into the service of utopia. Such optimism raised again old questions about the relationship between the intellectually equipped minority and the majority, precipitating tensions like the ones that can be seen in the work of Saint Simon, for instance.

Balancing the claims of the individual against those of society could be mitigated in utopian thought by the reconstruction of the individual's second nature, habituating him or her to new social norms and behavioural patterns congruent with the desired social outcome. This again reinforced the utopian tendency towards systemic or holistic solutions. All means had to be used to reshape the habitual behaviour and expectations of members of the ideal society. In consequence, we find throughout these utopian works a recurrent insistence on the importance of education. This is complemented by an equal insistence on law rigorously enforced as a means of containing and conditioning behaviour. If we think of education in a broad sense as equipping citizens for society, then the law and the judicial system, along with many other social arrangements and customary patterns of behaviour, become as much educational tools as the more formal institutions of learning. But law and a formally controlled, purposeful system of social education require an institutional framework to sustain and manage them. For this reason amongst others, the utopian imagination has to grapple with issues of constitutional and legal codes. How and by whom decisions are to be taken within those frameworks are questions that reinforce this political disposition inherent in utopian writing, and we see those issues reflected in almost all of the texts discussed here.

What is also striking is how many of these texts grapple with issues of equality and inequality. Even those that do not embrace total material equality are looking to modify hierarchical and/or patriarchal structures. In part, this may be because inequalities are seen as sources of conflict or of a materialist corruption distracting individuals and society from the true essence of the good life. However, it is also perhaps a question of the notion that, in an environment of limited satisfactions, social misery and alienation can only be mitigated, if not eradicated, by creating the conditions for a more equal society. In the process, the 'rights' of property begin to appear less fundamental and inflexible in utopian societies generally. Indeed the more general question might be asked as to whether, in the good society (at least, in the forms envisaged here), individual and corporate rights do not become conditional upon the greater social good. Is it true that the languages of civil rights, and a *fortiori* human rights, are conspicuous by their absence in utopian society? On the contrary, it might be argued that what to us seem like the natural rights of women or the poor were better provided for in Fourier's or Owen's vision than in the societies from which they sprang. But the question remains as to whether a language of rights could really function in the utopian ideal society.

Unlike the visions of natural abundance, or of easeful plenty, dreamt of in Cockaygne or Arcadia, utopian society and the individuals comprising it are to be found in an environment constrained both by the limitations that nature imposes on them and by the level of knowledge and understanding of the forces of nature which have been or are being achieved in that society. In other words, and again we see it illustrated in these utopian fictions, the relationship between humanity, nature and, where appropriate, God, the author of nature, remains pivotal. The quest for a 'practical science', whether it acknowledges or ignores God, appears as a key to social amelioration in Campanella's Solarian astrology, in Andreae's partnership of religion and science, in Bacon's natural philosophy and in the triumph of science and reason in Condorcet's writings. The elusive promise of progress can be recaptured in a well-ordered, educated and technologically equipped society but progress in turn poses the problem of the kinetic or 'non-Euclidean' utopia as explored by both Wells and Le Guin.

The societies that for the last five centuries have been most fertile in utopian imagination, and which remain amongst the richest on the planet, are now experiencing growing social and material inequalities, faltering free markets, a fiscal/welfare crisis, failed ideologies, incipient corruption, declining educational standards, massive personal and public indebtedness and the danger of being eclipsed by the non-Western economies they once dominated. Their utopian tradition may well not have the answers but it does appear to ask some of the right questions. We hope that this collection will encourage you to seek those questions out for yourself.

1

Systemic Remedies for Systemic Ills: The Political Thought of More's *Utopia*

George M. Logan

'Thus I am wholly convinced that unless private property is entirely
abolished, there can be no fair or just distribution of goods, nor can the
business of mortals be conducted happily. As long as private property
remains, by far the largest and best part of the human race will be
oppressed by a distressing and inescapable burden of poverty and
anxieties. This load, I admit, may be lightened to some extent, but
I maintain it cannot be entirely removed. Laws might be made that no
one should own more than a certain amount of land or receive more
than a certain income. Or laws might be passed to prevent the prince
from becoming too powerful and the populace too insolent. It might be
made illegal for public offices to be solicited or put up for sale or
made burdensome for the office-holder by great expense. Otherwise,
officials are tempted to get their money back by fraud or extortion,
and only rich men can accept appointment to positions which ought to
go to the wise. Laws of this sort, I agree, may have as much effect as
poultices continually applied to sick bodies that are past cure.
The social evils I mentioned may be alleviated and their effects
mitigated for a while, but so long as private property remains,
there is no hope at all of effecting a cure and restoring society to
good health. While you try to cure one part, you aggravate the wound
in other parts. Suppressing the disease in one place causes it to break
out in another, since you cannot give something to one person without
taking it away from someone else.'
'But I don't see it that way', I said. 'It seems to me that people cannot
possibly live well where all things are in common.'[1]

This passage occurs late in Book I of the two books of *Utopia*, in the
climactic pages of the broadly ranging dialogue on English and European
society and politics that constitutes that book. The speakers here are, first, the
fictitious character Raphael Hythloday (Hythlodaeus in More's Latin), who
in Book II reports on the island commonwealth of Utopia, newly discovered
somewhere off the coast of South America, and, in the second paragraph, More

himself – or, at least, a character who shares his name and biography, although the dialogue he takes part in is fictitious and in some passages of the work the author clearly holds his namesake at an ironic distance (as, indeed, he also holds Hythloday, whose name, based in Greek, means something like 'expert in nonsense' – though almost all of what Hythloday says is the opposite of nonsensical). The passage provides a key to understanding the most important facts about More's contribution to utopian thought and writing. But seeing how this is so requires some prior contextualization.

Evidently *Utopia* did not originally *have* a first book. In 1519 (that is, three years after the initial publication of the work), Desiderius Erasmus – the pre-eminent humanistic scholar of the era – wrote a brief but extremely interesting biography of More, whom he had known well for two decades, in a letter to the humanist and religious reformer Ulrich von Hutten. The rapid overview of More's writing included in this sketch reports that he had written Book II of *Utopia* 'earlier, when at leisure; at a later opportunity he added the first in the heat of the moment'.[2] In the mid-twentieth century, J. H. Hexter – the most brilliant critic of More's book – argued persuasively that the period of leisure must have occurred in the summer and autumn of 1515, the latter part of a period of nearly six months (early May to late October) when More was a member of a royal trade mission to Bruges.[3] By 21 July, negotiations were stalled and recessed (as More reports in the opening of Book I), and at some point More betook himself to Antwerp, where he met another of Erasmus's friends, Pieter Gillis (usually anglicized as Peter Giles), a humanist and practical man of affairs, city clerk of Antwerp. In one of the commendatory letters that buttressed the first and subsequent editions of *Utopia*, Giles hints broadly that the book originated in conversations between himself and More (120). He appears in Book I, whose opening recounts More's introduction to him and, in turn, his introduction of More to Hythloday. Giles is the third, albeit minor, speaker in the dialogue that follows, and a letter to him constitutes the preface to *Utopia*. Hexter also pointed out that the ur-*Utopia* cannot have consisted simply of the current Book II, since that part lacks the scene-setting of the opening pages of Book I and thus begins with an unidentified speaker addressing an unidentified audience in an unspecified location. So, he postulated, the original form of *Utopia* must have had an opening similar or identical to the early pages of what is now Book I, and More – as an afterthought, back in London – must have opened a 'seam' in those pages to insert the dialogue that became the rest of that book. Almost certainly this seam was at the point where More, as narrator, says that he will recount only what Hythloday said about the island of Utopia – but then suddenly veers off to the dialogue that occupies the remainder of Book I (12 and n. 15).

More, as he explains in the letter to Giles, had an extremely busy life in London and did not in fact finish the book until nearly a year after his return from Flanders. On 3 September 1516 he sent his manuscript to Erasmus, who was entrusted with seeing it through the press and with gathering commendations from fellow humanists and, if possible, also from 'distinguished statesmen'.[4] Erasmus shared the manuscript with Giles, who (as he says in his commendatory letter) added to it the marginal glosses – some 200 of them, ranging in length from a single word to a sentence – that form a running commentary on the book. And someone – one hopes it was More – gave it the title (converting from the Latin) *On the Best State of a Commonwealth and On the New Island of Utopia* (where 'and' creates an intriguing ambiguity), which is followed by the subtitle-and-puff (presumably by Erasmus or Giles) *A Truly Golden Little Book, No Less Beneficial than Entertaining, by the Most Distinguished and Eloquent Author Thomas More, Citizen and Undersheriff of the Famous City of London.*

From early on, editors and critics of the book have, in effect, often second-guessed More's decision to revise the ur-*Utopia* by adding Book I. Many of the early translations of *Utopia* into the European vernaculars either omit Book I entirely or abridge it;[5] and in a study of More's reception, Anne Lake Prescott has traced in English editions of the work from the first one, by Ralph Robinson (1551), through Bishop Gilbert Burnet's (1664), the process by which the elaborate title and subtitle-puff were gradually reduced to the single word '*Utopia*' – 'as though the island Hythloday describes in Book II had somehow colonized Book I and its discussions and debates: the part has become the whole ... From the mere object of a preposition in the first Latin titles, More's island would eventually become a solitary italicized name: *Utopia*'.[6] These developments testify to the fact that readers of More's book over the centuries have generally been more interested in the account of Utopia than in the dialogue that precedes it – a fact that is more a tribute to the special merits of Book II than to any deficiency in Book I, which has, at least for the last century or more, been held in high regard by many readers. Still, most criticism of *Utopia*, from 1516 to the present, has been focused primarily or exclusively on Book II. When Book I has come in for attention, it has often been treated – in a way that, after all, the compositional history would seem to justify – as largely independent of Book II. Hexter, especially, wrote that 'the published version of *Utopia* falls into two parts which represent two different and separate sets of intentions on the part of its author'.[7]

It is certainly true that *Utopia* can appear to be two largely discrete little books, not only in substance but in form. The primary disciplinary affiliation of Renaissance humanism was with rhetoric, whose classical Greek and Roman form the humanists revived, even as they revived the classical form of the Greek and Latin languages. More was a virtuoso rhetorician – his biographer Peter Ackroyd says that rhetoric was 'the basis of all his work. His wit, his ingenuity as a writer, his skill as an actor, and his public roles, were all part of the same dispensation'[8] – and the two books of *Utopia* constitute, in essence, brilliant examples of two quite different rhetorical species.

The dialogue of Book I consists mainly of deliberative oratory, the oratory of persuasion and dissuasion, associated especially with debate about public policy: the deliberative orator argues either for or against a course of action, most often with arguments based on one or both of the two great *topoi* of deliberative, *honestas* (honour/morality) and *utilitas* (utility/expediency).[9] The framing dialogue of Book I of *Utopia* is a debate, structured by these *topoi*, on the question of whether Hythloday should join a king's council – and thus, in general, whether a humanist intellectual should enter practical politics. Early in that debate – which often goes by the name Hexter gave it, the 'Dialogue of Counsel', and addresses one form of the ancient question of the choice between action and contemplation – Hythloday offers, in illustration of his claim that in fact it would be worse than useless for him to become a councillor, a verbatim report of a debate (that is, a dialogue *within* the dialogue of counsel) in which he took part, almost twenty years previously, at the dinner table of John Cardinal Morton (archbishop of Canterbury and Henry VII's Lord Chancellor) on the efficacy and morality of the current English policy of capital punishment for theft. Subsequently, he gives fictitious but solidly grounded accounts of the deliberations of two royal councils (of the King of France and then of the king of 'some country or other') on, respectively, foreign and domestic policy; that is, on the French king's desire to expand his domain by force and fraud, and the desire of some king or other (he would have put English readers, especially, in mind of the grasping Henry VII) to enrich himself at the cost of impoverishing his subjects. In all three of these included episodes, More wrote for Hythloday utterly splendid deliberative orations showing the immorality and folly of actual policies of European governments, just as he wrote splendid exchanges between Hythloday and himself on the topic of the encompassing debate on whether an intellectual can make things any better by entering politics. Hythloday's final remarks on this subject – which close with the first paragraph of the passage quoted at the head of this essay – reveal his belief that *nothing* can effect major improvements in human society unless private property is first abolished. That shocking revelation produces an immediate change of subject in the dialogue and leads quickly to Hythloday's lengthy account of Utopia, whose communistic society supposedly demonstrates the correctness of his view. Thus in Book II the form of the work abruptly changes from dialogue to monologue – from deliberative to demonstrative rhetoric, the rhetoric of praise (or blame) – as Hythloday describes in detail the commonwealth that, as he says in his peroration, he regards as 'not only the best but indeed the only one that can rightfully claim that name' (103).

But More's decision to preface his monologue with a dialogue was really neither surprising nor ill-advised. First, the topic of his book – 'On the Best State of a Commonwealth' (as given at the beginning of its full title) – had been associated with dialogue since the prototypical works on the topic, Plato's *Republic, Statesman* and *Laws*. Second, dialogue was More's best and most natural literary form. In addition to *Utopia*, two other of his greatest works – *A Dialogue Concerning Heresies* and *A Dialogue of Comfort against Tribulation* – are in this form. Dialogue came naturally to More because it was natural for him to see more than one side to a question (he was a superb lawyer), and because *acting* came naturally to him. There is a wonderful story on this facet of More's character in the biography by his son-in-law William Roper. At the age of about twelve to fourteen, More served as a page in Cardinal Morton's household. Morton was a patron of the early English drama – Henry Medwall, the earliest English vernacular playwright known by name,[10] was a member of his household – and plays were sometimes presented at his court, during which, Roper says, the young More would

> suddenly sometimes step in among the players, and never studying for the matter, make a part of his own there presently among them, which made the lookers-on more sport than all the players beside. In whose wit and towardness the Cardinal much delighting would often say of him unto the nobles that sometimes dined with him, 'This child here waiting at the table, whosoever shall live to see it, will prove a marvellous man'.[11]

As James McConica has written, 'a penchant for taking on roles, for adopting various voices, … was deeply imbedded in his nature'.[12]

But quite apart from More's special affinity for it, dialogue was appropriate to a work of this kind because it could, as had been evident since Plato, make philosophy, including political philosophy, much more interesting to read. If the passage that heads this essay were part of a treatise, it would summarize a position that is essentially Plato's and add in the next paragraph that Aristotle, in his critique of the *Republic* in Book II of his *Politics* (for that is where the arguments in this paragraph originated), made the following objections to Plato's position. How much more interesting it is to have the two positions attached to two sharply etched characters *arguing* – just before this passage, heatedly, with More expressing impatience and something close to contempt for what he sees as Hythloday's impractical idealism on the matter of counsel and Hythloday repaying him in similar coin, for what he sees as More's advocacy of morally unacceptable temporizing.

And yet More could not write *only* a dialogue, because his huge contribution to the study of 'the best state of a commonwealth' – the innovation that is definitive of the genre of utopian fiction – was to describe the alternative commonwealth not simply by dialectics but as if it already existed.[13] For this, he needed demonstrative rhetoric – here, something close to what we know as 'travelogue'.

Book I of *Utopia* is, in a complex and multi-faceted way that is characteristic of its author, the *introduction* to Book II. Its framing dialogue of counsel constitutes an astonishingly brilliant and balanced treatment of the problem of counsel: the essentially insoluble problem of assuring that rulers both get and take good, disinterested advice, in a situation where rule comes by inheritance or military conquest, to individuals who are usually habituated to sycophantic flattery from early childhood and are not infrequently deficient in intelligence or education or both, and where the self-interest of counsellors leads them to choose and expound their positions on issues with a view not to the public welfare but to besting their peers and flattering their superiors. For an intellectual of integrity, there are two possible responses in this situation. The first, powerfully espoused by Hythloday (it is also Plato's position; e.g. *Republic* 496c-e), is to keep out of politics. The second, equally powerfully espoused by the character More, is to participate but, though retaining one's principles, not to suppose 'every topic suitable to every occasion', instead cultivating an 'indirect approach': 'you must strive and struggle as best you can to handle everything tactfully – and thus what you cannot turn to good, you may at least make as little bad as possible' (34–5) – a solution that Hythloday regards as not only morally unacceptable but impracticable. This problem is, however, solved in the Utopian republic, in which all officials are drawn from a class of scholars, comprising individuals who 'from childhood have given evidence of excellent character, unusual intelligence and devotion to learning' (63), so that Utopia is an example of the only kind of state where Socrates says a philosopher should enter politics: one where the rulers are *themselves* philosophers (*Republic* 473c–e, 517b–520d).

The situation is the same with the other topics discussed in Book I. In the dialogue on crime and punishment that is embedded in the dialogue of counsel, Hitlodaeus develops a powerful argument that the ultimate cause of most crime is found in the inequitable distribution of wealth in a society polarized into paupers on the one hand and, on the other, the idle rich and their hangers-on. But in the highly egalitarian society of Utopia, where 'everything belongs to everybody' and where 'no one is poor …, there are no beggars, and though no one owns anything, everyone is rich' (103), there is no cause for theft, and such crime as remains is committed by a remnant of incorrigibles who act badly despite not being driven by need and despite the excellent education that all Utopians receive. Similarly, the militarism and greed of rulers that Hythloday powerfully satirizes in his accounts of two typical meetings of royal councils do not exist in Utopia, where war is 'utterly despise[d] … as an activity fit only for beasts' (85) and greed for money has been eliminated by the abolition *of* money.

Most fundamentally, though, Book I of *Utopia* introduces Book II by developing the method for the analysis of social problems and the formulation of solutions to them that underlies the design of the Utopian construct. In the dialogue on crime and punishment, Hythloday debates with an English lawyer who thinks that the cause of theft is simply the wickedness of thieves, and who therefore believes that the solution of the problem is simply to execute the thieves – and is thus 'amazed' by the fact that, despite the aggressive implementation of this policy, with thieves 'being executed everywhere, he said, with as many as twenty at a time being hanged on a single gallows[,][14]… so many thieves [still] sprang up everywhere' (15). To Hythloday, the explanation for this paradox lies in the fact that the primary cause of theft is to be found not in the character of thieves but in the polarization of society between rich and poor; and since the *problem* is thus systemic, the *solution* must also be.

This is also his view on counsel, and on every other problem he addresses; and it is clearly More's view as well: for the character More, who disagrees with Hythloday on the validity of one partial solution to the problem of counsel, expresses no disagreement with his social analysis. Hexter, among others, recognized the historic significance of this analysis. More's treatment (conveyed through Hythloday) of social problems is characterized by 'his capacity to see past the symptoms to the sources of trouble'; he sees 'in depth, in perspective, and in mutual relation problems which his contemporaries saw in the flat and as a disjointed series'.[15] This brings us back one last time to the passage at the head of the essay, whose primary significance is that it contains Hythloday's explicit discussion of the holistic view of social problems that underlies all his arguments in Book I and underlies the Utopian construct; the passage also states what, for him, is the main implication of this view, namely, that social justice can be attained only through the elimination of private property.

The metaphor that More has Hythloday use here to characterize this view of social problems and their solution is one of systemic disease. 'As long as private property remains', the largest part of humanity will be oppressed by poverty. Good laws can lighten this burden to some extent, but they can have only 'as much effect as poultices continually applied to sick bodies that are past cure'. Social evils may be 'alleviated' in this way,

> but so long as private property remains, there is no hope at all of effecting a cure and restoring society to good health. While you try to cure one part, you aggravate the wound in other parts. Suppressing the disease in one place causes it to break out in another, since you cannot give something to one person without taking it away from someone else.

Plato is fond of the metaphor of the statesman as physician (e.g. *Statesman* 293; Epistle VII 330c–331a), and his prescription is similar to Hythloday's: a complete reordering of society from the ground up, with a thoroughly communized ruling class at the top[16]. Indeed More *learned* the systemic approach to social problems and their solutions from Plato, and from Aristotle's *Politics*.[17] More's significance as a political philosopher inheres especially in his revival of this Greek approach and in his great innovations within it: first, in presenting his design for an alternative commonwealth as an account of a commonwealth that already exists; second (or so at least it seems to me), in his recognition that the fact that society is a complex network of mutually-affecting parts means that there can never be – even in the realm of theory – a *perfect* commonwealth, because there will always be conflicts between the full realization of different desirable social goals. In the case of Utopia, the consequences of these conflicts show up, not surprisingly, most clearly at or beyond its borders, that is, in Utopia's relations with its neighbours.[18] But this is not to say that best-commonwealth theory cannot provide a guide, both inspirational and practical, to making the social system 'as little bad as possible'.

2

More's *Utopia*: Colonialists, Refugees and the Nature of Sufficiency

Susan Bruce

*Each city, then, consists of households, the households consisting
generally of blood-relations ... To keep the cities from becoming too
sparse or too crowded, they have decreed that there shall be six thousand
households in each ... with each household containing between ten and
sixteen adults. They do not ... regulate the number of minor children in
a family. The limit on adults is easily observed by transferring individuals
from a household with too many into a household with not enough.
Likewise, if a city has too many people, the extra persons serve to make
up the shortage of population in other cities. And if the population
throughout the entire island exceeds the quota, they enrol citizens out
of every city and plant a colony under their own laws on the mainland
near them, where the natives have plenty of unoccupied and uncultivated
land. These natives who want to live with the Utopians are taken in.
When such a merger occurs, the two peoples gradually and easily
blend together, sharing the same way of life and customs, much to the
advantage of both. For by their policies, the utopians make the land yield
an abundance for all, though previously it had seemed too barren and
paltry even to support the natives. But those who refuse to live under
their laws, the Utopians drive out of the land they claim for themselves;
and on those who resist them, they declare war. The Utopians say it's
perfectly justifiable to make war on people who leave their land idle and
waste, yet forbid the use and possession of it to others who, by the law of
nature, ought to be supported from it. If for any reason the population
of one city shrinks so sharply that it cannot be made up without draining
others, the numbers are restored by bringing people back from the
colonies. This has happened only twice, they say, in their whole history ...
They would rather let their colonies perish entirely than allow any of the
cities on their island to get too small.*[1]

In episode one of 'The Promise' (2011), Peter Kosminsky's uncompromising
Channel 4 drama about the Israel/Palestine conflict, Erin, the naïve English
woman who's spending her gap year at the Tel-Aviv home of her rich Israeli

friend, is told a brief story by her friend's brother, Paul, about a lesson his father tried to teach him when he was a boy. 'When I was ten years old', he tells her,

> my father took me to see the border. The Jewish side was, uh, green and fertile, and the Arab side was brown, with a few goats, and then he said to me – and this was this big lesson he wanted me to remember – he said, 'look what they've done with the land in 2000 years. Look what we achieved in fifty'. And this is a good man, a liberal man. It took me years to learn how to question the assumptions behind the things he said to me that day. 'They are not as deserving as we are. They do nothing with the land. They are animals. They hate us.'[2]

Juxtaposing More's passage with this extract from 'The Promise' illustrates one way in which contemporary readers of *Utopia* might want to keep some Utopian practices at arm's length. Utopian foreign policy, as George Logan has argued, appears hard to distinguish from imperialism. Logan quotes several critics who reached the same conclusion, from the interpretative tradition of post-Versailles Germany noted by Russell Ames and Shlomo Avineri, to Avineri's own claim regarding the dependent relations between Utopia and its neighbours.[3] More recently, similar claims have been advanced by Andrew Hadfield, who remarks that the Utopians operate as 'displaced Europeans – English even – who have to confront exactly the same problems as their real counterparts, including the question of appropriating foreign lands to ease domestic pressures'.[4] Thomas Betteridge, similarly, reads *Utopia* as an encounter narrative which expresses a European fantasy of America as empty space.[5]

Perhaps these colonialist inclinations are unsurprising given the ways in which Utopia is modelled, at least partly, on More's own England. Utopia is a nautical island nation whose main city, Amaurot, has a geography similar to that of London's; it is separated from the mainland by a short channel of water, which Utopus created when he conquered the island, overseeing as he did so the digging of a fifteen-mile channel between Utopia and the mainland (43). The connection of the island's name with that of its first founder is a practice characteristic of early modern imperialism (witness Virginia, the Carolinas, Pennsylvania some years later, and America itself around the time *Utopia* is written). Hythloday had sailed with Amerigo Vespucci (10–11); and Jeffrey Knapp observes that although More 'seems markedly ambivalent about the very fact of America's discovery', *Utopia* 'represents More's attempt to turn England's classical nowhereness into a way of seeing England and America as destined for each other'.[6] More generally, the book is imbued with the dynamism of an emergent sense of nation. The myth of a founding moment – the birth of a nation – is exemplified in Utopus' act (Louis Marin, for instance, reads the destruction of the isthmus as akin to the cutting of an umbilical cord[7] and Knapp draws attention to theories that England too had once been attached to the mainland[8]). This sense of a nation founded, politically speaking, *ex nihilo*, marks the text as responding to the preoccupations of its own time, as does the transcription and transliteration of the 'Utopian' poem and alphabet which appeared in the 1518 Basel first edition of the text. Later 'rudely Englished' by the putative translator (with, the 1556 edition of the text is at pains to point out, 'simple knowledge and mean understanding in the Utopian tongue'[9]) the poem and alphabet and its subsequent 'translations', first into Latin and thence, in vernacular versions of the text, into English, Dutch and Spanish, amongst others, can be read as a palimpsestic representation of the text's relation to colonialism and to nation. In the poem, Utopia speaks itself, articulating its own existence – 'Uto-pus it was who redrew the map? And made me an island' – in the 'kingdom of its own language' as Spenser put it. Helgerson, who drew attention to the resonance of Spenser's phrase, points out that in most literature of that nature, the triangle between king, people and language is squared by the inclusion of the poet,[10] but in a typically Utopian twist, that role falls here to the translator, Utopian authorial agency elided, rendered as absent as the place itself. The transliteration and then translation of 'Utopian' into, first Latin, and then a series of vernaculars, echoes the response of real-life European travellers to the new languages encountered in the New World: they transliterated the vocabulary of these indigenous languages into European characters, and then translated them into English, or Portuguese, or Dutch.

In similar fashion, Book I opens by situating its 'characters' in national terms. Its opening paragraphs herald the spatial and political realities of a new, outward-looking European landscape and its burgeoning international networks, both humanist and diplomatic. England, Castile, Flanders, Bruges, Cassel and Antwerp are all mentioned in the first three paragraphs of *Utopia* (8–9) and the epistolary form of the book's paratexts perform the triumph of communication over distance, expressing a delight in the transcendence of national limitations through the power of intellectual exchange which is mirrored in the text's form, composed as it is of a dialogue between two foreign travellers (Morus[11] and Hytholoday) and their hosts. *Utopia* opens and proceeds by way of multi-national conversations, and with the buzz of excitement generated by a new *inter*nationalism. Yet a delight in overcoming the limitations of national boundaries gestures simultaneously to the concrete existence of those boundaries: internationalism presupposes the existence of nation. Indeed, the tension in *Utopia* between, on the one hand, a (new) patriotism expressed through the sense that one's own nation generally does things a good deal better than someone else's might, and, on the other, the pleasures afforded by new forms of European unions, is perhaps not worlds apart from some present day English attitudes to 'the Continent'.

To the traditional understanding of *Utopia* as linked to the emergence of early colonialist experiences, my juxtaposition of this passage with a more recent narrative may add other observations. Anachronous though they may be, the terms of these respective justifications of Israelis and Utopians are strikingly similar. The 'unoccupied and uncultivated land' of one's neighbours may be made green and fertile, 'yielding an abundance enough' for many, *if only people have the will so to transform it*, instead of being left barren, fit only to feed very few. Both passages voice the conviction that with sufficient labour, the most unforgiving of terrains can be made productive; and, by extension, that those willing so to exert themselves thereby earn the right to the terrain's use. But what each does *not* say is perhaps even more instructive. Both passages are deeply ideological accounts, a fact betrayed by what they omit to mention (which we will come to shortly) and by the drift of the censure embedded in them, from condemnation of the sloth of those who have indulged merely in subsistence farming to something more fundamental. Within a few phrases, the rhetoric of both passages quietly equates the laws of stronger nations with rather more transcendental legitimations. The Utopians insist first that the inhabitants of the land 'live under their laws', and, if they refuse, 'drive them out of the land they claim for themselves'. Utopian 'laws' being those which enable agricultural productivity, utopian law becomes first co-terminous with, and then indistinguishable from, the Law of Nature, which justifies expulsion just as, in 'The Promise', the Israeli narrative equates agricultural failure with the failure to be human, from which follows an irrationality implied to be the true source of the Palestinian conflict.

What is elided in language, then, becomes a crucial factor in its meaning, but material factors must also be suppressed if such imperialist accounts are to serve the ideological work they are designed to fulfil. Unmentioned in the Israeli account is any reference to the politics of water: to the technology and power necessary to bring water in, to control where it goes, and to ensure that its benefits fall to the Israelis, not the Palestinians. (All this particular story lacks, to make its application to Utopia complete, is a reference to its own 'River Anyder' – the waterless river.) And in Utopia, Hythloday's assertion that it is utopian law which enables the land's productivity obscures the resources that allow the Utopians to indulge in this periodic peripatetic population management in the first place. To that claim, we move in a moment. It will illustrate how, despite its ostensible simplicity, this passage exemplifies a fundamentally *Utopian* contradiction. But first, we make a brief digression back into Book I, which will complicate my reading of this passage as a proto-colonial moment.

This measured Utopian ebb and flow into and out of neighbouring lands is not the only instance in the text of references to movements of populations. Book I has its own instances, in the 'great train ... of ... servants' temporarily in the employ of the 'noblemen' of England who 'live idly like drones off the labour of others' and who are 'promptly turned out of doors' to wander through the countryside when they or their masters fall ill; or the mercenaries of France who overrun and destroy the land when they are no longer needed to fight (16–18). Most (in)famous of all are the vast throngs of 'wretched people – men, women, husbands, wives, orphans, widows, parents with little children and entire families' forced into vagrancy by the practice of enclosure (19). The itinerant poor populate the margins of Book I even when not explicitly invoked, ghostly presences attending the debates about the death penalty, the ills of private property, and the counselling of kings. It is the suffering of those subjected to the depredations of such 'hideous poverty' (20) which prompts Hythloday to articulate his account of an alternative social vision to that blighted European landscape wherein poverty 'exists side-by-side with wanton luxury' and vice – the beer halls, gambling and brothels which Utopia so clearly does without.

Our passage might then serve as Book II's Utopian solution to Book I's concerns with vagrant populations and the disorderly, shifting impermanence they inhabited and were believed more generally to herald.[12] Book I's images of superfluity, overflow and excess are countered in Book II with a model of managed containment, an economy of bodies forever shifting its surplus population somewhere else, or bringing it back again when deficiency manifests itself at home, in the interests of maintaining stasis within the Utopian nation. For if Utopia is 'like' England, it is also England's other, the place against which England and its ills can be thrown into relief. Situating this proto-colonial moment not merely in the historical context of the new imperialism, but also against the textual backdrop of an ethics of population control introduced (paradoxically) by its absence in the Europe of Book I, makes the meaning of this passage less straightforward than I have so far been suggesting. The foreign towns that the Utopians establish are not colonial enclaves in the sense that – say – Virginia was. They can be evacuated at a moment's notice, without any affective attachment to new landscapes having been established within the Utopians who have temporarily inhabited it. Even the founding of Utopia itself is not unproblematically colonialist. Utopia is created as a nation, not as a tributary or colony of another, and Utopus, although not himself Utopian, never goes home to wherever he first came from. Instead, like Hythloday, whose 'inheritance he has abandoned, giving it to his brother' (10), Utopus may be a figure for someone who finds an adoptive country and leaves his old one behind. Hythloday himself, 'Portuguese by birth', has abandoned his nation as easily as he has his patrimony. When we see him first, our attention is drawn to his 'sun-burned face ... long beard, and ... cloak hanging loosely from his shoulders' (9), and even the phrase 'Portuguese by birth' implies that his attachment to his native land is no longer as fundamental to his identity as it once was. Peripatetic, enigmatic, seemingly now nationless, Hytholoday is the original stranger, the consummate wanderer, drifting from Old World to New and back again only to promise to repeat the process anew once he has finished the telling of his tale.

There is a complex interplay going on in *Utopia* then, between the imperialist impulse to appropriate the agricultural wealth of other countries, justified by the concept of 'nation' embedded in the invocation of Utopian law, and the idealization in the text of figures able to shrug off their national identities and leave that birthright behind them, just as perhaps Morus himself does when the conversations of his European companions make him forget the family he's left at home (9). It is not, in other words, merely a question of exporting one's own law into new territory then claimed as an extension of one's own land. 'Growth', sanctioned though it may be by the Law of Nature when associated with agricultural productivity, is not in and of itself a Utopian objective or unmitigated 'good'. In this respect, the governing principle of Utopian expansion mirrors other Utopian practices. In Utopia, the desire to accumulate quantity is always countered by the notion of sufficiency, and the temptation to covet a commodity for its special qualities is limited by a social engineering which, precluding difference, proscribes affective attachment to objects. This phenomenon we see in the narrative of the Anemolian ambassadors, mocked by Utopian children for their attachment to the 'gaudy decorations' of glittering stones and to the fine thread of the wool they wear, which 'a sheep wore once, and still was nothing but a sheep' (64–5).

Another way of putting this is that privileging use – over exchange – value and dispensing with money and any other form of property serves the superficial function of protecting the Utopians from succumbing to the pleasures and dangers of commodity fetishism. Utopian communism controls the desire to accumulate many things, and the desire to possess any one, particular thing. But this distinction between Europe and Utopia wherein Europe is the locus of excess, the uncontained, the superfluous (and, therefore, the locus of desire) and Utopia the place of order, containment and the valorization of sufficiency (and, therefore, the locus of satisfaction), obscures the fact that underneath this rational, ordered surface and, indeed, shoring it up, is a very heightened sense of the intrinsic rather than conferred value of the commodity, and a constantly renewed surplus that Europe could only envy. As Halpern's brilliant reading of the Utopian attitude to gold shows, its logic is contradictory, 'shot through with the logic of the commodity' even whilst it pretends to eschew that logic. The ritual debasement of gold in Utopia, Halpern argues, 'suggests a desire that must be repressed ... invest[ing gold] with an innate desirability that transcends all social contexts ... and transform[s] social value ... into a quality of the thing itself', not to speak of the inconvenience of requisitioning all the chamberpots in wartime and simultaneously freeing all the slaves.[13] As for surplus: '[A]lthough they know ... how much food each city and its surrounding district will comsume,' relates Hythloday, 'they produce much more grain and cattle than they need for themselves, and share the surplus with their neighbours' (45). As Christopher Kendrick has pointed out: 'Utopian working arrangements are not calibrated to produce just enough, but much more' of the goods that they need.[14] Surplus – of corn, or cattle, or 'precious' stones – is what enables the Utopians to dominate their neighbours. It shores up their independence, provides the means to buy the things they lack (notably, iron),[15] and most usefully of all, pays their mercenaries to fight their wars for them. Perhaps it even underscores the subjugation of their neighbours, to whom some of that 'overplus' may periodically be donated. Why produce the surplus yourself if someone else is always giving it to you? For gift economies can act to keep your inferiors in their places, as many a potlatch king and his losing competitors have come in the end to recognize.

But all this leads us to a final irony, with which it's time to end. If a hidden surplus shores up the Utopians' ability to conquer their neighbours, that same hidden surplus also unsettles the ethical justifications with which we began, undermining the case for embarking on that agricultural appropriation in the first place. Halpern holds that the contrast between Utopia and England, between utility and waste, echoes the class division in English society between petty producers and aristocracy.[16] But who are the really petty producers in the larger, extended, imperial Utopian landscape? Isn't it in fact the mainlanders, those so roundly condemned as undeserving in the passage with which we began for their failure to work the land to make it produce more than they need? But that is what subsistence farming is: an agriculture that produces no surplus, only 'enough' to feed the farmers and their families, sufficient and fruitful for the maintenance of an indigenous population. So the really paramount question, which remains as pressing today as it was in the sixteenth century, concerns, perhaps, the nature of sufficiency. How much should we say is 'enough'?

3

Goodbye to Utopia: Thomas More's Utopian Conclusion

J.C. Davis

When Raphael had finished his story, I was left thinking that quite a few of the laws and customs he had described as existing amongst the Utopians were really absurd. These included their methods of waging war, their religious practices, as well as other of their customs; but my chief objection was to the basis of their whole system, that is, their communal living and their moneyless economy. This one thing alone utterly subverts all the nobility, magnificence, splendour and majesty which (in the popular view) are the true ornaments and glory of any commonwealth. But I saw Raphael was tired with talking, and I was not sure he could take contradiction in these matters, particularly when I recalled what he had said about certain counsellors who were afraid they might not appear knowing enough unless they found something to criticise in other men's ideas. So with praise for the utopian way of life and his account of it, I took him by the hand and led him into supper. But first I said that we would find some other time for thinking of these matters more deeply, and for talking them over in more detail. And I still hope such an opportunity will present itself some day.

Meantime, while I can hardly agree with everything he said (though he is a man of unquestionable learning and enormous experience of human affairs), yet I freely confess that in the utopian commonwealth there are many features that in our own societies I would like rather than expect to see.[1]

Following its brilliant reconstruction by J.H. Hexter,[2] George Logan notes in his essay earlier in this volume that the text of *Utopia* was probably written in a different sequence to that in which it was published. More, according to his friend Erasmus, first wrote the long and detailed account of the 'best state of a commonwealth and the new island of utopia', which now comprises most of Book II, in the Netherlands during the late summer and autumn of 1515. On his return to England, he composed the dialogue on counsel, with its penetrating indictment of contemporary politics, society and international relations, which was to become the substance of Book I. Finally, he added the bridging section between Book I and Book II, and the conclusion, part of which appears at the head of this chapter, and which, with its references both to the account of utopia and the dialogue which now precedes it, serves as one of those things which reunites the separately written sections. Our reading therefore takes off from what was probably the last section of *Utopia* written by More and the last that we encounter in reading it.

Almost every reader of a work of utopian fiction must finish the book's last section and close its pages with the 'So what?' question very much in mind. Perhaps this is especially true of those visions of an alternative society that we find appealing or deeply satisfying. We turn from an attractive world to the deeply flawed reality we inhabit and ask ourselves to note the apparently unbridgeable gap between the author's fiction and our reality. How should we react to what we have read? Utopian authors seldom offer guidance on what has just been 'reported' to us: how we should read the description we have just followed and what meaning we should draw from it. But Thomas More apparently does. As we reach the end of *Utopia*, the 'Thomas More' (Morus) depicted in its pages steps forward and pours cold water on what has been described to us. Much of it, he tells us, is absurd and ignoble and, even if there are some desirable features in it, we can have no sensible expectation of their realization. When it is not silly, *Utopia* is unrealistic – which is a by no means untypical response to reading utopian fiction. So More has anticipated the commonplace reaction to much of the modern utopian tradition which his masterwork is already inaugurating.

But, if we look more closely at these last two paragraphs, we begin to see that there is much more than what has become a conventional response to utopian fiction here. Morus gives four reasons for seeing *Utopia* as absurd. The first three are not, we are told, as important as the fourth. They are: the Utopians' manner of waging war; their attitude to religion; and 'other of their customs'. This last is a catch-all, too vague to be helpful. Their religious practice, essentially ignorant of Christianity and based on reason and an open-minded tolerance, might seem unacceptable to the contemporary Christendom of 1516 although the utopians have already shown a receptiveness to what they had learned of the Christian religion, especially as it appeared to endorse their own communism (96). They regard warfare 'as an activity fit only for beasts' (87; more generally see 87–92). Devoid of honour or glory, it is shameful and they only engage in it themselves as a last resort. Self-defence, driving invaders out of the territory of their allies, the liberation of an oppressed people and sometimes the avenging of previous injuries, are seen by them as justified causes for making war (87–8). Without shame in a shameless exercise, they prefer to raise sedition, use assassins or mercenaries to pursue international conflict when they must.[3] Why this is worse than the stratagems and 'crafty machinations' (29) of contemporary European statesmen outlined in Book I, or the 'many great cities destroyed, the states crushed, the republics beaten down, the towns burnt up' which Jerome Busleyden bemoaned as evils of sixteenth-century Europe (128), Morus does not tell us. It may, however, relate to questions of nobility, magnificence, splendour and majesty to which he soon turns.

The 'chief objection' of Morus to utopian life is their abolition of money and their communal living. Earlier in his debate with Raphael Hythlodaeus, Morus had rejected communism on Aristotelian grounds, namely that it robbed people of the incentive to work or to work well, that it led to confusion over ownership or use rights and thereby to disorder, and finally that equality undermined all authority (40).[4] Now these objections are dropped, raising the question of whether they have been answered by Raphael's description of Utopian life. The objection to a moneyless communism has shifted to the claim that it 'subverts all the nobility, magnificence, splendour and majesty (which in the popular view) are the true ornaments and glory of any commonwealth'. We are suddenly confronted with a double irony. The parenthetical qualification, '(in the popular view)', might be taken to suggest that Morus has abandoned the claim to speak to and for an elite of educated and sophisticated humanists, whose collaboration *Utopia* is a product of, in favour of the popular view. Second, nobility, magnificence, splendour and majesty have already been found to be deeply flawed criteria by which to judge society. They are expressed in terms of comparative advantage and disadvantage. The magnificent stand out only by contrast with those without the necessary attributes. Striving for them involves emulative competition, seeing others as rivals or even as enemies rather than as friends.[5] The vice which dominates European life, a 'pride, which glories in putting down others by a superfluous display of possessions' (56–7; see also 109–10), is rendered impossible and absurd by the Utopians' communist egalitarianism. Their scorn for the magnificence and splendour of material display is illustrated by the humiliation and conversion to Utopian ways of the Anemolian ambassadors who fail to impress with their richly gilded and bejeweled dress (63–4). The Utopians wonder at others' association of nobility with jewellery, dress, and gold and are appalled at the deference shown to the rich (65). The self-deluding fantasy of those who think themselves superior because of such things damages them because it snares them into the pursuit of false pleasure, and blinds them to the nature of true pleasure (71–4). It is at its most damaging when associated with majesty because it then leads princes to think that they can do anything they wish and nothing that they do not want to do (87). Towards the end of his discourse on Utopia, Raphael condemns European society as unjust in that it confers status on the idle, the greedy and parasitic while 'it makes no provision whatever for the welfare of farmers and colliers, labourers, carters and carpenters, without whom the commonwealth would simply cease to exist'. It is 'nothing but a conspiracy of the rich, who are fattening up their own interests under the name and title of the commonwealth' (108; the marginal note is 'Reader note well!'). Can this be defended as nobility, magnificence, splendour and majesty? William Budé in his letter to Thomas Lupset, which was printed with *Utopia*,[6] probed this question of justice. Budé, like More, was a practicing lawyer and, like many lawyers before and since, worried about the connection, or disconnection, between the law and justice. Some, he observed, argued that the law existed to serve and protect the interests of the rich, strong and powerful.

> The result of this logic is that it is now an accepted principle of the law of nations that men who are of no practical use whatever to their fellow citizens – so long as they can keep everyone else tied up in contractual knots and complicated testamentary clauses (matters which appear to the ignorant multitude, no less than to those humanistic scholars who live as retired and disinterested seekers after truth, as a vulgar combination of Gordian-knot tricks and common charlatanry) – such men, it is now agreed, should have each one an income equal to a thousand ordinary citizens, equal to a whole city, or even more. And naturally they also acquire impressive titles, as of honourable, munificent men, pillars of society.

So injustice, honour and nobility became inextricably linked in contemporary society.

> But the founder and controller of all property, Christ, left his followers a Pythagorean rule of mutual charity and community property; not only so, but he confirmed it unmistakably when Ananias was sentenced to death for violating the rule of community property.[7] By this arrangement, Christ seems to me to have undermined – at least among his own disciples – all that body of civil and canon law recently worked out in so many vast volumes. Yet this is the law which we see now holding the fort of jurisprudence, and ruling over our destinies. (118)

For Budé, it is *Utopia* that preserves 'by marvellous good fortune, access both in its public and its private life to the truly Christian customs and the authentic wisdom'.[8] It does so by adhering 'tenaciously' to 'three divine institutions': absolute equality; 'unwavering dedication to peace and tranquillity; and utter contempt for gold and silver' (119). So Budé, whose letter contains an interesting description of the circumstances under which he read *Utopia*, took from his reading of that work not a vindication of the nobility, magnificence and justice of contemporary society but of the justice and Christian quality of Utopian society. His reading comes closer then to Hythlodaeus's admiration of utopian society, than to Morus's dismissal of it.

But it is not only Morus's statement of his final conclusion which raises questions but his very manner of concluding his discussion with Hythlodaeus. His objection begins as a blunt, root-and-branch rejection of *Utopia*. Much of it is really absurd. Yet not only does he not voice these criticisms but he takes Raphael into supper 'with praise for the utopian way of life and his account of it'. The question of openness of mind and frankness of speech, which has been a theme throughout the book, is again re-opened. On one level Morus may appear to be engaging in a blameless hypocrisy, saying one thing while thinking another in order to avoid upsetting someone wearied after a long discourse. But, on another, his evasion reveals further misunderstanding of what Raphael with his 'unquestionable learning and enormous experience of human affairs' had taught him. Two lessons are in fact overlooked. The first relates to one of the keys of the utopian way of life, plain speaking[9] and open-mindedness. In sixteenth-century Europe flattery, envy, competition and a fawning condescension to the powerful have virtually eliminated good sense and truth speaking, as Raphael illustrates in recounting a discussion that took place in the court of Archbishop Morton (15–28). By contrast, the Utopians are distinguished by their keenness to learn from others, absorbing Greek and Roman knowledge when they have the chance, picking up the technology of print and exploring Christian theology (40–1, 77–9, 96–7). 'This readiness to learn', according to Raphael, 'is, I think, the really important reason for their being better governed and living more happily than we do, though we are not inferior to them in brains or resources' (41). In fact, by withholding his true opinion, Morus is judging Hythlodaeus by the standards of Europe rather than giving him the benefit of the standards of *Utopia* that his experience has taught him to admire. Only in the competitive and self-promoting conversations of European society would it be necessary to find fault with the arguments of others in order to enhance one's own reputation for wisdom (14). In the Utopian theatre of plain speaking and open-mindedness, it would be reasonable for Morus to voice his concerns, not to conceal them.

But the question of whether to be frank or not with Hythlodaeus also conceals a broader lesson which reverberates throughout *Utopia*. In concluding his description of *Utopia*, Hythlodaeus engages in a comparison between the dysfunctional society of Europe and the ideal society he has just been describing. In the former, men speak very freely of the commonwealth but pursue their own gain, but 'in Utopia, where there is no private business, every man zealously pursues the public business'. And then he adds the crucial rider: '*And in both cases men are right to act as they do*' (107; my emphasis). More sees the two societies as different theatres, performing different plays with different scripts and conventions. No individual could reject those conventions without wrecking the play. It is right to accommodate oneself to 'the drama in hand', acting one's part 'neatly and appropriately' (36).[10] The tragedy of More's England is that it is a theatre of misery, enacting injustice, engendering untruth, and productive of wasted lives, unhappiness and empty bombast. It may be right for its inhabitants to accommodate themselves to its play in hand since the only alternative is to fundamentally recast society, to enter a new and unknown theatre with new scripts, stage directions and conventions. Morus then responds like a man well accommodated to the theatre of contemporary society with its requirements of dissimulation and emulative competition in discussion. He would have been incapable of receiving the account of Utopia in an open-minded way and speaking frankly about it. Hythlodaus has already rejected that theatre as ineradicably destructive and unjust and has introduced us to to an alternative theatre, Utopian life, in which open-mindedness and the freedom to speak the truth in a world without emulative competition is paramount. Given this underlying confrontation, it is hard to see how More could have ended his *Utopia* in any other way.

So Raphael Hythlodaeus and 'Thomas More' (Morus) inhabit two different theatres. But before we leave it there, let us add just one note. As More himself wrote in his appended letter to Peter Giles, *Utopia* is a work well supplied with 'barbarous and meaningless names' such as, for example, Utopia itself (meaning both 'the place where things are well' and 'nowhere') (113), Anyder (the waterless river), Ademus (the prince without a people) and Amaurot (the phantom city). These names, comic and self-contradicting, have, at the same time, a serious point. They warn More's learned audience to be on guard, to read with utmost care. And foremost amongst the names which served this purpose were those of Raphael Hythlodaeus and Thomas More. Knowledge of Greek, Latin and the scriptures would have led More's first readers to note in the first of these names the uneasy juxtaposition of an angelic messenger (Raphael) and a teller of idle tales or a talker of nonsense (Hythlodaeus). But this also invited further scrutiny of the name of his fictional disputant, Thomas Morus. The apostle Thomas was so doubtful of the reality of the risen Christ that he could only be satisfied of its truth by plunging his hands into Christ's wounds.[11] And Morus would have reminded them of a work which Erasmus wrote while he was a guest in More's home in 1509, *Moriae Encomium* (1511) or *The Praise of Folly* as it was to become famously known in English. The Latin title, of course, punned facetiously on the Latin version of More's own surname. So, the book leaves us with two opposed verdicts on Utopian society. The positive one is that of a messenger from heaven who might also talk nonsense. The negative one is that of 'Thomas More', the sceptical fool. Dear reader, you have work to do.

4

So Close, So Far: The Puzzle of Antangil

Nadia Minerva

*An edict was issued stipulating that the fathers of the nobility of all the
provinces should ensure that the poor be fed, looked after and educated at
the expense of the rich, at no cost to the fathers and mothers.
That the wealthy would pay for their room and board according to their
fortune ... as valued by the President ...
In this way the wealthy are to pay for the sustenance of the poor as a matter
of course. So much so that the people hardly feels any burden or trouble.
As soon as the edict was delivered, everyone brought their children with great
joy stemming from the desire of the rich to see their children receive a good
education, at a lower cost than before; as for the poor, they were relieved of the
burden of their own children, with the hope that one day they would hold, like
the rich, a respectable office and rank, without any special treatment among
them, merit, wisdom and learning being the only criterion among them.[1]*

If the reader of *Antangil* anticipates the radical boldness of other utopias,
they will be disappointed. Nevertheless, in many respects, this utopia merits
attention. Set in the context of its time, its innovations still qualify it as the
first great French utopian novel. Inspired by Thomas More's *Utopia*, *Antangil*
appeared anonymously[2] in 1616, exactly a century after More's masterpiece
and some years before the *New Atlantis* by Francis Bacon and *The City of the
Sun* by Tommaso Campanella.

In *Antangil*, recourse to the utopian modality forged by More – assuming
and creating a reality opposite and symmetrical to the existing order – is
combined with the denunciation of the social evils and political contradictions
of France in the late sixteenth and early seventeenth centuries. That period was
marked, first by religious war, then, after the assassination of Henri IV (1610),
by insecurity and instability linked to the renewal of baronial conflict and by
the rekindling of religious hostility.[3] Responding to this state of conflict, the
narrator of *Antangil* offered the story of a nation where peace, security and
well-being reigned. Utopia tangibly replaces an unjust and broken structure
and stands as a place for the fulfilment of collective interests.

The story is an account of the daily encounters of the narrator with an
ambassador of the Kingdom of Antangil, during a visit to the island of Java in
1598, a date that emblematically recalls the Edict of Nantes and the return to

religious peace in France.[4] The work is comprised of five books. The first was dedicated to the geographic location of Antangil, followed by a description of the physical characteristics of the kingdom. The second book concerned its political and social system. The third was concerned with the organization of the army. In the fourth book, education and culture are dealt with (and the present chapter will focus specifically on this). The fifth described the kingdom's religion (surely protestant, although there was still a hint of Catholicism) and noted the absence of every form of zealotry. Religion there was not a source of conflict but contributed to the maintenance of a peaceful and ordered society.[5]

As is usual in utopia, the authenticity of this state is suggested by meticulous attention to the details of geographic location. Precise information was a fundamental element contributing to a sense of credibility. South of Grand Java, Antangil lies between 22 and 50 degrees south (1).[6] Its context is the powerful myth of 'Terra Australis'. In line with contemporary taste for the exotic and the legendary, the richness of the kingdom's natural resources, the blessings of God and nature, was described in detail. Another myth, that of the Age of Gold, renewed in accounts of voyages of exploration of the second half of the sixteenth century, was made tangible, as it was in many utopias.

The inhabitants of Antangil had opted for an elected monarchy, in which the king had a merely representative function: the antithesis of the absolute and hereditary monarchy in force in France at the time. Such a sovereign was no longer the incarnation of the deity and his only function was to delight the people with the magnificence of his dress and his residence, and with the pomp of his cortège. Legislative and executive power was in the hands of an elected body: a Council (in which an equal number of nobles, citizens and inhabitants of the villages take part) and a Senate, made up of 100 wise men, chosen not by birth or for their wealth but on merit. Private property had been abolished. The state owned all land and natural resources. This enabled the state to meet public expenses without taxing the population. The family provided the base of the social structure, and families were organized in a pyramidal hierarchy. The head of each level of family groups (ten, one hundred, one thousand, etc.), was responsible for checking the amount of assets of its members and for supervising their morality, modesty and industriousness. In Antangil, the poor or vagabonds did not exist. The family provided for orphans, widows, the elderly and those unable to work, while the care of the infirm was guaranteed by public hospitals. Should the family not be able to provide for its members because of poverty, it was the state that met their needs through a system of taxes, proportional to the wealth of the nobles and rich members of society. Finally, corruption was controlled by a prudent choice of dignitaries and magistrates who were required to have great moral integrity. After having shown how the highest responsibilities could only be achieved after a difficult apprenticeship during which the merits of each candidate emerged, the narrator concluded: 'Thus, gradually, they reach honours, not through purchases, sales, barter or favours, all of which bring misery, decline and disaster for states and republics' (156). It is an open attack on the venality of office in force in contemporary France.

The theme of education and culture was dealt with in the fourth book: 'On nurturing and educating the youth' (113–56). Education – a concern of all creators of alternative societies – often witnessed bold and impressive innovations in utopian writing.

Great importance was attached to education and culture as a means of promoting ethics and social discipline. The challenge of improving humanity was assigned to the process of learning: 'Entreaties, discipline, punishment are to little avail to make people better who are not first disciplined and educated: how indeed could a stupid, uncouth, treacherous or unmanly people, who are ignorant and unwise, ever value propriety, virtue and glory' (113–14). Man was not by nature inclined towards virtue. It was only thanks to an education system capable of correcting the naturally bad inclinations of humanity that people could be disciplined and improved, so enhancing their security, happiness and well-being. 'When she first shapes us, nature does not use the most vivid colours; nurturing and ruling need to be applied, even with the most willing and manageable minds' (114). Education was the means to accommodate citizens to the spirit of society. Anthropological pessimism met pedagogical optimism. The negative image of humanity, surely inherited from Judaeo-Christian traditions, was here balanced by faith in education, a legacy left from the Renaissance. Humanity is corrupt; but a good society could redeem it.

To this end, all citizens received an education, although the educational system was different for the two social classes, noble and rich commoners at one end and the common people at the other. The former were educated in a national Academy and in colleges in the provincial capitals where the best professors taught the arts and sciences (114).[7] They paid a fee according to their income and the excess was used to pay the fees of the poor. The length of study in the Academy was eighteen years, divided into three phases (126). In the first, from six to twelve years, the young learned to read and write, and studied grammar, poetry, history, music and some elements of geometry and cosmography. In the second phase, from twelve to eighteen years, the subjects were rhetoric, mathematics, dialectics, physics, metaphysics, medicine, architecture and fortification. In the third phase, from eighteen to twenty-four years, the same subjects were taught with the addition, for two years, of instruction in the law and the constitution. In this third stage, training in the law courts was foreseen. Theology was reserved for those who would have an ecclesiastical career. In order to follow such an intense programme, lessons absorbed for eleven hours a day, the author took care to provide some relief by alternating the teaching of theoretical and applied disciplines. Large classrooms and libraries and a rich programme of study made encyclopaedic knowledge accessible, while gymnasiums and open courtyards, where the young were expected to do hard physical exercises, guaranteed the development of healthy, agile bodies. Teachers emphasized the harmonious and gradual development of the young. Exercises were appropriate to the students' age groups and physical activities were chosen for the different age ranges so as not to damage young bodies and encourage concordant growth. Only when they reached twenty years of age were the students free to venture outside of the Academy to visit the city and the court and have their first experiences of life. When their studies were finished, the nobles and the wealthy were called to public office, first with a year's training in the provinces, at the end of which they received commendation or criticism. Knowledge and know-how were both harmoniously developed in *Antangil*.

The rest of the people, of both sexes (197),[8] were instructed in reading, writing, arithmetic, drawing and the catechism. However, the possibility of higher education, paid for by the wealthy citizens, was provided for the most gifted of them. Class and privilege were modified by the recognition of merit and a kind of solidarity amongst the social classes, in which the hegemonic class nonetheless retained their hold on power: 'all the chief offices, honours and ranks ... without the people objecting, for they are justly and equitably governed by them, and there being room for merit to pave the way to such rank' (156).

The Academy was like a city, which contained all that was necessary for the community living there, from storerooms, to a hospital and a cemetery. The segregation of young people was total, almost as if they were being defended from any contact with the outside world before the conclusion of the formative process, the aim of which, as has been seen, was to instil knowledge and the virtues, those of 'devotion' and 'obedience' (195), which alone could protect the state from bad government and corruption. Internal organization was rigorous and challenging and the system of discipline could be suffocating. The students' day was frantically full. Moments when they could relax and take their minds off study were rare. Austerity ruled even the food, the dress code and the living standards, which were extremely sober and characterized by a frugal well-being without any slackness, since 'what is done is meant to teach them frugality and prudence, and to make them intimate and open with everyone, without making distinctions except through personal merit, the most humble being treated there on an equal footing as the most important man' (132–3).

As in the platonic republic, higher education in *Antangil* was reserved for an elite, even if, with an adequate system of scholarships, the sons of the poor could join those of the nobles and the rich in the highest level of education, the Academy. On the other hand, in More's *Utopia* the working class had opportunities for exemption from manual work and admission to the status of intellectuals if they pursued a suitable education – devoting themselves to study in their free time. Nevertheless, there is a fundamental difference with More's *Utopia*. In *Antangil*, admission to the Academy was carefully controlled, while in Utopia the courses were free to everyone, including women.

The absence of Latin amongst the subjects taught should be noted; it is a sign of modernity. The presence of dialectics and rhetoric nevertheless signals a curriculum still marked by tradition. This relates to the controversies of the day about colleges and academies in France. At the time of Henri IV, schools were attracting growing numbers of students. In the colleges, six hours of grammar courses were taught as well as Latin rhetoric, for six long years of formal study. The university colleges and those of the religious orders (like the Jesuits with 14,000 students in the province of Paris alone) expected teachers and students to converse in Latin. In *Antangil,* the classics were translated into the vernacular. Suppressing Latin, the entire program could be rewritten.

Why did the anonymous author choose the formula of the Academy as the institution of education? The Academies of colleges, where equestrianism, fencing, dancing, mathematics and fortification were taught, were greatly criticized at the time. It was thought that they were not intellectually profitable and did not prepare students for conversation or debate.[9] In *Antangil*, instead, these skills were greatly prized and the young had various opportunities to develop them.[10] For example, it was required that all students should answer the teachers' questions in order to train themselves to be 'flexible and informed' (131). Every day, after lessons, students had to give an account of what they had learned, 'to make the mind sharp and perceptive, so as not to be without anything to say, but to become secure and determined in the face of objections' (135); they also participated in debates on the arts and the sciences, in fearless battles 'of words and explanations' (152), which were held around the table or during walks.

However, an oppressive atmosphere weighs on the young of Antangil, who are always under scrutiny. Even on Sundays, they are busy with supervised activities, 'since the young ones, in their restlessness … are bound to be up to mischief' (140). Entry into adulthood did not take the inhabitants away from the vigilant eyes of the censor who examined their behaviour and attitudes with mistrust. In fact, on leaving the Academy, the young Antangilians had not finished their education. They live in common, supervised residences because it is thought that otherwise they would become prey to their own wills, and 'may corrupt each other and spoil the good upbringing and discipline they have received' (151). In *Antangil*, the entirety of personal life was controlled, and appraised or criticized, publicly. Spying and informing were the instruments of a regime of suspicion from which none escaped.

The modern reader, aware of the rights and inalienable needs of the young, may be driven to judge this denial of liberty in general, and of children and adolescents in particular, negatively. Another aspect of *Antangil* seems, nevertheless, to redeem the darkest aspects of its educational imagination. Its aim was to make the whole of the existence a continuum of learning, of education and personal development. It was the idea of life-long learning, already expressed by Plato and Aristotle, and reinforced by More, which gave education a central role, a solid anchorage in the utopian imagination.[11] In this utopia, beyond a concern for the equal development of every individual, we may find the objective of social justice achieved through the offer of opportunities to everyone and allowing those capabilities which were not revealed initially to blossom.

> For the poor ... what also helps them greatly is the liberality of their rich colleagues and companions who hold nothing as expensive for their friends, since they share among themselves almost all possessions. There are no controversies leading to duels. On the contrary, there is agreement, benevolence, joy and entertainment ... when they leave the great schools to listen to rhetoricians, mathematicians, philosophers, doctors, lawyers and theologians, whom the king keeps near his palace, so that everyone can continuously learn new things, and consolidate what has already been learnt. (151–2)

Marked by its own blending of old and new, *Antangil* remains a moderate, bourgeois utopia. It had little of the subversive quality or the corrosive spirit which have been generally expressed by the genre since 1516. *Antangil*, with its sedate tones, still had space for the illusion of a political solution of the crises faced by civil society. Its proposed socio-political structure, rather than a revolution, offers, with appropriate reforms, to repair a fractured civil society. Utopia was therefore nearby and its realization was possible. Thus, as usual, the narrative strategies of the literary utopia generate distance: the journey, the Antipodes of the southern seas, the favourable natural environment. But there is a more profound strategy of distancing. The traveller had never reached utopia. He was not a direct witness who knew first hand and had experienced the otherness of what he reported. What we read is not his story but a story told to him by an ambassador. The space represented was in reality a mental space. Elsewhere is projected into a nowhere, but it fully retains its capacity to construct a socially positive model, here and now. Setting aside the utopian stereotypes, the reader's attention should be captured by the peacemakers' desire to mediate between religions, by the encouragement of participation in government, by the protection of the weak, and by public education. Of course, this all has a class orientation but it is balanced by equity and solidarity.

5

Microcosm, Macrocosm and 'Practical Science' in Andreae's *Christianopolis*

Edward Thompson

The fifth lecture theatre is claimed by Astronomy, which is of no less value to the human race than the other arts. For with incredible diligence it observes for us the movements and the slow rotations of the heavens, the paths followed by the heavenly bodies, and their eclipses and other changes, the position of the constellations and their dispositions and oppositions, even the number and size of the visible stars and the proportion between them. Indeed, astronomy now almost penetrates into the heavens themselves and makes them as it were pay tribute to this, our own realm ... But now let us consider those who look up at the skies no more thoughtfully than a beast would. As far as they are concerned, the sun might rise in the West, and they would not know the proper time to do anything if it was not set down in the calendar. If they claim to be above such things, they should be greatly despised for being unwilling to know about something which the holy patriarchs studied most industriously. Whereas if they claim that astronomy is beyond them, we should say of them that though they have been given the noble bones of humanity, they are reverting back to earth. Every excuse is discreditable which robs man of his humanity, or, if we may add this, which robs him of his divinity.
Clearly, if God had not lead the way humanity would never have climbed up to those superior planes on its own feet, nor would we have perceived the order within those most irregular movements. Hence it is that only the most noble spirits have an inclination to study astronomy. Ignoble and earthborn minds are satisfied if they have acorns and husks to feed on.[1]

Johann Valentin Andreae (1586–1654) studied and read widely at the University of Tübingen, and after a hesitant start had a distinguished career in the Lutheran Church. He is perhaps best known today as a probable joint author of the Rosicrucian *Fama* and *Confessio*, and for his utopian *Christianopolis*. His attitude towards many aspects of society anticipated values which are current today: he favoured education in bright, warm schoolrooms where children would learn by playing games; he preferred reform to revenge and would sooner make fun of human folly than punish it; he was the friend of scientists, and a lover of art and music; he took his pastoral role seriously, standing up for his parishioners against oppressive officials and using all his influence to rebuild his beloved town of Calw after its destruction in the Thirty Years' War (1618–1648).

At some time towards the end of his period at Tübingen, Andreae joined a Christian society whose aim was to reform religion and society. Its name varied from time to time – 'Societas Christiana', 'City of the Sun' and even 'My Christianopolis' – as did its membership and structure,[2] but out of this came a series of short works which he wrote between 1618 and 1628. While they varied in style, from the secular to the religious, they shared the utopian hope that society might be reformed by the example of a group of people united by faith and working together to a common aim. The most important of these for present purposes are *Imago* and *Christianopolis*, both printed in 1619.

Reipublicae Christianopolitanae descriptio is an account in 100 short chapters of an ideal community of scholar-craftsmen located on an imaginary island in a distant sea. It owes something to Campanella's *The City of the Sun,* although many other influences can also be identified. *Christianopolis* was published with etchings depicting a carefully worked-out plan and sketch of the community, with fully detailed measurements. It is square in shape, like the real-life mining settlement of Freudenstadt, which was designed by Heinrich Schickhard, uncle of Andreae's friend, the polymath Wilhelm Schickhardt.[3] Inside its defensive walls and moat, Christianopolis has three concentric square buildings, nested inside one another. These are the workshops of the community (where, for example, grain is milled, pottery is fired) and the accommodation of the people. Andreae emphasizes again and again that the work carried out here is an examination and exploration of the material universe. For example, working with metals

> is not done by men who are driven to mindless labour like beasts of burden, but on the contrary by men who have long been trained in an accurate knowledge of natural philosophy ... here is practical science ... That is, it is their practice to look into the operations of chemistry and help to carry out tests by various investigations. (168–9)

There is a virtuous circularity in this part of the community: the work of the people is made lighter and easier for everyone by the application of science, and the result is increased leisure time which can be devoted by everyone to scientific study.

Inside the area devoted to production and accommodation, which are separated by gardens and public spaces, stands a large square building which houses the college, the *primum mobile* of the community. This has the museum, the library and the laboratories of the community on the ground floor; upstairs there is a suite of lecture theatres, where the community educates its young men and women; and above that are dormitories for the scholars. The college is taller than the living quarters and workshops of the community, and inside is a large quadrangle surrounding the temple, the highest building of all.

Clearly the architecture of Christianopolis is intended to symbolize the relationships between the various spheres of activity it houses, and their relative importance. In this arrangement the college (science and education) is more important than the economy, and forms the interface between the material economy and religion. Andreae observes that Christianopolis may also be understood as a model of the ideal human personality, so its architecture also maps his view of the relationships between body, mind and soul.

So far as its contact with the outer, material world is concerned, science has a relatively modern character. It is experimental, or at least experiential – a hands-on activity founded on accurate observation and recording, rather than a body of immutable doctrine. So in the college in Christianopolis there is a large studio in which the visual arts are studied. In part this is because he believed that ideas enter our minds more easily through pictures than through words – an idea later taken up by Comenius in *Orbis pictus* – and so the walls in the college are covered in Campanellan style with instructive pictures and diagrams. The studio also functions to 'bring penetrating eyes to bear on everything, and hands that are skilled in copying, and – what is the chief thing – a judgement that is already equal to its task and trained' (214–15). This emphasis on observation and experience also explains why the library in this part of the community is relatively small. While the scientific methodology of Christianopolis favoured the recovery of lost knowledge, it also deprecated and distrusted classical authority and book learning.

Science is also a collective enterprise in which all the people of Christianopolis are expected to engage. It is not the province of isolated *virtuosi*; it is for everyone. Elisabeth Hansot and others have argued that science is not a collaborative activity in Andreae (as in, say, Bacon).[4] They are of course correct in the sense that for Andreae one may come to God's design as easily from a single leaf as from a forest of trees. This is perhaps implicit in the doctrine of the correspondence of microcosm and macrocosm, which suggests that there is a common pattern to all objects of study. But this view also requires us to ignore Andreae's other writing in which cooperative work is explicit. In *Imago* each researcher 'has such associates as can advance his discipline, and they can discuss their common business all the more certainly and more faithfully because they have agreed wholeheartedly in Christ to help each other'.[5]

There are, however, some limitations to science. Science was not a wonder-working activity for Andreae. Medicines, for example, may be discovered or improved, but they do not prolong life beyond its usual limits. Technical progress does not extend much beyond improved machinery and decent housing.

We may explore further the boundary between science and religion, or between the experimental and non-experimental forms of knowledge, by considering in more detail his view of astronomy and its related subjects.

Andreae was thoroughly familiar with the astronomy of his day: a friend and correspondent of Kepler, he had studied under Maestlin at Tübingen. Discussing sunspots in *Mythologiae* he refers to such authorities as Johann Fabricius, Christoph Scheiner, Adriaan Anthoniszoon, Simon Stevin and David Origanus, along with Galileo and Kepler;[6] in 1642 in *Subsidia* he listed the most eminent modern people in various fields, and chose the astronomers Copernicus, Tycho Brahe and Johann Kepler to represent mathematics, along with the Jesuit Christoph Clavius.[7] In his *Mathematical Collection* Andreae takes an even-handed view of the competing astronomical systems of Copernicus, Tycho Brahe, Nicolaus Reimers (Bär) and Helisaeus Röslin; but the outdated Ptolemaic system, which he illustrates, was merely of historical interest.[8]

Astronomy, for Andreae, is essentially a description of celestial bodies – sun, moon, planets, comets, stars – and their movements. It rests, like the other sciences, on accurate observation, measurement and recording; and of course on mathematical analysis. Next door to the studio for visual arts is the observatory of Christianopolis, which Andreae describes as 'an excavated place for astronomical instruments'.[9] This is presumably like the Stjerneborg annexe to Brahe's Uraniborg observatory – which Andreae illustrated in his *Mathematical Collection* (Plate 76) – in being dug into the ground to reduce wind-shake. Here,

> we observe the courses of the stars with various instruments, and set them down in writing; and it is a marvel that men can have both so much patience and so much perseverance as to arrive at various kinds of hypothesis. I shall not set out a list of the instruments at this point, since they are almost all to be found in the description of the most admirable Tycho Brahe. [In Christianopolis] They have added a few others, among which the most wonderful is the recently invented telescope. (215)

Andreae here shows that in his utopia astronomy is on the cutting edge of the new technology, and he separates himself from those who would drag their feet.

> But why do I describe these things? As if I did not know how ingenious devices are despised by the masses, who affect to have no ability to use mathematical instruments ... throwing away half of science and making themselves useless as contributors to human knowledge ... When they shall have recognised the instruments of science as the embodiment of human thought, and shall have used them skilfully for some purpose, then they must be honoured. But if, like strangers in a strange land, they contribute to mortal man no assistance, no advice, no judgement or explanation, they are contemptible and we shall come to the conclusion that they should be handed over to the herdsmen who look after sheep, oxen and swine. (215–16)

In the adjacent Astronomical Museum, which is designed as an educational resource, the heavens are represented, with their primary and secondary movements.

Here were displayed a map of the star-strewn sky, and a model of the whole heavenly host shining very brightly. Whether you wish to see the two celestial hemispheres in their convex form, or concave, or as a plane projection, nothing at all is left to be desired. The same is true if you wish to see very accurate drawings of individual constellations, or the harmony of the heavens and the wonderful proportions between them, or geographical charts of the earth. You were allowed to see accurate observations of celestial phenomena, and, what is more up to date, observations of spots on the planets, all displayed with incredible industry. (216–17)

Where the boundary between astronomy and astrology is concerned, Andreae held the standard view of educated people in his day that astronomy is a descriptive account of the movements of celestial bodies, whereas astrology studies relationships between earth and sky, the interdependence of macrocosm and microcosm: astrology is applied astronomy. As to astrology, he says, the effects on earth of 'the sun and moon are quite clearly evident' (237) but those of the stars are less certain. Weather forecasting is an instance of astrology, and it is in this context that he observes that 'anyone who does not know the use of astrology in human affairs, or who has the nerve to deny its usefulness is condemned to the opposite element – I hope he may have to dig and till the earth in unfavourable weather, and work for a very long time' (239).

Andreae's disapproval of those who are 'unwilling to know about something which the holy patriarchs studied most industriously' (237) was echoed – or perhaps quoted – a generation later when Beale wrote to Hartlib: 'I am of this heresy, that astrology is a most serious affaire, if it were handled with ancient sanctity, as I conceive, and finding [*sic*] anciently recorded that the holy patriarchs doe' (Sept., 1657).[10]

Andreae's treatment of astrology does not completely dismiss the possibility of celestial events having a bearing on human life. His illustration of his own horoscope, and of charts showing the purported relationship between, for example, the features of one's face and various planetary influences, comes with the advice that 'the reader must make up his own mind'.[11]

In *Turris Babel*, also published in 1619, where he was trying to draw a line under the recent Rosicrucian furore, Andreae couples the Astrologer with the Naometrian as two deluded self-deceivers.[12] In the section on 'Sunspots' in *Mythologiae*, however, he comes down on the side of hypothesis testing. A dispute is described concerning the effect on earth of these blemishes on the purity of the sun. Since the disputants were not able to place enough faith in the telescope, 'various religious, political, scientific and cultural blemishes were observed on earth and compared with those in the heavens'. The outcome of this was that no 'analogous correspondence appeared, and no regularities could be identified', leading to the conclusion that faults in human affairs are not the product of celestial imperfections.[13] The fault, as Shakespeare's Cassius remarked, is not in our stars, but in ourselves.

In Christianopolis the lecture theatres are arranged in groups of three, and it appears that while everyone goes through the two lower classes, the third is perhaps restricted to those able to benefit from the most advanced teaching. Thus arithmetic and geometry are followed by 'Mystic Numbers', natural history and civil history are followed by 'Church History', and study of astronomy and astrology leads up to 'The Christians' Heavens'.

This leads to the less progressive side of the regime in Christianopolis. Knowledge obtained by observation and experience from the Book of Nature is superior to that which comes from the written textbook, but it is inferior to the knowledge which comes from the Bible or which is obtained by revelation. The temple at the centre of the community rises above the college. The real reason why Christianopolitans do not fear astrological portents is not the flawed methodology of science, which may be improved by further study, but their confidence that there is a Christian Heaven above, which overrides the merely astronomical or astrological plane.

> In their view it is doubtful that everything depends on the first moment of existence or birth, and very doubtful that one should accept a judgement of life and death based on that. Therefore they are the more strongly inclined to study how the stars are ruled, and how they may through faith shake off the yoke of the stars, if such there be. (238)

Similarly, the reason why science is pursued as a collective activity is not so much because of synergy or the economy of massed resources, important though these may be, but because in the end 'Unity is divine, division is born of the demon; for there is one God, and countless demons'.[14] And in the last analysis the reason for studying the world and adding to scientific knowledge is to arrive at a deeper knowledge of the heavens – and so to come to despise the world. Those who take this to the highest level may end by rejecting all human knowledge in favour of a sacred simplicity, which he calls 'Christian Poverty' or 'Sacred Poverty'.

This is for those who 'unlearn everything, abandon everything and suffer everything' – but they turn away from conventional knowledge only after mastering it. 'No one is safer knowing nothing, than one who has penetrated the labyrinths of the sciences' (247–8).

Curiosity about the natural world is proper, then, and leads to an appreciation of its creator. Applied to the revealed truths of religion, however, it may become '*curiositas*' and thoroughly improper. Things known by the Light of Grace are not to be subjected to scientific inquiry. So in Christianopolis 'they do not subject everything to logic, least of all God' (225).

If knowledge from revelation is superior to knowledge inferred from observation of the world, why do we not rely entirely on revealed knowledge? Part of the answer is that Andreae would have his people exercise and make use of every talent that they have. Nothing is wasted or unused in Christianopolis.

For example, the defensive moat around the walls 'is full of fish so that it does not lie idle even in times of peace' and beside the outer walls of the community there are open spaces (to deny an attacker cover) which are 'stocked with wild animals, not for pleasure but to be made use of' (162).

A second part of Andreae's answer is that if someone is given a prophetic insight, 'the Christianopolitans do not reject it lightly. On the contrary, they test the revelation. So they have a School of Prophecy … a place where they can study the consistency and truth of prophetic inspiration' (251). The methodology may suggest the investigation of sunspots, but Prophecy is one of the third-level subjects, following on from Theology and its practice, so testing of revealed knowledge seems likely to be only for the most advanced students of theology.

There are then two sides to Andreae's utopia. If science lies between society and religion, it not only mediates between one and the other, it is also itself subject to the tensions that arise from being linked in two disparate directions. There are thus elements in Andreae's approach to science which are non-scientific or even anti-scientific. 'We really can not turn our backs on human knowledge,' he says, then adds the qualification 'provided that it is kept within the bounds of Christian simplicity, and it does not limit the freedom of our minds. In fact we should embrace it, if it reveals this universe to us and persuades us of the emptiness and imperfection of all things, and sends us away reinforced in our desire for heaven'.[15]

If Andreae's Christian utopia helped to create a climate of opinion in which bodies like the Royal Society could be established and were seen to be operating within stable Christian communities, it was perhaps also necessary for some aspects of his work to be rejected. Some of the achievement of Hartlib and his circle was perhaps that they seem to have succeeded in separating the more progressive elements of Andreae's work from those that would ultimately have hindered development.

6

Tommaso Campanella, *The City of the Sun* and the Protective Celestial Bodies[1]

Maurizio Cambi

They [the inhabitants of the City of the Sun] *believe that first the whole of life should be examined and then its respective parts. Therefore, when they founded their city, they set the fixed signs at the four corners of the world – the sun in the ascendant in Leo; Jupiter in Leo oriental to the sun; Mercury and Venus in Cancer, but so close as to produce satellite influence; Mars in the ninth house in Aries looking out with benefic aspect upon the ascendant and the apheta; the moon in Taurus looking upon Mercury and Venus with benefic aspect, but not at right angles to the sun; Saturn entering the fourth house without casting a malefic aspect upon Mars and the sun; Fortune with the Head of Medusa almost in the tenth house – from which circumstances they augur dominion, stability, and greatness for themselves. Being in a benefic aspect of Virgo, in the triplicity of its apsis and illuminated by the moon, Mercury could not be harmful; but since their science is jovial and not beggarly, they were not concerned about Mercury's entering Virgo and the conjunction.*[2]

In the sixth of the *Astrologicorum libri*, Tommaso Campanella recommended the founders of new cities to consult the stars in order to ascertain with precision the most propitious moment to begin their construction, when the heavens reveal the most benevolent astral conjunction which would thereafter exert its positive influence over the cities (and over the life of their inhabitants). This process is similar to the one applied by astrologers to determine a human being's astral horoscope (singling out the celestial bodies' positions in conjunction with the zodiacal houses at the moment of conception or birth) in order to foretell the subject's temperament, talents, natural inclinations and destiny. Yet individuals cannot choose at which moment (and under which stars) they are to be born, whereas the founders of a city can decide to build it, for instance, under *Leo in Medium coeli* (with the coincidence of the Sun and the Moon in a favourable aspect), so as to favourably determine its future.

In addition to setting the propitious point in time, the city builder or *Aedificator* can also plan the urban map of the city in such a way so that, like a talisman in its shape, it would be capable of attracting the beneficial influence exerted by Jupiter and so neutralize the nefarious influence brought on by the 'cold' Saturn. With this as its celestial map, the city would enjoy long life, wealth, honours and whatever might be needed for the well-being of its inhabitants.[3]

In 1602, a few years after the failure of the anti-Spanish plot he had inspired (encouraged by the extraordinary omens he had seen in the heavens announcing the world's renewal, as he would later confess), Campanella found himself in the role of the *Aedificator* – albeit only in literary fiction – entirely absorbed in the drafting of an ideal city's outline in the Naples prison cell where he was held. In those circumstances, Campanella created the most perfect city possible under the most favourable celestial conjunction and fully in keeping with his astrological beliefs.

A Genoese character – Columbus's helmsman and for us the narrator of a journey in which he happened to come across the community of the Solari – described the principles followed by the inhabitants of the City of the Sun when they began to build that city 'divided into seven large circuits, named after the seven planets'. In its urban plan, the city was laid out with the cardinal points clearly in mind – exactly as prescribed by the Philosopher in the *Astrologicorum libri*. As a result, entry into the city was gained through 'four gates facing the four points of the compass' (27). The text thoroughly analyses such details and reveals the reasons why and when the solar city's inhabitants decided to build the city. It is, however, difficult to understand by anyone not well versed in the science of astrology.

Thanks to their discerning choice when founding the solar city, the community would be looked after by the protective care provided by the celestial bodies in every single aspect of its life. It would, however, be naïve to believe that the horoscope on its own could completely determine 'the basic traits' (of a human being as well as of a city) or direct good or bad luck or that it could be fully relied upon 'to foretell coming events'.[4] This position had already been made clear in the *Tetrabiblos* by Claudio Tolomeo – the main authority in this supposed science, without whom, as Girolamo Cardano wrote, astrology would not have existed.

Campanella often disagrees with Tolomeo, but nonetheless agrees with him that the horoscope cast at birth does not determine anyone's destiny. The moment of birth is no more than an indicator of an individual's natural bent. Understanding the position of the stars and the figures drawn by the constellations at the moment of birth represents an invaluable resource by means of which the course of imminent events can be advantageously modified.

It therefore seems that the Calabrian friar behaves with regard to his imaginary city in exactly the same way as he would have done when drawing up one of the many horoscopes he had been required to make for over a decade by the most famous and powerful people of his time, ranging from Pope Urban VIII to Anne of Austria for her son (who would later become the Sun King, Louis XIV), along with Francesco Caracciolo and Tobia Adami.

The City of the Sun, written in 1602 and published in 1623, is generously endowed with astrological references and recalls the close relationship between the microcosm and the macrocosm. By observing the city's layout, one can readily see how the predominant role played by astrology lies behind the sites where its symbols are placed.

Carefully following the city's description, one notes that in the very centre of the city (thus within the smallest of the seven rings) there rises a temple which is 'perfectly circular ... [an] astonishing design'. Inside this temple, which is also the highest building (in other words, the closest to heaven), there are no sacred statues or paintings of traditional images, but only symbols of a higher natural religion. Within the place of worship,

> nothing rests on the altar but a huge celestial globe, upon which all the heavens are described, with a terrestrial globe beside it. On the vault of the dome overhead appear all the larger stars with their names and the influences they each have upon earthly things set down in three verses ... Seven lamps, each named for one of the seven planets, are always kept burning. (31)

One detail of the temple's structure is highly significant: 'The large dome has a cupola at its center with an aperture directly above the single altar in the middle of the temple.'[5] Through this opening, the Solari can gaze at the starry sky from the inside. In symbolic terms, it maintains open 'contact' between the stars and the community of men. Deciphering the signs of the heavens is the task of 'the clergy, who are forty in number', and who live in the cells located 'around the cupola at the top of the temple ... and above the cloister' (31). Another twenty-four priests stand quietly above the temple's dome. Their duty is 'to gaze at the stars and, using astrolabes, note all their movements and the effects these produce. In this manner, they learn what changes have taken place or are to take place in every country' (103).

The Sun – the city's main political and religious authority – discusses all the information received from the heavens with the priests. Through such news, he obtains a universal overview, allowing him to take the most effective decisions for the community over which he rules.

He has been appointed as the Prince-Priest because he is acknowledged to possess superior competence. Well read in metaphysics, an acute theologian, well-versed in 'the theory and practice of every art and every science', the Sun – like Campanella – 'must study astrology and the prophets carefully' and therefore will be in a position to differentiate 'the degrees of being and their correspondence to celestial, terrestrial, and marine things' (45).

However, not only the most diligent visitors to the temple (the Sun, the religious authorities and the priests) have knowledge of the celestial language, but all the City's inhabitants know this very useful ancient science whose main principles are available to everybody – as for any other discipline – by means of an extraordinary illustrated encyclopaedia entirely written in images drawn on the inner walls of the seven circles which defend the city, making it impregnable. Unlike the religious men, the population learn about these occult sciences derived from the heavens, but not its predictive aspects (for which calculation and advanced technical skills would be required). They learn, however, the means to take practical advantage of the correlation between the *res naturales* and the bodies which animate the celestial spheres in accordance with the fascinating procedures of astral medicine set out by Marsilio Ficino in the third volume of *De vita*.

> 'On the inner wall of the third circuit every kind of herb and tree to be found in the world is represented ... with explanations as to where they were first discovered, what their specific powers are, what their relation is to the stars, to metals, to parts of the body, and how they are used in medicine' – uses also authorized for all Roman Catholics by the Council of Trent (35).

The Solari read the stars even when they have to make relatively unimportant decisions. Before any agricultural task, 'the winds and propitious stars are consulted',[6] and before providing any kind of medical treatment, they previously 'observe the stars, inspect herbs' (83, 93).

All of them have chosen their occupation 'because the particular inclination of each person is seen in his birth, and in the division of labor no one is assigned to things that are destructive to his individuality but rather to things that preserve it' (81). They would thus form an entire people who are laborious, kind and inclined to virtue; in a word, a population of well-tempered human beings. The reason for their attitude, very different from the real world's inhabitants, can once more be found in the heavenly bodies.

As with the city in the act of its foundation, arrangements are made so that everyone is born under a favourable star. According to the criteria of a 'rudimentary' eugenics, an experiment is conducted in Campanella's city to enhance the race over the generations. The Solari ask 'the Astrologist and the Physician' to set the right time to have sex. Together they choose favourable alignments and above all avoid adverse ones:

> 'Most frequently they seek a time when Virgo is in the ascendant, but they take great care to see that Saturn and Mars are not in the angles, because all four angles, with oppositions and quadratures, are harmful; and from these springs the root of vital power and of fate, which are dependent upon the harmony of the whole in relation to its parts' (55–6).

Thus protected by the stars, children will be born fit in body and strong in spirit. The aim of choosing with whom (and when) to copulate is intended to produce the most robust physical constitution in coming generations. This is the main reason why only a harmonious body can generate virtues. 'The Solarians say that a pure nature wherein virtues thrive cannot be acquired through study and application, that moral virtue is fostered only with difficulty where there is no natural disposition to favor it ... Care in mating, is a matter of major concern' (57).

The application of these measures will lead to compatibility of character, by engendering a generation of newly born without any great differences and with a similar bent for the good ('since those of the same age are all born under the same constellation, they tend to be alike in ability, habits, and appearance. This accounts for the concord and stability in the state and encourages the citizens to love and help each other' (59)).

To sum up, the people of the City of the Sun are inclined to obedience, solidarity and cohesion. They are a population that is easy to rule. Insubordination and rebelliousness, due to an excess of passion, are unlikely to manifest themselves among these people. They are built similar to one another, sound in mind and body, because they were born under the same stars.

Having placed their trust in the stars' protection and the messages from the planets, which are 'translated' into political choices, the Solari are very different from the inhabitants of Thomas More's *Utopia*. Although the Utopians have 'learned to plot expertly the courses of the stars and the movement of heavenly bodies' and have even 'devised a number of different instruments by which they compute with the greatest exactness the course of the sun, the moon and the other stars that are visible in their area of the sky', 'as for the friendly and hostile influence of the planets and that whole deceitful business of divination of stars, they have never so much as dreamed of it'.[7]

It should be emphasized that Campanella's thinking did not tend towards a strict astral determinism (as asserted by Arabian astrologers), which would have denied the free will of man and entered into a direct conflict with the Christian religion. If Campanella had supported the theory of the planets' tyranny, he would have undermined the meaning set out in the descriptive relevance of his utopia, leaving the quality of life of the entire community in the hands of the stars rather than in the hands of a human political project.

In *The City of the Sun*, the Italian philosopher also coherently confirms his belief, previously expressed elsewhere in his work, that heavenly bodies can only produce tendencies in individuals, who are by no means bound by them and can, on the contrary, always correct the course of events by means of the arts and science, or by praying to God, who is above all things (fate included). Knowing how to read the language of the heavens thus becomes a skill which cannot be renounced in order to remedy the misfortunes which the stars foretell.

Summoned by an anxious Urban VIII, Campanella reassured the worried Pope, whose death had been foretold as imminent in various predictions made from 1628 to 1630, that even the most fatal of predictions could be avoided as 'God allows no evil to mankind without proper remedy'.[8]

The repeated astral consultations conducted by the solar city's inhabitants to foretell the future, however, were legitimate and in line with Christian orthodoxy and even within the limits set by Sixtus V in his Papal Bull *Consitutio coeli et terrae* (1586).

No trace of superstition can be found in the Solari's attitude. On the contrary, God is the one and only supreme ruler and mankind has but to read the signs that can be found in Nature, which reveal God's plan (as he states in *Senso delle cose e la magia*, 'onto the stars God wrote the laws and orders ruling over corporeal creatures'[9]). The optimum regimen for the people governed by the Sun arises from the continuing effort to make human prospects conform to the divine plan.

Looking at the living universe, in which every single being bears messages from God, the inhabitants of the ideal city search for signs and symbols to guide their choices and to prepare them for imminent events ('after the appearance of the new star in Cassiopeia, there will be a great new monarchy, reformation of laws and of arts, new prophets, and a general renewal' (123)). From this perspective, the stars only constitute privileged signs foretelling what is likely to happen (*probabiliter*). In this regard, Campanella writes,

> the earth is a great beast and we live within it as worms live within us. As a consequence we stand under the providence of God and not that of the world and of the stars because, with respect to these, we exist by chance; but with respect to God, Whose instruments they are, we are foreknown and foreordained. Hence we are under obligation to Him alone as Lord, Father, and all. (113)

This interpretation of the natural universe allows us to purge astrological beliefs from any heretical connotations. As a matter of fact, celestial bodies do not have within themselves any independent powers. They are merely instruments used by God to manifest his might in connection with humankind. Is it not written in the Holy Scriptures (Gen. I: 14) that God 'made celestial bodies and stars to be signs over the seasons, the days and the years'? Moreover, did not Luke (21: 25) state that there would be 'signs in the sun, in the moon and in the stars' to foretell the coming of the 'Son of man'?

Those priests who constantly scrutinize the skies on top of the dome actually 'serve as mediators between God and humanity'. God's message reveals itself through the stars; the solar priests interpret it and pass it on to the Sun who can then decide whether and how to use it for political purposes. In an explanatory passage (containing Thomistic hints) the philosopher does away with any doubts and makes clear the appropriate correspondence between the cause (God), the instruments (celestial bodies) and the inhabitants of the ideal city. He states how the latter had understood better than anyone else the role played by the celestial bodies in the grand scheme of things.

> They honor the sun and the stars as living things, as images of God, and as celestial temples; but they do not worship them, though they honor the sun above the rest. No creature but God do they deem worthy of *latria*, and Him they serve under the sign of the sun which is the symbol and visage of God from Whom comes light and warmth and every other thing. For this reason their altar is shaped like a sun, and their priests pray to God in the sun and in the starts as

though these were His altars, and they pray to Him in the sky as though that were His temple. They say that angels, who dwell in the stars which are their living abodes, are reliable intercessors, and they declare that God most clearly revealed His beauty in the sky and in the sun, His trophy and His image. (109)

What in some passages could have seemed to portray the excessive power of the celestial bodies reveals itself, upon a deeper analysis, to be a mild and indirect influence of distant bodies made powerful only by the use God makes of them. They do nothing to diminish the final responsibility of man.[10] The stars, as Albertus Magnus and Thomas Aquinas stated, can exercise an influence over the body, the animal spirit and its moods, and only incidentally on an individual's free will.

Campanella underlines this point further in the last part of his work, recalling the dramatic personal experience he suffered when, under torture, he pretended to be mad in order to escape the stake. 'Know this: that these people believe in the freedom of the will; and they say that if a man, after forty hours of torture, will not reveal what he has resolved to keep secret, then not even the stars working so far off can force him to do so' (127).

7

'A Dark Light': Spectacle and Secrecy in Francis Bacon's *New Atlantis*

Bronwen Price

> *God bless thee, my son; I will give thee the greatest jewel*
> *I have. For I will impart unto thee, for the love of God and men,*
> *a relation of the true state of Salomon's House. Son, to make you*
> *know the true state of Salomon's House, I will keep this order. First,*
> *I will set forth unto you the end of our foundation. Secondly, the*
> *preparations and instruments we have for our works. Thirdly, the*
> *several employments and functions whereto our fellows are assigned.*
> *And fourthly, the ordinances and rites which we observe.*
> *The End of our Foundation is the knowledge of Causes, and*
> *secret motions of things; and the enlarging of the bounds of*
> *Human Empire, to the effecting of all things possible.*[1]

The utopia offered in Francis Bacon's *New Atlantis* (1627) alludes to and departs from the earlier models of Plato and More. It signals generic hybridity, drawing on the travel narrative genre by beginning with the arrival of a crew lost at sea at the remote island of New Atlantis or Bensalem, and relating the workings of this unknown society through the unfamiliar eyes of its European narrator.[2] Presented as a 'fable' in William Rawley's preface to the work (151), *New Atlantis* also intersects with the practical concerns of *Sylva Sylvarum*, Bacon's collection of scientific experiments, to which it was appended; it evokes Old Testament wisdom, yet its depiction of Salomon's House, Bensalem's ancient institution 'dedicated to the study of the Works and Creatures of God' (167), is often viewed as offering the projection of an advanced scientific research institute.[3] It is indeed this moment, the 'relation of the true state of Salomon's House' (177), anticipated in the preface, referred to from early in the narrative and comprising the last and longest part of the text, that appears to represent the core of its utopian vision and marks its difference from any previous 'Feigned Commonwealth' (174).

This essay will argue that *New Atlantis* pulls the concept of utopia in opposite directions, particularly through its representation of Salomon's House, and that this is highlighted through the apparently conflicting modes of spectacle and secrecy.

Numerous commentators have noted that while its concealed elements contribute to Bensalem's quasi-religious resonance, they also produce a sense of disquiet about its utopian features.[4] However, while this is true, little reference has been made to *New Atlantis*'s theatrical attributes and how these underscore its areas of secrecy. Although, as Brian Vickers demonstrates, theatrical imagery pervades Bacon's writing,[5] this aspect of *New Atlantis* has not been explored in depth.

Each central episode of the text is indeed punctuated by a sense of the performative: from the 'thick clouds' that lift like a curtain to reveal the unknown island (152), to the detailed accounts of the inhabitants' clothing and gestures; from the description of the 'spectacle' of the 'pillar of light' viewed by Bensalem's citizens from boats that 'stood all as in a theatre' (159), signalling New Atlantis's conversion to Christianity, to the elaborate social rituals and ceremonies that underpin Bensalem's society more generally and its artificial manifestations of all things natural. These features are, moreover, delivered to a captive audience, the European crew, which is, in turn, subdivided into further sets of selected spectators in a way not unlike the internal audience of Prospero's manipulative 'magic' in Shakespeare's *The Tempest* (c. 1611). And, as in *The Tempest*, such theatrics, which are given a similarly semi-divine air on an island thought by the crew members to be 'somewhat supernatural' (162), unsettle the efficacy of what is presented and how it is interpreted by the narrator.

These theatrical layers of Bensalem's society prepare for what appears to be the text's central utopian moment when Salomon's House, introduced as being 'the very eye of this kingdom' (159), at last takes centre stage. Significantly, this event is heralded by the rare, spectacular visit 'in state' by one of its Fathers, 'the cause' of whose 'coming' remains 'secret' (175). Only after a fulsome description of this public ceremony are the activities performed in Salomon's House revealed in 'private conference' to the narrator (176). The inner workings of Salomon's House are indeed only gradually and partially disclosed: it sees, but remains largely unseen; it surveys, but its operations are shrouded in secrecy.

The Society's name itself indicates ambivalence. We learn from the governor of the Strangers' House, where the crew members are initially lodged, that its founder was the kingdom's ancient law-giver, King Solamona, whose name obviously bears a close resemblance to the Biblical law-giver King Solomon, renowned for his wisdom and set up as an example throughout Bacon's work. However, as Susan Bruce indicates: '[T]he precise relation between the biblical Solomon and King Solamona is left opaque ... as is the relation of the name of Salomon's House to both Solamona and Solomon.'[6] The governor explains that 'Some think' the Society 'beareth the founder's name a little corrupted' (167), but this is never established, thus signalling the uncertain relationship between signs and meanings that Bacon himself notes in *The Great Instauration*, for 'words are the tokens and signs of notions'.[7]

Salomon's House is first mentioned during the description of Bensalem's conversion to Christianity when one of the society's 'wise men' interprets the pillar of light's arrival as 'a true Miracle' and a sign of God's sanction to allow its members 'to know thy works of creation, and the secrets of them; and to discern ... between divine miracles, works of nature, works of art, and impostures and illusions' (160). They are thus required to distinguish between immanent signs of God, which is how the crew members continually interpret New Atlantis's manifestations, and empty or false signs. But the text also provokes the reader to ponder over this process of discrimination when presented with Bensalem's workings, particularly those of Salomon's House. While Bensalem is described as 'the virgin of the world' (173), being unknown to the rest of humanity and untainted by 'received systems' of knowledge, which for Bacon 'are but so many stage plays, representing worlds of their own creation',[8] its own operations, as we've seen, are repeatedly described in theatrical terms. Perhaps this is partly a self-referential strategy, reminding us that *New Atlantis* is a fable rather than a straightforward scientific exposition. But it also has the effect of inciting the reader to explore the substance of signs.

In this regard the spectacle marking the Father of Salomon's House's arrival, which follows one of the text's many unexplained interruptions, is especially striking. Initially it appears as a solemn, quasi-religious ceremony. Preceded by what seem to be two ecclesiastical figures, one holding a crosier and the other 'a pastoral staff', the Father himself adopts a priest-like bearing or role of divine mediator: he 'had an aspect as if he pitied men', holding up his hand 'as blessing the people' (175–6). But the procession also seems to incorporate civic hierarchy as 'Behind his chariot went all the officers and principals of the Companies of the City' (176). In these and other respects, the spectacle resembles the lavish state pageants orchestrated by James I, which demanded its spectators behold, marvel at and succumb to the patriarchal authority they witnessed. Bacon himself connects James I directly with Salomon's monarchic wisdom in, for example, 'The Epistle Dedicatory' to *The Great Instauration*, and draws on this link in seeking James's support for his scientific programme.[9]

But the Father, if a patriarchal figure, is not of course a monarch and, as David Colclough notes, the Fathers' 'specific place in the social hierarchy and the precise extent of their authority remains unclear'.[10] Indeed, while the precision with which the narrator documents the event both produces the effect of verisimilitude and suggests emblematic import, like many of the island's rituals, the reader is left asking exactly what it connotes. Such details seem to demand interpretation, but remain enigmatic; connections are signalled but left unexplained.[11] The reader is left in the position of continually looking beneath the text's surface in order to gain illumination, but frequently remains in the dark.

Yet what is perhaps most notable when examining the spectacle is the scrupulous attention given to surface detail – the sumptuous clothing and rich materials through which its effects are primarily produced: from the Father's 'shoes of peach-coloured velvet' to the 'hats of blue velvet; with fine plumes of divers colours' worn by his fifty male attendants (175) – all are recorded with sensuous precision so that superficial adornment seems to empty out substance. Indeed, when explored in depth, the whole event seems stagey and is even described as 'the show' (176).

It is this show, which seems both to signify and be vacuous, to be sacred and glossy, that acts as a prologue to the disclosure of the secrets of Salomon's House and the perspective placed upon them. At this point the performance shifts in scene and tone when the Father invites the European crew 'to his presence' 'in a fair chamber'. Once again, clothing, furnishing and gesture are emphasized: the Father is 'set upon a low throne richly adorned' (176). He resembles a king without actually being one, while his apparently divine role is described in performative terms when he offers the 'posture of blessing' to the crew (176). All but the narrator then depart and it is within this private, but no less theatrical setting, that the reader seems at last to view the 'Light' represented by Salomon's House, being privy to the Father's revelations to this exclusive audience of one.

It is also within this cloistered context of display that features explicitly resonating with the scientific programme Bacon advocates elsewhere find fullest expression. *The Great Instauration*'s assertion that 'human knowledge and human power, do really meet in one'[12] is echoed in the Father's twinning of knowledge and power when he defines 'The End of our Foundation' as being 'the knowledge of Causes, and secret motions of things; and the enlarging of the bounds of Human Empire, to the effecting of all things possible' (177). In identifying each specialist research area within Salomon's House, the Father highlights its overall empirical, inductive approach, in which artificial aids and experiments are constructed to improve sense perception and whose underlying purpose is to promote 'the relief of man's estate',[13] providing the means to enhance nutrition, health, medicine and longevity, as well as generating Christian virtue and civic order. Moreover, the activities of Salomon's House appear to follow Bacon's model 'of scientific inquiry as a collective, collaborative, and social enterprise',[14] supported by the State and granted divine sanction recommended in *The Advancement*. In all of these respects, Salomon's House certainly resembles Bacon's conception of an ideal scientific community presented in his other writings.

However, some details remain ambivalent, especially when viewed from the perspective of the theatrical preliminaries. The Father's disclosures are indeed encased within yet another performative process, being initiated by a ritualized act of gift-giving. He introduces them by declaring that 'I will give thee the greatest jewel I have' (177) and, having bestowed this treasure, grants the narrator the reward of disseminating his findings: 'I give thee leave to publish it for the good of other nations' (185). Having cloaked Salomon's House's operations in secrecy throughout, the fable's final lines entrust the narrator with making them public. Furthermore, as if both to symbolize and seal this gift, the narrative concludes with the Father assigning 'a value of about two thousand ducats, for a bounty to me and my fellows' (185). But what exactly is being given and in what ways does it illuminate Salomon's House's 'Light'? Certainly, the Father's inventory of its advanced instruments and investigations, together with his explanations of their beneficial uses, give the impression of both enlightenment and utopian vision.

When examining the Father's disclosures further, however, what is withheld is as striking as what is revealed. The materials used in each research area are often too vaguely identified to be of use to the audience to whom this information is imparted. For example, when the Father states, 'We have also great variety of composts, and soils, for the making of the earth fruitful' (177), he gives no indication of the particular types of material employed or how they are produced. The effects are highlighted, but the specific methods of achieving them remain unclear. Nor is any information given about how the members of Salomon's House are chosen or selected for particular roles.

Elsewhere, the Father makes explicit how some areas remain veiled as the Society's members 'take all an oath of secrecy, for the concealing of those which we think fit to keep secret: though some of those we do reveal sometimes to the state, and some not' (184). However, the premise on which such judgements are made are not divulged, nor is the decision-making process for the publication of 'new profitable inventions' (185). The description of Salomon's House presents a show of revelation, but a sense of uncertainty prevails. Moreover, these apparent polarities of spectacle and secrecy are strangely consonant with those manifestations of knowing questioned as being 'Seeming Wise' in Bacon's essay of the same name. Here he warns: 'Some are so close and reserved, as they will not shew their wares but by a dark light; and seem always to keep back somewhat' and would 'seem to others to know of that which they may not well speak. Some help themselves with countenance and gesture, and are wise by signs'.[15] While *New Atlantis* never directly queries the Fathers' wisdom, it nonetheless resembles both of these extremes in some respects and thus provokes further investigation.

Notably, as the Father's description of Salomon's House progresses, so it becomes increasingly as much an assertion of authority and superiority as about imparting 'Light' to its expectant audience. The narrator's early observation of Bensalem's supplementary qualities reverberates in the Father's 'better than' claims for the inventions of Salomon's House. Each section of his description is prefaced by the cumulative 'We have ...' in contradistinction with the reiterated negatives 'which you have not', 'to you unknown' (182), so that the surface spectacle of gift-giving is underwritten by an insistent reminder of what the audience lacks and cannot reciprocate. Like all acts of largesse within Bensalem, the conventions of gratuity are denied to the recipient and thus reaffirm the benefactor's primacy. Indeed, having previously been in thrall to Bensalem's account of itself, the narrator is now struck dumb until the final paragraph, subject to the Father's authoritative discourse, to which he seems willingly to succumb. This, again, is supported by a theatrical gesture in which the Father stands 'and I, as I had been taught, kneeled down' (185), suggesting both an act of blessing and submission.

It is significant, however, that, while surrounded by show, the description of Salomon's House is one of the least empirically-centred parts of the text. The narrator does not actually witness the scientific stage-sets – the artificial re-creations of the natural world – that comprise Salomon's House's array of specialized areas of knowledge, but relies solely on the Father's account of them. Ironically, while highlighting Salomon's House's practical approach, the Father discloses its activities through narration alone and, moreover, indicates the limitations of this when he explains why he will not provide details about the 'excellent works' of 'our own' 'divers inventors', for 'since you have not seen, it were too long to make descriptions of them; and besides, in the right understanding of those descriptions you might easily err' (185). The Father himself identifies discursive communication as being partial and unreliable, even while giving the narrator licence to publish what he imparts.[16]

However, as I've suggested throughout, the reader is placed in a more active role than the narrator. Bruce indeed argues: 'More and more systematically, the text establishes a split between its narrator and its reader.'[17] Being located at one remove from the Father's address, he or she is enabled to read 'over' the narrator's restricted viewpoint and examine his interpretation. This invokes the more participatory, but also 'self-distanced',[18] reading position that Bacon advises in his essay 'Of Studies': 'Read not to contradict and confute; nor to believe and take for granted; nor to find talk and discourse; but to weigh and consider.'[19] Here the reader is expected not to be wilfully censorious, nor passively uncritical, nor simply to recount what is presented to them, but rather to take an approach that is both judicious and probing, one that may recognize the merits of Salomon's House without taking them at face value.

It is the insistent repetition of theatrical tropes that highlights this process, as they encourage the reader to look beneath surface gloss and discern the text's ambiguities and their refusal to produce a straightforward reading of New Atlantis. In particular, display rarely simply reveals, but rather signals what is hidden, obscure and puzzling so as to demand further enquiry. Just as the core of Bensalem's operations, Salomon's House, is only partially displayed, so New Atlantis as a whole is presented as being 'A Work Unfinished' (151), offering itself as a starting point for, rather than a comprehensive account of, an ideal society. It thus remains open to recreation and transformation. Through its theatre of partial disclosure and secrecy, Salomon's House elicits an interrogation of New Atlantis's utopian vision at the moment of its inscription.

8

Gerrard Winstanley's *The Law Of Freedom*: Context and Continuity

John Gurney

*And indeed the main Work of Reformation lies in this, to reform
the Clergy, Lawyers, and Law; for all the Complaints of the
Land are wrapped up within them three.*[1]

The Law of Freedom in a Platform: Or, True Magistracy Restored (1652)
was the last of Gerrard Winstanley's published works, and the one for
which he is best known. It has generally been regarded as a utopia since 1895,
when Eduard Bernstein described it as such in the first modern account of
this long-neglected work, although there have been some dissentient voices.
In recent decades much has been made of the work's singular nature and of
the contrasts between it and Winstanley's earlier writings. For many scholars
the work is proof that Winstanley's early optimism had largely evaporated
by 1652, following the defeat of the Digger venture two years earlier. There
are, however, grounds for questioning the work's singularity and the extent to
which it stood apart both from contemporary debates and from the main body
of Winstanley's *oeuvre*.

Gerrard Winstanley (1609–1676) had come to public attention in 1648
when he published his first four, highly original, theological tracts, in which he
argued for general redemption and universal salvation and equated God with
Reason.[2] Following the appearance in early 1649 of his tract *The New Law
of Righteousnes*, Winstanley became briefly famous when he led the Diggers
on to waste ground at St George's Hill in Surrey, where they worked the land
in common and called on all to join them. The Diggers, true to the spirit of
millenarian excitement which followed the execution of Charles I, hoped that
through their example humankind might be persuaded to abandon private
property and buying and selling, and to make the Earth 'a common treasury,
without respect of persons'.[3] Winstanley's writings in 1649 and early 1650
were concerned chiefly with promoting, defending and justifying the Digger
experiment. His final Digger publication, *An Humble Request*, appeared in
print in April 1650, the same month that the Diggers were driven off the Surrey
commons. This was the last of Winstanley's works to be published before the
appearance of *The Law of Freedom* almost two years later.

It is clear that a significant shift in Winstanley's thinking did take place from 1650 to 1652.[4] In *The New Law of Righteousnes* and in his Digger writings, the transformation he envisaged was essentially millenarian, and would be brought about primarily through a process of internal regeneration, or 'Christ rising in sons and daughters', as all submitted to the law of righteousness and came to abide by the Golden Rule and to accept the necessity of community.[5] Although Winstanley's arguments were never wholly consistent, he was, it seems, in no doubt that the impending 'work of restoration' would be total and that the curse would be lifted from the whole creation: 'Christ must rise, and the powers of the flesh must fall'; there 'shal not be a vessel of humane earth, but it shal be filled with Christ'.[6]

In *The Law of Freedom*, by contrast, much greater emphasis was placed on the need for state action and for proper laws and constitutional arrangements to be put in place to preserve commonwealth's government and to maintain 'true freedom'.[7] The work was dedicated to Oliver Cromwell, who was urged to make use of his unrivalled power to advance righteous government (2: 278–92). Much of the text was taken up with utopian descriptions of the complex system of office holding, education and rewards and punishments that would be required in a society from which private property, buying and selling and organized religion had departed (2: 315–42, 348–52, 354–63, 366–7, 368–78). Throughout the work, the need for laws to control the 'confused and disordered' body of the people, and to counter 'the spirit of unreasonable ignorance', was insisted on (2: 293, 302, 312, 315). Office holders should enjoy an effective degree of power, for 'if there were not power in the hands of Officers, the spirit of rudeness would not be obedient to any Law or Government, but their own wils' (2: 329). Laws must be faithfully executed, for 'herein lies the life of Government' (2: 304, 305, 323). Whereas Winstanley had, in his earlier writings, denounced 'imprisoning, whiping and killing' as 'but the actings of the curse', in *The Law of Freedom* he provided for a series of penalties for transgressions, including temporary servitude for 'such as have lost their Freedom' and the death penalty (1: 481, 515, 523; 2: 45, 331, 370–1, 373–8). There must, he emphasized, 'be suitable Laws for every occasion, and almost for every action that men do' (2: 304).

All commentators would agree that *The Law of Freedom* marked a change in emphasis in Winstanley's argument, but there remains disagreement about the precise nature of that change and the reasons behind it. One way of approaching *The Law of Freedom* afresh is to focus less on the extent to which the work differs from Winstanley's earlier writings, and more on the specific context in which it was produced. The key here is Winstanley's prefatory address to Cromwell, in which he insisted that 'indeed the main Work of Reformation lies in this, to reform the Clergy, Lawyers, and Law; for all the Complaints of the Land are wrapped up within them three' (2: 283). It is no doubt significant that it was in this address that Winstanley – who normally claimed that his ideas came from the spirit within rather than from book learning – made one of his rare, positive references to a work by another author. This was to Hugh Peter's *Good Work for a Good Magistrate*, which had appeared a few months before *The Law of Freedom*, and which sought through 'honest, homely, plain English hints' to offer advice on the advancement and preservation of true religion, mercy and justice.[8]

Peter's *Good Work for a Good Magistrate* was a product of the movement for social and religious reform which was such a vigorous feature of English political debate in late 1651 and 1652. Peter was an early nominee to the Hale Commission on law reform, and from January 1652 he became one the most enthusiastic participants in its work. *Good Work for a Good Magistrate* was published in June 1651, but its message gained added significance in the wake of Cromwell's victory at Worcester, an event that helped to increase the stability of the commonwealth regime and fuel the conviction among radicals that major reforms were imminent.[9] Several writers were encouraged to join the debates about how best to proceed, and each offered their own prescriptions for reform in the hope that Cromwell, Parliament or the Hale Commission might heed their advice.[10] A number of them dedicated their work – as Winstanley was to do – to Cromwell, who was praised as someone whose 'heart was bent for the publique good' and whose 'Genius runs full and fast that way'.[11] In *The Law of Freedom* Winstanley expressed his approval of the suggestion by Peter and others 'that the Word of God might be consulted with to finde out a healing Government', and he acknowledged that it was this that lay behind his decision to complete a work which otherwise may have lain dormant (2: 287). There is every reason to see *The Law of Freedom*, in its finished version, as a conscious contribution to the reform debates in which Peter played such an important part.

Peter, in assessing the relative importance of his themes of religion, mercy and justice, concluded that the last was 'more necessarie to the immediate subsistence of a Common-wealth then the two former', for 'without Justice, no Commonwealth can long subsist'.[12] A substantial part of his tract was given over to setting out a 'model for the law' and rules for justice.[13] Peter also helped to further define the terms of the debates by addressing the need for a strong militia – for 'Justice cannot bee executed without Power' – and the question of poverty and idleness.[14] His arguments were backed up by copious biblical quotation and by many references to current Dutch practice, which for Peter best demonstrated the way forward for a prosperous, commercially minded republic.[15]

In places *The Law of Freedom* reads like a commentary on the proposals by Peter and other participants in the reform debates, and an attempt to provide a persuasive alternative to Peter's vision of a society driven by commerce and wealth creation. The repeated emphasis on laws and government, which to some readers seems so striking in comparison with Winstanley's Digger and pre-Digger writings, was consistent with much of the pamphlet literature of the time. Winstanley's criticism of costs and delays in legal proceedings, his advocacy of county courts or senates and his concerns about the effects of stopping 'the current of succeeding Parliaments' also chimed with what others at the time believed to be important.[16] His insistence that laws should be 'few and short, and often read' reflected the concerns of many that the legal system's complexity encouraged costly suits and benefited only the lawyers.[17] In advocating the use of peace-makers to settle disputes, Winstanley was making use of one of Peter's core proposals, a proposal that was supported by other writers keen to free potential litigants from the clutches of lawyers.[18]

The influence on Winstanley of particular writers can be detected. Winstanley's support for successive parliaments, frequent elections and rotation might at first sight appear to show an awareness of Marchamont Nedham's celebrated editorials in *Mercurius Politicus*, which ran from September 1651 to August 1652 (2: 290, 315–18). It seems certain, however, that the writer whose work Winstanley was following most closely was the Independent and future Quaker Isaac Penington junior, from whose 1651 tract *The Fundamental Right, Safety and Liberty of the People* Nedham borrowed heavily and without acknowledgement in his *Politicus* editorials.[19] Winstanley was evidently familiar with Penington's tract and with his earlier *A Word for the Common Weale* (1650): their influence can be seen not only in Winstanley's admittedly rather hazy constitutional proposals but also in several of his statements on law and government.[20] Winstanley's advocacy of easily comprehensible laws and his insistence on fit officers and on the faithful execution of the laws could all be found in Penington's works, and were expressed there in similar words. Like Winstanley, Penington argued for laws that were 'cleare and easy to be known'; he maintained that 'execution is the life of the law' and that without a due and faithful execution even the best laws were to little purpose.[21] He also insisted that those who execute the law should be guided by clear rules and not be swayed by their own 'apprehensions and judgements', and that parliaments too should be bound by clear rules.[22] Penington was, like Winstanley, anxious to define 'true freedom' and in *The Fundamental Right* set out to list its main components.[23]

Winstanley had always paid heed to other writers, however reluctant he was to refer directly to them or to acknowledge their influence. The shifts in argument from his earlier to his later Digger writings – including his adoption of Norman Yoke theories, his increasing focus on the concept of kingly power and his use of arguments drawn from necessity and contract theory – all point to his capacity to absorb the arguments of others and to re-use them in highly original ways.[24] Commentators have noted how the contents of *The Law of Freedom* show some engagement with the Hobbesian arguments that were making headway in 1651, but they seem above all to reflect Winstanley's awareness that the current of radical argument had shifted since the days of digging, and that radical hopes were now increasingly channelled towards the cause of structured legal, religious and constitutional reform.

Winstanley seems to have been quite clear about the value of restating his commitment to community in the context of the reform debates of the early 1650s. Historians have often been puzzled by the appearance in early 1652 of quite lengthy extracts from *The Law of Freedom* in newsbooks (the precursors of modern newspapers) and other publications. These extracts appeared anonymously, and were highly selective in the arguments they advanced.[25] It is sometimes thought that a pre-publication manuscript may have fallen into the hands of unscrupulous publishers who made use of it without the author's consent and in ways that differed markedly from his intentions.[26] What is often overlooked, however, is that similar selections had been made of some of Winstanley's earlier Digger writings.[27] It is quite possible that Winstanley was fully aware of what was taking place with the publication of passages from *The Law of Freedom*, and even had a hand in it. This would certainly have been an effective way of reaching new readers, and Winstanley may well have been pleased when Cromwell unwittingly endorsed some of his proposals which were presented to him in April 1652 as a set of anonymous propositions for 'the better regulating of the Law'.[28]

We should not exaggerate the differences between *The Law of Freedom* and Winstanley's earlier writings. The stated aim of the work was to advance the cause of community, or 'commonwealth's government', and if we strip away those passages which reflect most the concerns of participants in the reform debates, there is much that is consistent with the arguments of Winstanley's Digger and pre-Digger writings (2: 278, 291). In particular, there are several hints in Winstanley's earlier works that the system of law and government set out in *The Law of Freedom* was not an aberration, and did not necessarily represent a major retreat from his earlier principles. Winstanley had always insisted that he was not against law or government.[29] The Diggers were, he claimed, slandered by the accusation that 'we deny all Law, because we deny the corruption in Law'; 'True Government is that I long for to see' (2: 83, 198). Even in *The New Law of Righteousnes*, the work in which Winstanley stated most forcefully and optimistically his belief that righteousness would come to rule in everyone, and that all would be persuaded to live according to the Golden Rule, he acknowledged the possibility of disobedience and recalcitrance. Provision would have to be made to deal with those who broke the law of righteousness, those who 'steal or whore or become idle and wil not work'. Such offenders would, he suggested, be set to work as servants for others, and they would lose the privilege of sonship until such time as they repented (1: 508, 514–5, 520).[30]

Winstanley was concerned in *The New Law of Righteousnes* with proclaiming imminent change and urging action, and there was no good reason why he should devote space in that work to elaborating upon the mechanisms needed to deal with transgression in a future society; there was similarly little scope for this in his Digger pamphlets. But the problems had been noted then, as had the accusation that community of property would inevitably lead to idleness, community of partners or lawlessness (1: 507–8; 2: 121–2). Writing *The Law of Freedom* enabled Winstanley to address in much greater detail questions that had been raised in his earlier works, and to offer answers that had been anticipated in them. The reform debates provided him with the opportunity to make his voice heard once more, and to restate his commitment to community, in language that would have been familiar to other participants in the debates. Like many other writers he dedicated his work to Cromwell, but it is doubtful whether he hoped of more from him than help in advancing commonwealth's government by making available commons, wastes and confiscated lands for the use of the poor (2: 291–2). Winstanley's chief hopes were, it seems, still pinned on the 'spirit of universal Righteousness dwelling in Mankinde, now rising up to teach every one to do to another as he would have another do to him'. This was the 'great Lawgiver in Commonwealths Government'. As he reminded Cromwell, the 'spirit of the whole creation (who is God) is about the Reformation of the World, and he will go forward in his work' (2: 280, 311). Seen in this context, *The Law of Freedom* might appear less of an aberration in relation to Winstanley's earlier works, and more of a determined attempt by Winstanley to reiterate his communist message in the changed circumstances of 1651–2. It is perhaps the author's desire to address current radical concerns, rather than his utopianism, that is most striking about this work.

9

'De Te Fabula Narratur': Oceana and James Harrington's Narrative Constitutionalism

J.C. Davis

Tantalus a labris sitiens fugientia captat
Flumina: quid rides? mutato nomine, de te
Fabula narratur.
(Horace)[1]

James Harrington's *Oceana* (1656) is at once one of the most important political and constitutional works to be produced in the course of what we commonly call the English Revolution and yet it has proved one of the most difficult to digest and to arrive at consensus on its final meaning.

Its importance relates partly to its influence on constitutional thinking in both the American and the French Revolutions and the development of both Country and Whig ideologies in eighteenth-century Britain. It was also instrumental in the adaptation and transmission of ideas of civil life and responsibility developed in classical city states and Renaissance cities or small principalities to the larger landmasses of the transatlantic world.[2] Additionally, Harrington alerted those who wished to put their political and constitutional prescriptions into an historical context to the necessity of looking beyond the surface of events, to identifying and analysing the changing social forces that shaped political possibilities, limitations and outcomes. Something like that outlook and approach came to dominate much of the historical and political thinking of the nineteenth and twentieth centuries. So, there are strong claims to be made for *Oceana*'s importance. At the same time, many of Harrington's contemporaries, and readers since, have found the work overly complex, a slog to read and difficult to digest. Looking for constitutional proposals, they expected and expect lists of rules, laws, *ordini*. To find them they have to wade through what amounts to a prose romance[3] and when they do encounter *Oceana*'s orders, it is to find that they too are more like narratives of scripted performances rather than the legalistically informed requirements of traditional constitutional documents. It is a work that has influenced generations of readers while throwing others off balance and engendering irritation. The argument of this essay is that *Oceana* should be read as a narrative – '*de te Fabula narratur*' – and that, in approaching the text in this way, it is important to understand why, in a moment of profound crisis, Harrington chose to tell a story, partly historical, partly fictional, to his compatriots.[4]

Harrington conceived and wrote *Oceana* in the aftermath of the worst civil violence his country ever experienced. Casualties and physical destruction were, on a per capita basis, on a par with, or in excess of, those of the First and Second World Wars. Between 1640 and 1656, England experienced three civil wars and three invasions. Like Tantalalus, the nation sought relief but found it forever out of reach. Wartime negotiations had proved frustratingly fruitless. Bitterly divided political and religious groups multiplied. The Church of England had been abolished but mutually intolerant protestant groups could not effectively implement a replacement. In 1649, the king had been tried and executed, the monarchy and the House of Lords were abolished and England was declared a commonwealth or 'Free State'. But victory, revolution and conquest saw peace and stability remain elusive. In the seven years since 1649, there had been five 'parliaments' and four parliamentary systems and, when *Oceana* was in the press, a fifth was under consideration. Tension between the military and civilian politicians remained high against a backcloth of high taxation, resented, if spasmodic, interference by the soldiers in civil governance, and a 'government in exile' watching and waiting for the commonwealth's terminal collapse into disorder.

The *Instrument of Government*, imposed by the army in December 1653, had offered 'co-ordinate' government with an interdependent Lord Protector (Oliver Cromwell), a Council of State and a single-chamber, triennially elected Parliament. Hostility towards it was intense. In 1654, its first parliament had to be purged if there were to be any hope of progress and even so progress was not forthcoming. In 1656, a second parliament, due to meet in the autumn, saw measures taken to prevent a substantial number of elected members from sitting. The *Instrument* had failed and needed to be replaced. The question was what should it be replaced with, and how could its replacement liberate England from the tantalizing, frustrating and destructive cycle it had been locked in for over a decade and a half. Like others, Harrington thought he saw a way forward to permanent stability. Unlike others, he recognized that yet another list of proposals was not enough, that an analysis had to be developed which saw beyond immediate events to the underlying forces that held political actors captive and rendered them virtually impotent. Above all, unlike them, he realized that, if they were to command widespread assent, his proposals had to reconcile all parties and enable them to imaginatively participate in a new and complicated system. They had, therefore, to be presented in a different way. The way he chose was narrative. Why?

There were four principal reasons. The first was a preference for deeds over words. In 1641, the collapse of controls on the press and preaching had led to a dramatic expansion of the quantity and variety of printed material in wide circulation, a 'print revolution'. Coinciding with both physical conflict and a war of words escalating into bitterly partisan politics, the result by the 1650s was a pervasive sense that language was exhausted, an anxious perception that a language of shared meanings was lost. Behind Harrington's choice of the narrative form lay the assumption that the constitution could be more readily stabilized in deeds rather than words; that a good constitution was not what we say but what we do. Accordingly, the enactment and stabilization of the Oceanic constitution was through an annual series of scripted performances. 'To philosophise further upon this art [of constitution making], though there be nothing more rational, were not worth the while, because in writing it will be perplexed and the first practice of it gives the demonstration' (89–90). Acting was, for this purpose, better than writing; deeds better than words. Focusing on things acted, deeds, could be seen as not only mitigating the ambiguities inherent in words but also as dealing a blow at hypocrisy, the divergence of words and deeds. But the best way of conveying deeds and action was through narrative.

A second reason for narrative was that constitutional provision adequate to the task of ending chronic instability required some radical innovation and technical complexity. Describing that in words could be complex and confusing but, once citizens became accustomed to acting out the new requirements, they would seem like second nature to them. Harrington recognized that the technical details of his thirty orders could be daunting but rejecting them would be as foolish as sailors neglecting the latest aids to navigation simply because they were hard to understand. They might be 'very many and difficult' but 'what seaman casts away his card because it hath four and twenty points of the compass? And yet those are very near as many and as difficult as the orders in the whole circumference of your commonwealth' (145). Every day, without a second thought, we perform routine functions which it would be time-consuming and complex to have to describe. Harrington wanted to use narrative to cut through that barrier. But, thirdly to achieve this he had to engage his readers' imaginative participation. To believe in the possibility and practicality of what he proposed they had to 'experience' it, if only through following the detailed story which Harrington told. So that, for example, the annual recreation of civil society through ritual assemblies of citizens in parishes, groups of parishes ('hundreds') and counties ('tribes'), scripted by Harrington in considerable narrative detail, would soon in practice make the 'four days' election in a whole year (one at the parish, one at the hundred, and two at the tribe)' seem 'like milk for babes' (165). Throughout *Oceana*, he gave priority to collective acting in time and space with a repetitive regularity that would lead to the establishment of customary behaviour. Ultimately, *Oceana* was about the establishment of new local, regional and national narratives for a nation whose old collective narratives had been shattered and which continued to flounder in their absence.

But the transition from the old dysfunctional narratives to which people would irrationally cling, despite the misery involved, to the new narrative of a perfect and immortal commonwealth which *Oceana* offered, would require access to power and this meant recourse to Oliver Cromwell, and *Oceana* was accordingly dedicated to him. Enlisting his agency, however, involved not only persuading him to back the transition but to do so in a disinterested way. Ambiguity governed his contemporaries' perception of Cromwell. Was he the godly servant of the 'good old cause' or was he the ambitious and unscrupulous agent of his own rise to power?[5] Was he Caesar, waiting his opportunity to overthrow the republic and set up his own rule or was he Lycurgus, or even Timoleon, the disinterested lawgiver, wanting to lay the basis of stability and then withdraw from active politics? Meanwhile, the nation struggled to escape two dilemmas. First, was there no escape from the dark alternatives of dehumanizing civil war, on the one hand, or a tyrannical and corrupt peace, on the other? Second, to enjoy the benefits of a republican political culture England needed the appropriate republican institutions to sustain it; but, to achieve such institutions, it needed the appropriate political culture. How was it to escape this chicken and egg situation?[6] The Lord Protector's power and prestige might be the instrument to break both these cycles but only if he could be led to efface, rather than to aggrandise, himself. Instrumental in Parliament's victories in three civil wars and the conquest of Ireland and Scotland, Cromwell's prestige after the battle of Worcester (3 September 1651) was so great that he was the obvious candidate when there was a return to 'a single person' under the *Instrument of Government*. Nevertheless, the narrative of his rise from obscurity, of his military prowess and of his providential agency, had run into difficulties as the constitutional provisions of the Instrument revealed their weaknesses, and in the wake of the defeat at Hispaniola in 1655 when God seemed to have turned his face against him.[7] By 1656, Cromwell's personal narrative of greatness had run into a cul-de-sac. Through the narrative of *Oceana*, Harrington offered him an alternative ending to his story. By setting up the Oceanic commonwealth and then retiring from the scene, he would be immortalized as:

> The Greatest of Captains.
> The Best of Princes.
> The Happiest of Legislators.
> The Most Sincere of Christians. (266)

Oceana was divided into four parts:[8] the Preliminaries, giving an analysis and an historical account of the principles of government; the Council of Legislators, recounting the fictional setting up of an ideal way of devising a new commonwealth; the Model of the Commonwealth of Oceana, which was a fictional account of the constitution and institution of a perfect and immortal commonwealth; and the Corollary, which narrated the history and consequences of the first fifty years of such a government. Within this grand narrative framework, many other stories were told but they were essentially held together by two master narratives. The first delineated the vulnerability of all past governments to the unregulated flow of history around two principles of analysis, Empire and Authority. The second showed how the flow of history could be brought under regulation by the erection of an entirely new polity, an Equal Commonwealth, which would be perfect and immortal.

Empire, or power, in any substantial rural society (such as England was in Harrington's day), was a function of landownership. If one person owned all of the land, absolute monarchy was the natural form of government. Such government was always vulnerable to an externally or internally generated coup. If a few owned all of the land – and this had been the situation in England from the Norman Conquest until the early sixteenth century – aristocracy, or limited monarchy, was the natural form of government. Here the great landowners would compete against one another for dominance. They might establish a monarchical umpire but there would also be recurrent baronial struggles to win control of that figure. Hence, both of these two distributions of Empire entailed instability. Since the early sixteenth century, the policies of Henry VII and Henry VIII (particularly the latter's secularization of church property) had tipped the balance of landownership on to a popular basis and hence democracy was possible. The political ramifications of this shift of Empire had been ignored by the later Tudors and their Stuart successors. They had tried to rule through the barons when the balance of Empire of power had shifted to the people. Consequently, they had in the end to rule by force without having the resources to make such rule effective. The result was instability, violence and eventual civil war. Any pretence of minorities – civil, religious or military – to rule against the popular balance of Empire could only result in further instability/violence. Here was the explanation of England's tantalizingly prolonged suffering. Only if the political superstructures (or constitution) were brought into alignment with the popular balance of Empire, could some form of stability and peace be restored. But the narrative building blocks were not quite yet in place and Harrington turned to examine the principles of Authority. What made a good or legitimate authority? Once more the classical options of the one, the few and the many were brought into play. The interest of the one almost invariably turned out to be a selfish interest. The interests of the few were sectional interests, often divided in selfish struggles for pre-eminence. However, the interest of the many came closest to the interest of all and therefore to right reason and the will of God. Harrington's claim in 1656, and in the face of a seemingly intractable on-going set of crises, was a truly ambitious one: namely, that the distribution of power/Empire within England made it possible to establish the most authoritative form of government, a popular commonwealth or democracy.

At the same time, his comparative analysis of all previous republics or commonwealths, including that of Israel, showed that they had, without exception, been flawed and had failed. Something special, something new, was required which would, through a feat of political architecture, build on the popular distribution of power a stable and authoritative republic reflecting the will of all, a perfect and an immortal commonwealth. This structure, which Harrington called an Equal Commonwealth, was a unique combination of essential elements and his great contribution to constitutional design. It was to be established along two pivotal axes. The horizontal one was its core principles of operation. In essence, these were fourfold: an 'equal Agrarian'; the ballot; bicameral legislation with the separation of debate and decision; and the rotation of office. Harrington's agrarian law was designed to stabilize the distribution of property on a popular basis while preserving a leisured aristocracy. Only the latter would have the time and resources to travel and study and so attain political wisdom. Their representatives would populate the Senate and have the exclusive right of debate and proposal. But the popular will embodied the common interest and therefore the popular assembly had the sole right to decide on the propositions proposed to it by the Senate and it took those decisions in silence, without debate. This bicameral specialism ensured that the wealthy had a role in politics without being dominant and that the people took political decisions in light of the wisdom of an educated and well-travelled minority. The secret ballot devised by Harrington was essential to maintaining this balance, both because it enabled ordinary citizens to escape the claims of deference and because it liberated them from the claims of party. All office was elective and subject to limited periods of tenure followed by vacation from office. The effect of this rotation was to prevent the domination of any one group or party and to ensure the most extensive experience of office-holding. Over a triennial cycle, more than half of the elders of Oceana would be called to office and there were severe penalties for refusal. The absence of any political or religious tests meant that Oceana was an invitation to all to bury their differences and reconcile themselves to a system in which all could participate and which would serve the interests of all.

The vertical axis of the new commonwealth was in its annual reassembly in performances (scripted in considerable detail) ascending from the parish, through the hundred to the county, or tribe, and then on to the national level. At these assemblies, those citizens over the age of thirty elected office-holders at the appropriate level and deputies to represent them at the next level. Those aged from eighteen to thirty had similar assemblies for military service, drill and the election of officers. Out of this emerged a national citizen militia, which was both committed to the maintenance of the commonwealth's liberties and which bestowed a capacity on the republic which made it an expansionist 'commonwealth for increase' that could deliver those liberties to a wider world. The nation which had been bitterly fragmented by civil conflict was to be re-divided along non-partisan lines and literally re-assembled in these performative cycles. In many senses, *Oceana* was a utopian vision of reconciliation and inclusivity and it was roundly criticized by other republicans for being so inclusive as to risk the whole republican project.[9] But, in its attempt to establish a narrative which could lead the English out of the political misery to which they had become habituated, in its complex facing of the difficult issues and risks which such an attempt involved, and in its attempt to provide the living picture of the new polity in which his fellow countrymen could imaginatively participate, Harrington provided in *Oceana* a classic example of the utopian genre.

10

An Island with Potential: Henry Neville's *The Isle Of Pines*

Gaby Mahlberg

At length one of our men mounting the Main-mast espyed fire,
an evident sign of some Countrey near adjoyning, which presently
after we apparently discovered, and steering our course nigher,
we saw several persons promiscuously running about the shore,
as it were wondering and admiring at what they saw: Being now
near to the Land, we manned our long Boat with ten persons,
who approaching the shore, asked them in our Dutch Tongue
Wat Eylant is dit? *to which they returned this Answer in English,*
That they knew not what we said. One of our Company named
Jeremiah Hanzen who understood English very well, hearing
their words discourst to them in their own Language; so that in
fine we were very kindly invited on shore, great numbers of them
flocking about us, admiring at our Cloaths which we did wear,
as we on the other side did to find in such a strange place, so many
that could speak English, and yet to go naked.[1]

At first sight, the reader witnesses a typical colonial encounter: Western Europeans arriving on the shores of a remote island in the Pacific meet the native population. The nakedness of the natives epitomizes the savage, uncivilized and unprotected state of the islanders. Their wonder at and admiration of the Dutch visitors immediately establishes a hierarchy of the discoverers over the discovered, who had never seen 'a thing called a Ship' (6). Due to the perceived superiority of the Dutch it is not the islanders who command the intruders to declare themselves, but the sailors who ask the natives to identify their country. Again the islanders are at a disadvantage because they do not understand Dutch, while the sailors recognize that the natives speak English, and are able to converse with the islanders in their own tongue. Here the familiar colonial narrative ends. Once it has been established that the islanders are of English descent, there is a background story to be told which connects the discoverers with the discovered. Both England and the United Provinces were sea-faring states in the north west of Europe. As Jonathan Scott has pointed out, they were to a significant extent defined by their geographical location and proximity to each other, their shared Protestant religion and economic ties. They had shared for several centuries a similar maritime culture, although the fortunes of the English and the Dutch turned out in rather different ways.[2] The encounter with the Dutch as a narrative frame for the story of the marooned English people, read out by the Isle's current ruler, Prince William, is thus loaded with meaning.

According to this story, William's grandfather, the English accountant George Pines, had been shipwrecked on the island during Elizabeth I's reign when he was sailing to the East Indies. He managed to save himself together with four women, including his master's daughter, two maids and a black slave. Finding themselves alone on an island with a pleasant climate, shelter and food in abundance, the five began to populate it, and George settled his descendants in four tribes on different parts of the island, which served to maintain order until after his death. This core narrative of *The Isle of Pines* had originally been published on its own with a licensing note of 27 June 1668. Its author, the Civil War republican Henry Neville, subsequently published a separate letter purporting to be by the Dutch ship's captain Cornelius van Sloetten and narrating the discovery of the Isle by the Dutch in 1667, before issuing the full version of the pamphlet with a licensing note of 27 July 1668.[3] The publication of these pamphlets coincided with Neville's return to England after a period of exile in Italy, where he had sought refuge from the Restoration regime.

The Isle's core text with George Pines' narration can be read as an Arcadian work, in which humans are at one with nature, and civilization and domination of the country are implicitly rejected.[4] The framing narrative and the description of the Dutch encounter, however, end this romantic vision of a state of nature and innocence and bring the Isle back into the context of seventeenth-century European competition for overseas trading posts and possessions, where good government of land and people was the key to success. Due to the lack of such a government, subsequent generations of islanders had failed to uphold the harmonious co-existence of the initial settlers. Their innocence was lost when George first took possession of the women and entered into sexual relations with all four of them in a recreation of The Fall. Yet the consequences of his transgression only became fully visible in the third generation when 'wantonness' among his descendants had come to replace the 'necessity' (17) which forced the first generation of sons to 'marry their sisters' (14). This degeneration of society caused by a 'neglect of hearing the Bible read' and characterized by 'whoredoms, incests, and adulteries' was temporarily contained by the exemplary punishment of 'the grandest offender' (17), the second son of the black slave, and the institution of a code of law by the new king, Henry. The Fall of Man had made government necessary. It was, as Thomas Paine was to say, 'like dress ... the badge of lost innocence'.[5] Loosely based on the Ten Commandments, Henry's laws imposed the death penalty on blasphemers, absentees from the monthly religious assembly, rapists and adulterers, while there were also physical punishments for assault, theft and the defamation of the governor. Like More a century and a half earlier, and Harrington in the previous decade, Neville acknowledged that law and order had to be imposed and maintained if any utopian project was to succeed. Yet, Neville's Isle never reaches a state of organization comparable to either Utopia or Oceana because any attempt by the ruler is thwarted by the unruliness of the people. George Pines is no great legislator like King Utopus or Olphaus Megaletor, and certainly no early modern Lycurgus. Bringing order to the Isle's unruly society happens by piecemeal reform. Without the right foundations, the ideal society could not be achieved.

The succession of rulers on the Isle roughly corresponds to the governments of England. The patriarchal rule of George Pines represents the early Stuarts, while Henry as the founder of a new order with its own code of scripturally inspired law which follows a period of civil unrest echoes Oliver Cromwell and the Interregnum regimes. The present ruler, William Pines, meanwhile, a thinly disguised Charles II, faces renewed unrest caused by two competing factions inside the State representing the Restoration government challenged by a radical underground that continued to disrupt the civil peace. Incidentally, Neville himself had left England for Italy after having been implicated in the Northern Rising of 1663. The Isle was a warning to Charles that all was not well in his kingdom. Factionalism on the fictional island leads to insurrection when a tribal ruler and descendant of the black slave rapes the wife of a leading representative of another tribe, thus threatening 'ruin to the whole State' (26). Only the intervention of the Dutch with their superior arms and authority saves the island from a collapse of order. It is the Dutch who reveal the shortcomings of the islanders.

Their arrival on the island is the defining moment that changes the whole dynamics of Neville's *The Isle of Pines*. The narrative pitches representatives of two European sea powers against each other, leaving the English looking increasingly embarrassed. The colonial (as well as the utopian) project is concerned with the efficient government of resources, such as land and people, for economic growth and the establishment of civilization. Yet, the first thing the Dutch notice on their arrival is the islanders' primitive living conditions. The 'Pallace of their Prince' is only the size 'of one of our ordinary village houses', covered with boughs to 'keep out the … Rain' (4), while the majority of the people live in 'little … Huts … under Trees' (20). The islanders admire the Dutch sailors' dress, but Prince William's wife only wears 'rags', the 'Relicts of those Cloaths … of them which first came hither' (4), despite the fact that the textiles production in their country of origin far exceeded demand in Restoration times. The islanders offer their visitors food, which is scorned due to a lack of 'materials' (4) to season it. The Dutch meanwhile are successfully involved in the spice trade, exchanging 'Knives, Beads' and 'Glasses' for 'Cloves and Silver' in Madagascar (2). The islanders in contrast do not have 'any ships or Boats' and are 'strangers to ... shipping' (5), missing out on trading opportunities, even though their English forefathers had been pioneers in the East India trade. They also lack the most basic tools and gratefully receive from the Dutch 'some few Knives' and 'an Ax' to cut timber as the axe their ancestors had saved from the shipwreck was now 'quite blunt' (5). All this marked the contrast between England's former glory and the Island's regress into a barely civilized state. The republicans' utopian projects of the 1650s had been aborted with the Restoration. Instead of realizing a Harringtonian 'commonwealth for increase' England had been thrown back into the confines of a monarchy.[6] While the English had descended into political and economic insignificance, the Dutch had risen to become the new international sea and trading power in Europe. Neville blamed the inertia of the Restoration regime.

Given that the colonial encounter between the two nations is set in the aftermath of the Second Anglo–Dutch War in the summer of 1667, it is hardly difficult to see the author's point. That fateful summer for English fortunes saw the Medway disaster, in which the United Provinces destroyed much of the English fleet at Chatham, the loss of Surinam to the Dutch in the Treaty of Breda as well as the ceding of Pola Run, which gave the Dutch significant advantages in the Spice Trade. The 1651 Navigation Act, originally intended to favour English shipping, was also modified in favour of the Dutch, now allowing them to transport German goods to England. The decline of the English as depicted by Neville, however, does not just refer to their trading power, but also to their lack of industry and their military weakness. The islanders are naked also in the sense of being unarmed. They take to their heels at the mere sound of a gun, and even their ruler wonders at 'the strange effects of Powder' (25). The military and naval insignificance of the English Pines under Prince William (and the later Stuarts) stands in contrast to the military and naval power of the England his grandfather George had left late in Elizabeth's Golden Age, one year after the defeat of the Spanish Armada, and in a period known for the exploratory travels of Drake and Raleigh. Neville bemoans English military decline under the early Stuarts when financial constraints and political conflicts at home meant that foreign policy took a back seat. His narrative reveals nostalgia for the naval success and military greatness, when republicans such as Arthur Hesilrige, Henry Marten, Thomas Scott, Thomas Chaloner and Neville himself were in charge of the Rump's diplomacy (1649–53). Then, England could still match the Dutch, whom English republicans considered as their natural allies. However, the United Provinces' failure to recognize the regicide regime of the Commonwealth provoked England. The republicans broke off negotiations and went to war with Dutch in 1652. That war ended with English naval victory and the loss of numerous warships and merchantmen on the Dutch side. This first Anglo–Dutch War (1652–4) was about trading rights as well as ideological issues, such as the legitimacy of the English government. Yet, this did not prevent English republicans from continuing to see the Dutch as more natural allies than the French. Neville emphasizes this point by referring to the Dutch sailors explicitly as 'friends' (5).

Not only do they build a palace for William Pines, they also help him put down an insurrection of his own people. They never contest the English possession of the Island, and they present the Pines with useful tools. With their model behaviour, the Dutch invite emulation. The contrast between status quo and ideal that characterizes utopian writing here is not between England and the Isle, but between England/the Isle and the United Provinces. In that sense the utopian project of the Isle is unfinished. Yet, the Dutch relationship to the English is not one of open hostility, but of friendly competitiveness. For English republicans, the Dutch and the English were still natural allies. It was in England's best interest, Slingsby Bethel argued, to ally with the Dutch and ward off the threat of French 'universal monarchy'.[7] Neville stresses his preferred alliance in his reference to the Amsterdam merchant Abraham Keek – a contact of the English republican underground – who is the ostensible author of the 'Two Letters' to 'a Credible person' in London's Covent Garden which preface the work, reporting on the discovery of the English Pines (f. A2v). Like More's fictitious epistle to Peter Giles introducing Utopia, the letters are to give credibility to the story and authenticate the existence of the island. Yet, to an attentive reader familiar with More's work, the fictional device could equally signal that the Isle was a utopia written to criticize the Stuart regime in ways otherwise impossible under restored censorship regulations. The same is true for the deliberately vague information on the Isle's location, which Keek initially describes as 'about 2 or 300 Leagues Northwest from Cape Finis Terre', while later admitting possible mistakes 'in the number of the Leagues' and 'exact point of the Compass'. The letters also suggest that the ship that 'fell in' with the Isle was initially thought to be French, while the actual pamphlet reveals its Dutch provenance (f. A2v). Neville thus hints that the English were mistaken in their judgement of who their real friends were. The Stuart government might think English salvation was to be found in an alliance with the French; the republicans favoured a partnership with the United Provinces.

Charles II's performance as a monarch disappointed Neville, especially in foreign policy terms. Yet, he also made a point that the Isle, and by implication the English motherland, had unused potential: its people. As Harrington had remarked, the people were the 'materials of a commonwealth'.[8] In Oceana they would help perpetuate the political system through their participation; on the Isle they only perpetuate the English race but have no obvious sense of purpose or direction. George Pines, the accountant, is obsessed with the propagation and numbering of his people. He even has a rota to impregnate his four women in turn, and is proud to report that they brought him thirteen, seven, fifteen and twelve children respectively. The first generation of children on the island amounts to 47 people, while the island population counts 1,789 at the end of George's life. Yet, the English islanders neither make anything of their geographically convenient situation off the European trading routes nor of their growing population. Contemporary economic theory, represented by the works of Petty and Graunt, stressed the importance of a strong population for national wealth creation. Petty in particular emphasized that it was 'the number, arts, and industry of [a] people, well united and governed', not the extent of a territory, that was responsible for 'the greatness and glory of a Prince'. Both 'Labour and Industry' and a country's geographical location held the key to success, while Locke's 'labour theory' would stress that the acquisition of land was justified by its cultivation and efficient use.[9] Neville's theory of colonization and wealth creation went beyond the mere possession of land. It was also about the efficiency of its cultivation, the use of labour and the trade with its excess produce. *The Isle* points towards colonial policies the Whigs would develop in more detail after 1689.[10] Yet, Neville implies that the English are not ready to embrace the task. The Pines suffer from laziness and 'idleness', and their favourite pastime is to 'lay abroad on Mossey Bankes' (12–12 [*sic* 13]), thus fulfilling the common stereotype among republicans that warmer climates produced inferior, effeminate peoples, unable to build up significant military or colonial power.

The Dutch in contrast do everything the English settlers have failed to do on their arrival at the island or any time since: they survey the land, take measurements, and assess the geography for accessibility for shipping, for fresh water supplies and natural resources, such as 'veins of Minerals' (22) in the ground. They appreciate the island's 'fertile' (21) soil, trees and fruits, and the suitability of the animal population for food provision. Most importantly, the Dutch know how to assert authority, discharging just 'three or four Guns' (26) to restore order on the island. In the light of contemporary works on colonialism, the Isle becomes an illustration of missed opportunities, or as Adam Beach puts it, a case study for 'English degeneracy and Dutch supremacy'.[11] However, Neville's work is not as profoundly pessimistic as Beach suggests. For the Isle of Pines is an island with potential for economic growth. It has everything it needs 'by ... Nature'. However, with 'the benefit of Art ... it would equal, if not exceed many of our Europian Countries' (21). The Dutch captain reassures the reader in his 'Post-Script' that 'time will make this Island known better to the world', if its inhabitants learn to make use of 'Natures abundance' (31). As much as the first institution of government with Prince Henry's law code brings some degree of political civilization, the 'art' of agriculture and the production of goods for trade would bring civilization in economic terms. Only if the English Pines transform their island to make it properly their own will they become known around the world and respected as a great power. The Isle thus remains a work in progress, a utopia in the making. Neville meanwhile calls on his English readers to reconsider their constitution at home and England's role in the wider world.

In our post-colonial age, the acquisition and economic exploitation of foreign territories has rightly come to be seen in a critical light. For seventeenth-century republicans, colonization was a way of propagating wealth, spreading ideologies of civilization, and of experimenting with alternative forms of government and utopian settlements. The competition for overseas territories was also a continuation of inner-European competition on a new scale. If the English Pines made this island their own by cultivation, and wholeheartedly entered into the colonial venture, the riches of the island would provide new opportunities for the export of agricultural products, shipping and trade. Neville's verdict was simple: the English would have to become more like the Dutch, or would eventually be overtaken by them and perish, marooned on the wide, open seas. It would be another few decades before English governments embraced this controversial challenge.

11

The Persian Moment in Denis Veiras's *History of the Sevarambians*

Cyrus Masroori and John Christian Laursen

*I should grow too prolix, were I to recite here all that is written
of this great Man, whose wise Conduct, and worthy Actions,
wou'd furnish Materials for many Volumes. I shall therefore pick out
some of the most remarkable and essential Parts of the History of
this happy People, who ascribe all their Felicity to the Care and
Prudence of their incomparable Legislator.*
*He was Persian by Birth, and of a very ancient Family, being descended
from the Parses, of whom there are still several branches in Persia,
distinguish'd by this Name from the Tartars, who possess'd themselves
of that ancient Kingdom. These Parses are the true Aborigines of the
Country, and have retain'd many of the Customs of their Ancestors, of
which, that of worshipping the Sun, and Fire, is one of the principal: For
they are not Mahometans, as the Sophi, and the rest of his Subjects are. So
that Sevarias, being born a Parsis, was brought up, from his very Infancy,
in this Religion of his Fathers. He was called, in his own Country, Sevaris
Ambarces, being the eldest Son of a Lord, whose Name was Alestan
Hosser Ambarces, who, among those of his Religion, was acknowledged
High Priest of the SUN. The Place of his Birth and Abode, was not far
from that Part of Persia which stretches along by the Gulph; where his
Family had maintain'd their Credit and Reputation during all the Wars,
and notwithstanding the Persecutions of the Tartars, till the time of this
Alestan; when it lost much of its ancient Splendor, by the malice of certain
Powerful Enemies which Envy had rais'd up against them.*[1]

The founder of the ideal city in Denis Veiras's *L'Histoire des Sevarambes* of 1677–9 was a Persian Zoroastrian. Part Three (1677–8) tells the story of Sevarias, a Zoroastrian aristocrat who is subject to persecution in Persia and flees to the south, eventually conquering Sevarambia in what is now Australia, settling there, and building a civilization where he rules as the Viceroy of the Sun. The questions cry out: Why a Persian? Why a Zoroastrian? What did the seventeenth century know about them? Why would a European writer attribute his utopia to a Persian?

Given the turmoil of the Reformation and continued religious tension, it is not surprising that religion occupies a central part in early modern utopian discourse. Religious violence was going to have to be suppressed if a utopia was going to be possible. But where most utopian authors of the time took it for granted that a utopia could be constructed within Christianity, Veiras offers an alternative religion capable of promoting and sustaining social coherence instead of causing the conflicts and corruption frequently associated with Christianity. He seems to suggest that while religion cannot be entirely rationalized, an ideal society demands a less irrational religion than Christianity.

This chapter shows how Veiras used exoticism from Persia as a foil for a subversive undermining of Christianity. We start with a brief mention of the references to Persia in Thomas More's path-breaking *Utopia* (1516), which set the model for later writers. Then we explore the travel literature available to Veiras, and draw attention to elements of it from which he may have drawn. And finally we expand upon the ways in which Veiras drew ideas about Persian religion from the neo-Platonists which enabled him to undermine Christianity. We conclude that Veiras's ideas about religion were closest of all to deists such as Herbert of Cherbury, and that he disagreed with Spinoza in fundamental ways.

Unfortunately, we know very little about Denis Veiras.[2] He was a French Huguenot who spent a number of years in England, where he was evidently a member of the Duke of Buckingham's circle and may have been an acquaintance of John Locke. The first version of Veiras's utopia was published in English as *The History of the Sevarites or Sevarambi* in two parts appearing in 1675 and 1679 respectively. From 1677 to 1679 the French version of the book, *L'Histoire des Sevarambes*, was published in five parts. *The History of the Sevarambians* (hereafter *Sevarambians*) is the English translation of this French version, first printed in London in 1738. That Veiras's utopia was well received is evident from Dutch, German, Italian and English translations and the responses to it by dozens of European intellectuals of the seventeenth and eighteenth centuries including Bayle, Leibniz, Montesquieu, Hume, Rousseau and Kant.

The first English version claims that the utopia is a part of Paradise transported 'upon the shoulders of Angels', but in *Sevarambians* the utopia is established by a Persian as a successor to a dystopia.[3] Its religion centres on worship of the sun; there is a Hymn to the Sun (225 f.), and the ruler rules as Viceroy of the Sun. And this Persian's utopia bears little resemblance to the real Persia at the time. It is more technologically advanced, such that this work has been taken as an early piece of science fiction. Aerial tramways cross the mountains and the author shows a special interest in irrigation, hydraulics and fountains. It is also a highly regulated society, with special attention to marriage and the regulation of sex; clothing that indicates rank; and equal living arrangements for everyone. Dispersed throughout the narrative are swashbuckling adventures and stories of romance and human passion.

There are only a few references to Persia in More's *Utopia*. In Book I his main character, Raphael Hythloday, says that he has travelled in Persia and praises some policies of the Polylerits, a 'well-governed nation' that paid tribute to the king of Persia in return for protection.[4] In Book II, he reports that the Utopians' language 'resembles Persian' (125) and that their supreme deity is 'known by all as Mithra', which many readers would have recognized as a Persian god (145). The association between Persians, sun worship and Mithra (or Mithras) was established as early as Herodotus (c.490 BC–425 BC), who wrote that the Persians 'worship the sun, moon, and earth, fire, water, and winds, which are their only original deities'.[5] Later, the Greek geographer Strabo (64 BC–c.24 AD) refers to Persian worship of the sun, 'whom they call Mithras'.[6] Greek and Roman understandings of Persian religion often associated it with fire and sun worship.[7]

Note that the Greek and Roman understanding was probably not very close to reality. The ancient Zoroastrians believed in Ahura Mazda as the Supreme God, and their texts are clear about the superiority of Ahura Mazda over Mithra.[8] What probably misled the Greeks was that there was often an association of Mithra with the Sun.[9] Also, worshipping the Sun was common among various ancient Middle Eastern people.

Christians admired Cyrus the Great of Persia for allowing the Jews in captivity in Babylon to return to Jerusalem.[10] However, Christians were naturally more hostile to Zoroastrianism and its legacy, and More must have known this. Justin (103–165 AD) labelled followers of Mithras 'wicked devils', accusing them of imitating Christians 'in the mysteries of Mithras'.[11] Archelaus (third century AD) added: 'Barbarian priest and crafty coadjutor of Mithras, you will only be a worshipper of the sun-god Mithras.'[12] Perhaps More did not elaborate on his utopia's Mithraic cult because he did not really mean to promote it as a religion: it was only a mirror.

Later sources available to More include the pioneering work of the neo-Platonist Marsilio Ficino (1433–99), who surveyed the ancient sources and asserted that Zoroaster was the first of six great theologians of which Plato was the last and greatest.[13] Giovanni Pico della Mirandola (1463–94) developed some of Ficino's ideas, using the divine inspiration of Zoroaster as a way of proving that pagan philosophy is a way to true wisdom.[14] More was undoubtedly influenced by the neo-Platonists, but his few and superficial references to Persia and Mithra make it unlikely that he was doing anything more than adding a touch of exoticism to the idealized mirror in which his contemporaries could recognize their weaknesses and his call for reform.

There were at least two bodies of literature on Persia and Zoroastrianism from after More's time that were available to Veiras. One was the travel literature, and this seems a likely source for some of his ideas. The second was the philosophical and theological work of erudite scholars such as Herbert of Cherbury's *De religione gentilium* (1663).[15]

The travel literature bloomed in the decades before Veiras. A French translation of a Spanish ambassador's report, *L'Ambassade de D. Garcias de Silva Figueroa en Perssee* of 1667, observed that

> there have remained a number of those ancient and true Persians who ... have ... not ceased to hold steadfastly to their original way of life, their customs and their religion. Thus they venerate to this day the sun, as did the Persians of old when their empire was the greatest in the world, and, following their example, they keep a fire always burning in their homes.[16]

Veiras may also have borrowed from *L'Ambassade de D. Garcias* the narratives of hunts and animal fights as entertainment in both versions of his book (84, 97, 174f.).[17]

In 1671 Jean Chardin referred in passing to the 'Guebres', or infidels – which is what the Muslims called the Zoroastrians – as 'the ancient Persians or Fire Worshippers', observing that 'they were a miserable sort of People, and under great distress'.[18] Chardin's book, *Le couronnement de Soleimaan, troisiéme Roy de Perse de cette nomme*, may have provided a model for other things in Veiras's book. The better part of the work is a description of court intrigue very much in a Tacitean or Machiavellian mode. Every person's decisions are made with self-interest in mind, and no-one's word is trustworthy. This is a feature of many of the vignettes in Veiras's work, ranging from the intrigues Sevarias uses to gain power (212ff.) to the very realistic and unromantic considerations a woman takes into account in choosing to be one of the wives of the Viceroy instead of remaining faithful to her betrothed (296ff.).

Other details also could have been lifted from Chardin. For example, the idea that in utopia sexual infidelity would be reflected in a person's face (60, 68) could have been taken from Chardin's description of venereal disease as that 'nauseous Distemper ... [that] displays itself in the Faces of the Diseased, and publishes with Ignominy their frequent Converse with lewd Women' (2). Veiras's Viceroy chooses the most beautiful women for his wives (294–9), just as the King of Persia 'caus'd all the handsom women to be taken up, and brought to his Haram' (114). The Persian King was styled 'the Lieutenant of the true Sovereign [God]' (34, 66), just as Sevarias does not call himself a king but the Viceroy of the Sun (229, 237, 252, etc.). In their inauguration, the Persians demand that 'his Majesty may always appear surrounded with glory like the Sun' (47). The late king of Persia is credited with respecting 'the Liberty of mens Consciences' (48), just as the Sevarambians do (301). Finally, the coronation speeches and descriptions of coronation and wedding ceremonies in Veiras echo the many such descriptions in Chardin's work.

At times, the Safavid kings imposed compulsory migration policies on minorities, including the Zoroastrians. This and other sorts of persecution led some Zoroastrians to flee to Surat and Gujarat in India, where they prospered. Henry Lord wrote about them in *A Display of Two Forraign Sects in the East Indies … Part II, The Religion of the Parsees* (1630), which was also available in French in Veiras's day as *Histoire de la religion … avec un traité de la Religion des anciens Persans ou Parsis* (1667). Here we have the spelling of the word that Veiras used to describe his Zoroastrians: Parsis (plural: Parses) (203, 205, etc.). Those who settled in Surat and Gujarat found more wealth and power than those who stayed home in Persia. The experience of these exiles is such a close parallel to Veiras's account that it may have been his source.

The other main body of work on Zoroastrianism available to Veiras was the scholarly neo-Platonism after Thomas More, which also drew on Marsilio Ficino and Giovanni Pico della Mirandola. Some of it remained Christian, like the Cambridge Platonists, but some of it eventually became what we now refer to as 'deism'. One of the key early figures in the latter movement was Edward Herbert of Cherbury, whose book, *De religione gentilium* (1663), might well be a source for Veiras. Chapter 4 is a survey of peoples who worshipped the sun, with substantial attention to Zoroastrians.[19] Herbert drew on G.J. Vossius's *De theologia gentilium* (1642), which argued that sun worship was the oldest form of religion.[20] Herbert also suggested his own minimum core of a universal religion, just as Veiras reported of both the public religion of the Sevarambians and of the intellectual, Scromenas (301–13, 353–8). The Platonic heritage is clear: Scromenas draws on Plato, but also on Pythagoras and other Greek, Arabian and Indian philosophers (353). For Herbert, the core beliefs are: there is a supreme God; this God should be worshipped; virtue and piety are the principal elements of that worship; we should repent of our sins; and we will be rewarded or punished in the next life. The core of the Sevarambians' religion is similar (301–13). Richard Baxter observed of Herbert what could also be observed of Veiras: there was no place for Christ in these accounts.[21] But things get worse for Christians: Scromenas's core beliefs include only the first four of Herbert's: there is no next life in his account (355).

It is worth observing that the tradition of sun-worshipping utopias also had an anti-Christian background: Julian the Apostate tried to make the sun the supreme god in order to undermine Christianity.[22] In any case, Herbert is credited with being the founder of English deism, and it is clear that Veiras follows him closely, if not exactly.

The question that the utopian authors of Veiras's era faced is this: given that modernity has unleashed unprecedented forces and opportunities with potential to build a substantially better life for Europeans, why is Europe experiencing turbulence unseen since the fall of Rome? It is in response to this question that Veiras, like a number of other utopian authors, finds himself compelled to turn to experiences other than those of modern Europe. In other words, if Europe, ravaged by war and persecution, is the dystopia, utopia can only be in faraway lands and rooted in other cultures.

At least in part, it is to find an alternative to this European dystopia that Veiras turns to Persia. The choice of a non-Christian and non-European to be the founder of the 'paradise on Earth' is apparently a vote of no confidence in modern Europeans. Further, the story is a daring rejection of the potential of Christianity to establish the ideal city. In More's *Utopia*, there is a mass conversion to Christianity upon introduction of that religion, and Bacon's *New Atlantis* is a Christian community. In Sevarambia, however, the population has been exposed to Christianity since the time of Giovanni but very few have converted to it (307–9). In fact, some shipwrecked Europeans choose to convert to the Sevarambian religion (358).

Our most ambitious claim is that Veiras may be using a Zoroastrian to criticize Christianity as a whole. Stroukaras, the ruler of Veiras's dystopia, for example, claims to be the Son of the Sun, the supreme deity of the land. Stroukaras and his priests commit acts of deception, debauchery and cruelty similar to those that some Popes and Cardinals of the sixteenth and seventeenth centuries were accused of by Protestants. But if the analogy of Stroukaras as Son of the Sun to the Christian Son of God is intentional (and it is hard to imagine otherwise), Veiras's criticism is directed at Christianity as a whole and not just at one or another Christian sect. Also, similar to the way that the injustice and intolerance of the Muslim Persians against the Zoroastrian minority deprived Persia of a rare talent like Sevarias, persecution in Christian Europe had deprived it of many talented individuals like Veiras. In fact, Veiras could be comparing Christianity (the religion of Stroukaras) to Persian Mithraism (the religion of Sevarias).

Neo-Platonism includes Christian Platonism, but that is clearly not what Veiras has in mind. Cambridge Platonist Henry More's *An Antidote Against Atheism* (1651) cited apparitions of men fighting on the ground and in the sky as proof of a supernatural spirit world, drawing on Maccabees, Josephus, English chronicles and contemporary sources.[23] When these 'reports cannot be suspected to be in subserviency to any Politick design, [they] ought in reason to be held true, when there have been many profest Eye-witnesses', he wrote (244). Veiras's narrator reports that the Sevarambians figured out that such apparitions were optical illusions, reflections from the clouds of distant events, and thus not proof of any spirit world (310–11). This sort of observation positions Veiras not as a Christian, but as a deist Platonist.

Neo-Platonic deism is not the same as Spinozism. Jonathan Israel has asserted that Veiras's story is 'a Spinozist utopia'.[24] There are elements of agreement, such as the critique of miracles and priestcraft. But Veiras is certainly not fully Spinozist: Spinoza would presumably not approve of his endorsement of censorship, communism, political absolutism and political Platonism. That makes it more likely that he is best understood as a neo-Platonist deist, not a Spinozist.

Denis Veiras's *The History of Sevarambians* is not only one of the longest, most innovative and most articulated utopian accounts of early modernity, it is arguably the boldest account of that genre in the seventeenth century. Veiras reconstructs Persians and Zoroastrianism not to justify European superiority or pave the way for colonialism, but to suggest that non-Europeans are as capable as Europeans of creating an ideal society. In doing so, he overcomes Eurocentric prejudice.

At the same time, as a neo-Platonist Veiras demands that Christianity be subject to the tests of reasonableness that were the intellectual spirit of his time. While most of his contemporaries either rather unsuccessfully attempted to demonstrate the reasonableness of various Christian principles or excused Christianity from the test of reason, Veiras implied that in fact Christianity was not capable of passing such a test, and therefore was unfit to be the religion of a society where reason rules.

12

Nature and Utopia in Morelly's *Code De La Nature*

Claudio De Boni

*The only vice that I perceive in the universe is Avarice; all the
others, by whatever name they be known, are only variations, degrees,
of this one; it is the Proteus, the Mercury, the basis, the vehicle,
of all the vices. Analyze vanity; fatuousness; pride; ambition;
duplicity; hypocrisy; dishonesty; break down most of our sophistic
virtues into their component parts, and they all resolve themselves
into this subtle and pernicious element, the desire to have.
You will even find it at the bottom of disinterestedness...
I dare to conclude here that it is almost mathematically demonstrable
that all division of goods, whether equal or unequal, and that
all private property whatever these portions is, in all societies, what
Horace calls 'material for the highest evil'. All moral and political
phenomena, are the effects of this pernicious cause; through it
can be explained and resolved all theorems or problems about the origin
or advancement of, the connection or affinity between, the different
virtues and vices, disorders and crimes; about the true motives behind
good or bad actions; about all the resolutions or perplexities of the
human will; about the depravity of the passions; about the ineffectuality
of precepts and laws that are meant to contain them; about the very
technical faults in these lessons; finally, about all the monstrous
productions that come from the aberrations of the mind
or the heart. I say that the grounds for all these defects can be seen
in the general tendency of legislators to allow the primary link of all
sociability to be broken by the usurpation of the resources that should
belong in common to all humanity.*[1]

Morelly's *Code de la Nature* has long been read in a controversial way, both for criticism and historiography. The work was published in 1755 anonymously, a common strategy to escape censorship, and with the attributes of a fiction, as was also common at the time. But the combination of anonymity and fiction led immediately to heated debate about the authorship and significance of the work.

The Abbé Raynal was of the opinion that the encyclopaedist Toussaint was the author, while, for Grimm, it was a work by Rousseau, interpreting the criticism of civilization as similar to that in Rousseau's *Essay on Inequality*. *La France Littéraire* identified Diderot as the writer of the *Code*, noting the text's radicalization of the idea of equality which was then spreading among followers of the Enlightenment. Only in the nineteenth century, and more definitively in the twentieth, was the author established as being Etienne-Gabriel Morelly, who at that time was a teacher at a local school in a small town in Champagne: Vitry-le-François.[2]

Within Morelly's *oeuvre*, the *Code* opened a new debate, noteworthy in the history of utopias, but which can only be touched on here. *Code de la Nature* was indeed based on a strict communism, but it presented a political model different from the one celebrated in Morelly's other utopian work, *Basiliade*, published just two years earlier.[3] Some of the themes of Morelly's *weltanschauung* were also expressed in *Basiliade*: the belief that human nature has a drive towards harmony; faith in a form of social organization that would make men mutually supportive and moderate in their consumption of the goods provided by Nature itself; and a prospect of the end of conflicts between men, primarily due to the elimination amongst them of the right to private property. Nevertheless, the political government of the ideal society defined in *Basiliade* was not a communist one. According to the most widespread political theories of the eighteenth century, the best ruler was an enlightened Prince. The Prince was always connected with his citizens, more as an educating father rather than as a dictator, and his main task consisted in reducing government to simple legislation, in line with natural principles. Within two years, however, and in a surprisingly swift manner, Morelly lost faith in the political schemes typical of the Enlightenment, and switched to a coherent and total communistic system in the *Code de la Nature*. At the beginning of the *Code*, he explained that the fundamental purpose of *Basiliade*, which was the same as the *Code*, was the goodness of all humankind. If in the earlier novel the Prince stood out in the character of a prince-hero, it was mainly a matter of genre, because in that case, the novel was an allegorical tale.

Let us return to the *Code*. It is divided into two parts. In the first, and longest, Morelly presented the key elements of his vision of the world, in the form of a philosophical essay. In turn, this philosophical section could be divided into two parts: one presenting the elements of the natural order, and the other showing that the distortions of history have been the cause of the human separation from an original harmony. All of this had a conclusion, almost like an appendix, which was the real focus and the real novelty of Morelly's argument: the 'Model of legislation conforming with the intentions of Nature' (189). Here he presented a perfect society with an ideal system of laws which, for the first time in the utopian genre, came very close to the drafting of an imaginary Bill of Rights.

In line with the utopian tradition, the *Code* is constructed as a pedagogical text, but it begins by recalling some of the topics the author had already dealt with in his early works on education.[4] His aim was to combine empirical and utilitarian views of human action in the hope that the individual can be motivated to pursue happiness as expressed within a harmonious social framework. The starting point of this theory lay in his conviction that both the ideas and the behaviour of men depended upon external, sensory impressions. Using an image similar to the one coined by his contemporary Condillac about an inanimate statue, in both his early writings and in his mature work, Morelly argued that, before receiving sensations from external motions, the human soul was like 'a canvas on which the painter has not drawn any sign yet'.[5] Ideas and actions did not come from abstract rationality, but from the concrete repetition of impressions that affect humans, causing pleasure or pain, according to circumstances. The formation of ideas depended on such sensations. As a result of human ability to remember and to catalogue the sensations which had been previously experienced, we were able to foresee the likely effects of our own future actions. The stimulation of feelings also depended on these sensations, enabling one to obtain as much pleasure as possible from one's own behaviour, while minimizing pain. Human nature had not only provided us with a rational system, but also with passions, which continuously drove us towards the pursuit of happiness.

This quest for happiness is both common to humankind and productive of social cohesion. Love for oneself might be the first feeling perceived, driving one to protect one's own existence and to make it as pleasant as possible. Nevertheless, humans showed a significant diversity when it came to the objects that made them happy, depending on their age, mental and physical character, tastes, environment and social organization. Such differences are usually a matter of primary concern for utopian writers. Morelly, on the contrary, underlined the propitious overlapping of unity and variability in human nature. The basis of a society founded on a common law was our common desire for happiness. Because individuals have different expectations, it is less likely that there will not be enough goods to satisfy their diverse wants. In the previous century, Hobbes had instead depicted this situation as one of inevitable conflict for the same goods between members of the human race. So, for Morelly, passions in themselves are not in themselves bad: Nature had endowed us with them to encourage us to take care of ourselves. In the context of the Enlightenment, he believed that passions should be moderate, and should not induce behaviours adverse to the ones of our fellows and to the social order.

Hence people were equal because they all had feelings (the first being love for oneself) and they all had needs. This egalitarian situation made people understand the rightness of the idea of equal rights and the necessity of shared work to meet everyone's needs. The different conditions of people (tastes, abilities, strength, etc.) made everyone's desires vary according to the specific situation. This, in turn, encouraged a mutual exchange between individuals, so that no one should be willing to keep things they did not need. What was not useful for one person could be of use to another and vice versa. So it may happen that the sum of desires at a certain point might be greater than the actual resources available. But this is not a bad thing in itself. It could be the key to cooperation among people, who understand that, only by working together more and more, can they easily achieve what they need. Nature wills that

> the sorrow and the difficulty of attending to our needs, since when acting alone they are beyond our reach, make us understand the importance of turning to others for help. It inspires affection, if it is helpful. Hence our distaste for the abandonment of loneliness, and our love of the pleasures and for the benefits of being part of community and society. (25–6)

In Morelly's text, the idea of natural harmony combined with the critique of history, comparable to that in Rousseau's *Essay on Inequality*, which was written in the same period. The natural order, as a combined satisfaction of everyone's needs, may be known by people in a state of nature, but it has been swept away by a civilization progressively based on principles far from natural ones. As in Rousseau, demographic expansion was seen as the basis of such a negative process. Increasing in numbers, humanity had to deal with scarce resources and then often left their homes in order to be able to survive. But in so acting they discovered and somehow absorbed the spirit of competition instead of collaboration. In this way, they lost the concept of natural relationships. During this long historical process, the vices of individualism replaced feelings of solidarity. In Morelly's opinion, greed or avarice was the worst of these vices. By recognizing private property, greed had been consolidated in legal systems. So, in the *Code* such greed is subject to attack. This was clear in the passage quoted at the beginning of this chapter. It could also be seen in the passages where Morelly argued against those legislators, past and present, who had failed their task as educators and guides to their people. By doing so,

> they have stifled the causes of affection that are necessary to create the link between human beings, as well as having turned mutual agreement and mutual aid into undesirable divisions aimed at separating the great body of humankind into different parts. Besides they have stoked the fire of a burning greed and whetted the appetite of an insatiable and demanding avarice, by the several agitations opposing each other stimulated by those confused and divided parts. (35–6)

As is typical for many Utopians, Morelly's vision of past history is as a series of errors which pit individuals one against the other. Assuming that it would be possible to escape from this, the only way out might be a kind of return to original Nature as a source of truth.

People are the corrupt ones, not Nature. Man abandons the Truth, but the Truth never vanishes. And everything disputed in this respect would never affect my thesis; every nation, wild or not, can or could be redirected to the laws of Nature, maintaining what they allow and eliminating what they disapprove. (45)

In order to improve humankind, such a return to the natural order would bring together three tools disastrously separated by history. The first of these is Politics, as the capacity to lead individuals towards social harmony; the second is Legislation, because the truth has to become a codified norm; and the third is Morality, as a criterion leading human acts to the common good.

On the basis of such a critique of civilization contrasted with the natural order, Morelly concluded his work with the drafting of a legal system, laying the conceptual foundations of a perfect communistic society. At the same time, he presented this social ideal through legislation embracing all aspects of the usual planning of utopias: government, economic organization, employment, the cultural environment and social customs. Three laws, 'fundamental and sacred', underwrite Morelly's perfect society. In his opinion 'they are designed to cut the roots of all the vices and evils of society'. They are the abolition of private property, except for goods for purely personal use; the consideration of every citizen as a 'public individual, fed, supported and employed at public expense' (190); in return, third, for the duty of work as everyone's contribution to public necessity.

On such foundations, the new, natural society was characterized by the centralized distribution of the common product and by a common obligation to work applied to the production of only those goods specifically necessary for its citizens. Work as a duty had an educational meaning as well as economic implications. All citizens, at least for one specific period during their lives, devoted themselves to agricultural production, in a form most suited to the needs of the community. Morelly's ideal society was, however, neither poor, nor purely rural, as many cities and artisanal activities are encouraged. Nevertheless, any aspiration to luxury was excluded. Every form of social expression had to rest on egalitarian values producing a uniformity extending to architectural and urban structures, based on the geometric regularity of the road lines and of the building sizes.

The system of political representation was based on both democratic and paternalistic principles. Representation had its origin in the family and in the political role of the household leader. It extended to local institutions and to the Senate which was identified as the focus of the State. The social importance of the family was emphasized by legislation specifically dedicated to the marital system, subjecting marriage and divorce to strict regulation. In selecting those who would take political roles, the principle of election from below was important, but managed in such a way as to give prevalence to seniority. Indeed, it was not the function of political authority to outline new directions in the management of public affairs, but to preserve what the laws of Nature prescribed. For such a role the wisdom and the prudence bestowed by age were regarded as more suitable. Morelly, as a pedagogue, described the educational system of his ideal society in depth. Removing young men from the family was fundamental. They were first to be educated in boarding schools and then in the fields and in the factories. Like many other utopias, the *Code* described the social welfare services very fully, covering public health, care for the elderly, care for the disabled, etc. The result was a social system transmitting a feeling of great organic unity to the reader; maybe too much. The account of the secondary variability among people given in Morelly's first writings seems to give way to a desire for uniformity in which differences of status and of preferences between individuals dissolved into a single, general idea of happiness. This is a feature of utopian writing that we could observe not only in Morelly but even in many other utopias.

Morelly definitely shares the tendency of utopian writers to an analytic and complete planning of a society alternative to the existing one. His effectiveness lies primarily in shifting the description of a perfect world into the language of legislation, the highest form of morality and politics (whether reformist or revolutionary) that is condensed in the writing of a new constitution. It was along these lines of thought that Babeuf was to take the *Code de la Nature* as a model of action (even while believing that Diderot was its author). In reference to the social ideas of the Enlightenment, Engels would reserve for Morelly, along with Mably, a very important role in the long line of 'precursors' of contemporary socialism from the authors of Renaissance utopias to the contributions of Saint-Simon, Fourier and Owen.[6] In a similar way, a great historian of the late nineteenth century, André Lichtenberger, would consider the *Code* to be 'the great socialist book of the eighteenth century'.[7]

13

Sinapia, A Political Journey to the Antipodes of Spain

Miguel A. Ramiro Avilés

Veracity or verisimilitude, this republic is very worthy of praise, since it has succeeded better than might have been expected or, at least, has set an example for those who wish to succeed.[1]

*T*he *Description of Sinapia, a peninsula in terra australis* (henceforth *Sinapia*) summarizes the anxiety and pain felt by the authors of the Spanish Enlightenment contemplating the decadence of their country, its institutions and people. It reflects an Enlightenment interest in the improvement both of the human condition and of forms of government. *Sinapia* is an account of an imaginary Spain located in *terra australis* where the best remedies for the reform of souls and institutions have been implemented. It is an invitation to consider the distance between how things are in Spain and how things might be in its antipodes, Sinapia.

Sinapia is a rare text because, although it is not the first Spanish utopia, like More's *Utopia* it uses law and the formal institutions of government as a basis on which to build the ideal society. The text was lost until the 1970s when it was discovered in the archives of Pedro Rodríguez, Count of Campomanes. Its close links with *Utopia*, and some other utopian texts, are most obvious in its reiteration of common ideas or its reproduction of passages, a practice which lessens the sense of its own originality – '[the prince] directs surplus population to the colonies, and orders the return of colonists when population declines' (91/20).[2] The text's long disappearance means that even today we do not know who the author is or when the work was written.

Scholars have discussed whether Campomanes was the author or if one of his close circle wrote *Sinapia*.[3] We should perhaps recall that utopian writers have often been close to power. The discussion in Book I of *Utopia* is on precisely this: whether philosophers should be the counsellors of kings and princes.[4] James Harrington and Gerrard Winstanley both dedicated their utopias to Oliver Cromwell.[5] Utopian writers often formulate a vision of the best society and hope to insinuate their ideas by indirect means, as Thomas More proposed in *Utopia*. They long to find an educated or enlightened prince or patron who will assume the responsibility of implementing their proposals.[6] In *Sinapia's* case that might be Campomanes, who was President of the Council of Castille from 1786 to 1791 and planned, with Pablo de Olavide, Intendent of Seville, the repopulation of the Sierra Morena, restoring a traditional agrarian society of small peasants.[7]

The passage selected above contains, I think, two ideas which may be useful in reading *Sinapia* afresh. First, it is the author's intention that a fictional story – the description of the institutions and customs of the republic of Sinapia – should be considered a true or plausible account, one possessed of verisimilitude. Second, the way in which Sinapia is socially and institutionally arranged should be thought of as an example to be followed in undertaking the reforms necessary to transform reality in Spain.

The author does not want *Sinapia* to be read 'as a novel' (70/1) in which monsters and unlikely situations are described since the aim of the book is not to discover man-eating Lestrygonians but something even more strange and unusual – one republic wisely governed.[8] His desire is that *Sinapia* be considered as a true story and a practical model in ethics and politics. Maybe he wanted to evade the censorship exercised by the Council of Castille and the Inquisition and maybe this is the reason why he made use of the literary form – making his utopia look like an avatar for the genre of the novel.[9] In those same years, José de Cadalso confessed: '[T]he spaniard who publishes his works today writes them very carefully, and he trembles when he manages to print them … At that point many men, whose compositions would be useful for them and confer honour on their country, hide them.'[10]

Sinapia could be read as a sketch of a social and political culture turned inside-out, one where the author hides behind the mask of an impartial critic engaged in the analysis of the customs and practices followed in Sinapia. Impartiality was a quality much appreciated by Spain's Enlightenment authors because they considered, to use Cadalso's words again, that 'this just balance is what assures us that a man has the full use of his reason'.[11]

The utopian literary form allowed the author of *Sinapia* to avoid presenting his readers with reform policies to be legitimated and adopted. Instead, the readers were offered a political project already implemented and legitimized by the rationality, fairness and justice of its arrangements as they were vividly experienced in the lives and characters of the populace. The republic of Sinapia was a microcosm set in motion as an entire and functioning society, as complex as the real macrocosm, and with a plausible life (verisimilitude). 'The method of describing a functioning society, with all its components and details, only emphasizes their practical and realistic intentions: the fabricated authenticity makes ideas into concrete, believable facts.'[12]

Verisimilitude was achieved both by populating the account with real facts[13] and by proposing reforms which depended neither on the transformation of human nature and the natural environment nor on supernatural force but which were solely dependent on human capacity and activity. In this sense, it was a hypothesis about the possibilities of human action.[14] It was possible to implement the reforms described, to imagine them as possible options confronting the *status quo*, even if they could not be accommodated in current conceptual language and would not be adopted as active policies in the current political climate.[15] The utopian text then inhabits a space in which it was free to develop a theory transformative of the material conditions which could underwrite fundamental social change.[16]

Verisimilitude, or plausibility, then went along with *estrangement* because one object (the kingdom of Spain) was represented in such a way (as republic of Sinapia) that it could be easily recognized but, at the same time, it was unfamiliar to the readers due to the scale of social, political and legal change.[17] For example, the author observed that people raised under a system of private property ('mine and yours') could barely be persuaded that people could live in perfect community and perfect equality (70/1).

The plausibility of its proposals reflects the political content of *Sinapia*. It is a wisely governed republic, with implications for the reform of the social, economic, religious, political and legal conditions of contemporary Spain. It is a union of diverse peoples – 'malay, peruvian, chinese and persian' (72/3) – in which 'the monarch is the law, the nobles are the magistrates and the people are the families' (86/13). *Sinapia*'s author follows the republican formula of a perfect government combining the rule of the one, the few and the many, where nobility is not hereditary but by election, and magistrates, including the prince, are chosen 'by the nomination of those who are to obey and by the election of those who are to command' (119/28).

Founded by the persian prince Sinap, the persian patriarch Codabend and the chinese philosopher Si-Ang,[18] the republic of Sinapia, previously named Bireia, is not only antipodean to Spain in a geographical sense – 'the climate of this peninsula is like Spain's but the seasons are reversed, with the longest day of the year about Christmas and the shortest about the festival of Saint John' (72/2) – but also socially, economically, religiously, politically and legally. The Australasian location facilitates its conversion into the perfectly reflected inversion of its model.

That reversal is indicated from the very first pages. In Sinapia it is shocking that European societies follow the teachings of Tacitus and Machiavelli in their politics, forgetting that 'the practice of Christian virtue is better suited to building a flourishing republic and a blessed nation' (69/1). Christianity had arrived with the Persians, 'who brought the light of Gospel and true politics with it' (73/3).

The prince presides over the Senate and the General Assembly, and the patriarch is the head of the Synod. These three institutions are entrusted with all important government functions: legislation; the sending and receiving of embassies; the making of war, peace and alliances; the naturalization of foreigners; the liberation of slaves; approving and monitoring all office-holders, including the prince; allowing or forbidding all types of innovation and publication; establishing new colonies; and regulating the welfare of the people and the shortage or abundance of things (90–1/20, 110/25). The reform of the customs, canons and laws shows that in Sinapia the *leggi* can be changed but the *ordini* remain unchangeable; a certain flexibility is possible while the fundamental laws remain unaltered. Some practices against the *ordini* had been attempted 'but this had been checked by prompt punishment of the few who had this opinion, because since childhood they are well-educated in the advantages of this form of government' (134/33).

Despite its possible side effects, science is very important in the republic of Sinapia:

> This College has really been of great utility to the nation, because, by their means, every day they make advances in natural sciences to a point which will be difficult to believe in Europe, with very useful inventions for the conservation and alleviation of human life, closing the doors to harmful innovations and inventions that could be spread by communication with foreigners, while, at the same time, acquiring an adequate knowledge of all the works of merit of the other nations ... and, with the help of the translations that are allowed with great prudence ... saving the republic from every thing that is harmful and useless.[19] (126–7/30)

One of the distinguishing features of Sinapia is that 'mine and yours is cast out' because private property is seen as the root cause of every social dispute. For this reason, they have formal institutions to provide the people with 'whatever they need' (91/21). At the end of the book, the author defends the community of goods against those who could use Aristotle's ideas saying that the power of education in Sinapia and the example of the parents and magistrates are the key elements (132/33).

Another important aspect of Sinapia is the reform it has undergone to make the Christian religion 'rational and pious' (75/3). In particular, the training and election of its priests, who must have served as deacons for ten years, guarantees their fluency in Hebrew and Greek, and their command of Holy Writ and ecclesiastical history (94/22). In Sinapia 'the christian religion is the only faith but one without hyprocrisy, superstition or vanity' (93/22) and they strive to restore primitive Christianity as embodied in 'the discipline observed in the third and fourth centuries'. It is forbidden to probe into the mysteries of the faith and people must be content to simply believe them, 'without indulging their curiousity'. Thanks to these reforms, 'religion [is] free of error and superstition. Care is taken to avoid all novelty and tenuousness in the doctrines of faith. They escape any kind of violence and excessive roughness in their religious discipline and limit the clergy to only the essential, and those proven, learned, without private possessions and employed only in the ministry' (133/33).

Another principal area of reform is that of the structure and laws of the republic: '[B]uilding the settlement and laws of their republic, they were prudent legislators introducing reforms not at a blow, which was impossible, but step by step' (76/3). With legal and institutional transformation, the causes of many crimes disappeared, but they remain necessary tools. The solution is not the absence of laws (*anomia*) but new, fairer laws and institutions. The utopian solution is to simplify the complexity of the legal system, creating legal certainty by a schematic system of laws. The people are instructed in their laws every day in the morning (103/24) so that everyone knows the rules which govern their lives and to which they owe their social peace (99/23). Sinapia is a law-based utopia where there is *eunomia* because the system comprises few laws, which must be published and clearly written in the vernacular so that everybody can understand them.[20]

> The book of Sinapian law, made by the three founders of the state and supplemented and amended by the General Assembly of the nation (which alone has this authority) is written in the native language, in a pure style, and in free verse. The laws are brief, clear, giving no cause for contention but commanding and forbidding absolutely and the date of the law's origin is noted in the margin. Whenever they add a law, another is repealed, in order not to increase the number to be observed.

The interpretation of doubtful laws is done by the Senate but such decisions are valid only for one particular case and cannot be appealed to in other cases in the future (116/26). Legal rules in the law-based Utopia are usually interpreted in the simplest way and literally, 'the bare letter of the law'.

In the administration of justice, they draw a distinction between ecclesiastical and civil jurisdictions: 'Any jurisdiction exercised by prelates, whether over the laity or the clergy, is restricted to matters of conscience and the spiritual penalties of excommunication or privation of clerical status. In civil cases everyone is subject to the magistrates' (96/22). The tempo of justice is reinvigorated: '[A]ll judgements are summary, circumstantial evidence is taken as proof and witnesses are under oath, and for the slightest offence they can be condemned, without appeal, to perpetual slavery' (114/26). The anonymous author has a good knowledge of court proceedings because he knows that proof derived from circumstantial evidence should not be adequate to condemn anyone, and he resolves the problem of perjury with a very hard penalty. Judges cannot increase or diminish the punishments set by the laws (115/26). They can only apply the law, being, as Montesquieu stated, 'the mouth that pronounces the words of the law, mere passive beings, incapable of moderating either its force or rigour'.[21]

The rationality of the legal system can also be seen in the proportionality, defended by Beccaria, between crimes and punishments, applied equally to slaves and foreigners, and the gravity of the crime also influences the right of appeal against the penalty's imposition. They have almost succeeded in dispensing with capital punishment and have prohibited torture, judging it 'inhuman and uncertain' (114/26).

The other cornerstone of the republic of Sinapia is education, on which depends 'the conservation and the well-being of the republic' (116/27). The author professes a belief in the power of education and knowledge to mould better people and thus a better society.[22] Sinapia is inhabited by people who, in the main, voluntarily and spontaneously follow the rules, leaving only a minority of recalcitrants. This kind of general observance of the laws allows them to be seen as no more than customary behaviour. Usually, law-based utopias do not seek to gain compliance with the laws through force as a permanent instrument, because such a strategy could weaken the legitimacy and stability of the system in the long term. Its aspiration is rather that the people should agree with the content of the laws, an objective which could be achieved by developing an educational system infused with the same principles. The emphasis here is on the importance of duty: 'To realise genuine honour and true delight ... can only be achieved when our conscience is assured that all our duty has been done' (134/33).

Moderation, fairness and the subordination of the self to society are the norms which are defended in Sinapia. The idea of happiness for everybody, as a goal attainable through mutual understanding, prevails. 'All doubt comes to an end when we consider the aim that this republic has in its foundation – to live with moderation, devotion and fairness in this world awaiting the promised bliss with the glorious coming of our great God, so that no means are more appropriate than life in common, equality, moderation and work' (70/1). *Sinapia* is, therefore, one product of the Enlightenment but in Spain that had not the same reach as elsewhere in Europe – 'the reception of a more critical Enlightenment discourse was not easy for those who kept abreast of the new ideas in Spain. Often alien ideas had to be decontaminated or tranformed'.[23] *Sinapia* illustrates the contradiction besetting Spanish Enlightenment authors: intellectual loyalty to the ideals of the Enlightenment as against emotional loyalty to the national tradition. The author seems to look outwards from Spain in search of critical norms but he is also looking towards Spain as the only context where he can find some personal and human identity.[24]

14

Condorcet's Utopianism: Faith in Science and Reason

K. Steven Vincent

If man is able to predict, with almost complete assurance, the phenomena of which he knows the laws; and if, even when these laws are unknown to him, he is able, because of the experience of the past, to foresee, with great probability, the events of the future; why would one regard as a fanciful project, tracing, with some pretense to truth, the picture of the future destinies of the human species on the basis of its history? The sole foundation for belief in the natural sciences is this idea that the general laws, both known and unknown, which organize the phenomena of the universe, are necessary and constant; why should this principle be less true for the development of the intellectual and moral faculties of man, than it is for the other operations of nature? Finally, while some opinions, formed because of the experience of the past, relative to objects of the same order, are the sole rule of conduct for the wisest of men, why should the philosopher be prohibited from supporting his conjectures on this same basis, provided that he does not attribute to them a certainty superior to that which is justified by the number, the constancy, and the accuracy of his observations?

Our hope for the future condition of the human race is able to be reduced to three important points: the destruction of inequality between nations; the progress of equality within each nation; finally, the real perfection of man...

The time will come, therefore, when the sun will no longer shine on the earth on any but free men, who recognize no master but their own reason; when tyrants and slaves, priests and their stupid or hypocritical instruments will no longer exist except in history and in the theaters; when one will think of them only in order to pity their victims and their dupes; in order to support ourselves in a useful vigilance by thinking of the horror of their excesses; in order to recognize and to stifle, under the weight of reason, the first germs of superstition and of tyranny, if ever they dare to reappear.

In perusing the history of societies, we shall have had the occasion to observe that often there exists a great difference between the rights that

*the law recognizes for citizens and the rights that they actually enjoy;
between the equality that is established by political institutions and
that which exists among individuals: we shall have noticed that this
difference has been one of the principal causes of the destruction of
liberty in ancient republics, of the thunderstorms that troubled them, of
the weaknesses that delivered them to foreign tyrants.*

*These differences have three principal causes: the inequality of wealth;
the inequality of the conditions between those for whom the means of
subsistence is assured for themselves and is transmitted to his family,
and those, on the other hand, for whom the means of subsistence is
dependant on the length of life, or sooner on that part of life during
which he is capable of work; finally, the inequality of education.*

*It will be necessary therefore to show that these three species of real
inequality should continually diminish, without however disappearing;
because they have some natural and necessary causes, that it would
be absurd and dangerous to wish to destroy; and one would not even
be able to try to make the effects of them entirely disappear without
opening up even more fertile sources of inequality, without carrying to
the rights of man more direct and fatal blows ...*

*The various causes of equality do not act in an isolated manner;
they unite, combine, mutually sustain each other, and their combined
effect results in an action that is stronger, surer, and more constant. If
instruction was more equal, it would give birth to a greater equality
in industry, and therefore in wealth; and equality of wealth would
contribute necessarily to equality of education; while the equality
between nations and within each nation would be mutually reinforcing.*

*Finally, well-directed education corrects the natural inequality of
abilities, rather than strengthening it, just as good laws remedy the
natural inequality of the means of subsistence; and just as in societies
where institutions have realized this equality, liberty, though subject to
a regular constitution, will be more widespread, more complete than in
the independence of the savage life. Thus, the social art has fulfilled its
goal, to assure and to extend to all the enjoyment of common rights, to
which they are called by nature.*

*The real advantages that ought to result from this progress, of which
one comes to have an almost certain hope, are not able to have any
other end than the absolute perfection of the human species; since,
to the extent that diverse genres of equality are established to better
provide for our needs, for a more extensive education, for a more
complete liberty, the more this equality will be real, the more it will
embrace almost all those truly interested in the happiness of mankind.
It is thus by examining the progression and the laws of this perfecting
that we shall be able to know the extent or limit of our hopes.*[1]

Condorcet's utopianism was built on his faith in the power of human reason and science, on his belief that social and political reform could be placed on as firm a basis as the natural sciences, and on his conviction that modern history would witness the inscription of humanity's dreams and hopes. Condorcet believed that the methodology emerging with the scientific revolution – in particular observation and mathematics – would lead to progress of our understanding of the world and, beyond this, to inevitable improvement of the condition of humans on earth. He had a roseate vision of human nature and human rationality, which provided the foundation for a resolute confidence in the cumulative dynamics of progress, and the basis for a future-oriented vision of human perfectibility. Frank Manuel cogently captures the utopian aspects of such claims when he writes: 'The leap from a rationalist statement of scientific methodology to wishing is not so rare in the science of society ... but the ingenuousness of the transition in Condorcet is truly disarming.'[2]

Condorcet's faith in the sociopolitical application of science and reason was present from his first writings and speeches. In an address delivered to the *Académie Française* on 21 February 1782, for example, he expressed confidence in the ability of humankind to discover truth and to progressively extinguish darkness and error, proclaiming: 'It is true that ignorance and error still breathe, but these monsters, the most formidable enemies of man's happiness, bring with them the mark of mortality which has struck them, and even their cries, which frighten you, only prove how sure and terrible are the blows they have received.'[3] Such faith in progress grew as Condorcet became familiar with the calculus of probabilities and confident that this could be used to subject political decisions and the contingencies of life to mathematical rule. He came to call this new science 'social mathematics'.[4] As David Williams has pointed out, there was a 'crucial linkage between his mathematical researches on probability theory and his non-mathematical essays and treatises on political, social, constitutional and economic issues'.[5] During the early phases of the Revolution, Condorcet attempted unsuccessfully to get accepted constitutional and educational reforms based on his understanding of 'social mathematics' that, he believed, would channel passionate popular political agitation into a hierarchy of assemblies that would allow enlightened rational choice to emerge.[6]

Condorcet's confidence in the cumulative dynamics of progress was expressed most starkly in his *Sketch for a Historical Survey of the Progress of the Human Mind* written while in hiding during the radical phase of the French Revolution. In this work, he claimed that 'there is no term to the perfection of human faculties; that the perfectibility of man is truly indefinite; and that progress of this perfectibility, henceforth independent of any power that might wish to stop it, has no other limit than the duration of the globe upon which nature has thrown us'.[7] He goes on to argue, as the excerpt from this work printed above reveals, that 'the future condition of the human race can be reduced to three important points: the destruction of inequality between nations; the progress of equality within each nation; finally, the real perfection of man'[8].

Belief in progress, underpinned by a belief in science and reason, was not unusual during the late eighteenth century. Many of Condorcet's contemporaries of the late-Enlightenment had high hopes for science and reason. Most, like Condorcet, did not endorse Rousseau's attack on the arts and sciences, and rejected his dystopic view of modern humanity's descent into inequality and *amour propre*. Belief in the efficacy of science was especially strong in the ranks of Physiocrats, also known as the *économistes*, a group of thinkers who had a deep and enduring influence on Condorcet. The Physiocrats claimed that they were able to establish scientifically the key elements of economic doctrine, and argued that this science proved that only agriculture (rather than manufacturing and trade) produced value, and that the function of government was to protect property and limit intervention in commerce. Condorcet was deeply impressed with Physiocratic scientism, and with the general claim that it was possible to discover 'perpetual and immutable laws' (the phrase is that of François Quesnay).[9] He was a close ally of Turgot, a Physiocrat who, as Controller-General from 1774 to 1776, introduced a series of reforms that liberalized the grain trade, suppressed the guilds and more generally undermined the historically sanctioned power of the *parlements* and other traditional bodies of French Old Regime society.

Condorcet was exceptional, however, in the degree to which his utopian vision became the filter for assessing historical becoming. In his *Sketch*, the ultimate significance of historical eras and individuals is judged from the perspective of the improvements already achieved and, even more striking, from the perspective of positive aspects of the utopian future that Condorcet imagined. In sum, history is in the service of the utopia whose realization it promises and for which it works. 'It is in arriving at the last degree of the chain [of the history of the progress of the human spirit]', he writes,

> that the observations of past events, like knowledge acquired through meditation, becomes truly useful. It is in arriving at this term, that men can appreciate their real claims to glory, or enjoy, with a sure pleasure, the progress of their reason; it is only there that one is able to judge the true perfection of the human species. This idea, of relating everything to this last point, is dictated by justice and reason; but while it would be tempting to regard it as chimerical, it is not.[10]

Given the surrounding violence of the Revolution during the period in which Condorcet was writing his *Sketch* (1793–4), and given the personal dangers Condorcet was facing (arrested on 27 March 1794, he died in prison the following day, probably from taking poison to avoid the dishonour of the guillotine), such an assessment of the past, and such optimism about the future, is striking. Bronislaw Baczko has observed that the end of the Terror in France in 1794 led to an important re-evaluation of the temporal dimension by many actors and observers of the Revolution.[11] Before Thermidor, many proceeded as if change were a straightforward linear process pointing toward a luminous future that would fulfil hopes for human happiness and regeneration. After Thermidor, the traumas of the Terror had to be incorporated into any understanding of change; and the result was a more complex framework that viewed history as an agonistic process. On this continuum, Condorcet shared the pre-Thermidorian mindset, even occupying its radical optimistic extreme. As he put it in his 'Fragment de Justification', written in 1793 while hiding from the revolutionary authorities:

> Persuaded for a long time that the human species is infinitely perfectible, and that this perfection follows necessarily from the current state of knowledge and society, and cannot be stopped by the physical revolutions of the globe, I regarded the task of hastening progress to be one of the sweetest occupations, one of the first duties to man who has fortified his reason by study and meditation.[12]

On another continuum, Condorcet is similar to later thinkers like François Guizot and Karl Marx, who also viewed history as a secular unfolding that would realize the society of their dreams. While these later thinkers viewed historical becoming as more troubled than Condorcet, with periods of painful regression, they all shared a perspective that assessed the present and the past in terms of a future utopia. That is, each judged contemporary possibilities as positive or negative depending on whether they contributed to the superior society of the future or retarded progress towards it. For a philosopher like Hegel, the conflation of possibility and actuality was retrospective; the 'owl of Minerva' flew only at dusk; consequently, past forces could be assessed only in terms of what had come to be realized in fact. For Condorcet, Guizot and Marx, the conflation of possibility and actuality was prospective rather than retrospective; past and present forces were assessed in terms of the utopian society to be realized in the near future.

From the perspective of the early twenty-first century, Condorcet's utopia has many attractive aspects. It is more appealing than Guizot's vision of the triumph of the middle class; and it is more concrete than Marx's elusive vision (in the *Communist Manifesto*) of an 'association, in which the free development of each is the condition for the free development of all', and/or Marx's suggestion (in *Capital*) that self-actualization in 'the true realm of freedom' will no longer require enervating labour.[13] Condorcet imagined more familiar reforms. Before and during the French Revolution, he supported the establishment of inalienable, inviolable 'natural rights'; the implementation of just and equitable laws; the abolition of slavery; the emancipation of women; the overthrow of religious fanaticism; the redistribution of wealth; the creation of a system of social insurance. As Stuart Hampshire has pointed out, the *Sketch* was 'the first and most complete statement of that radical programme which was gradually to be translated into fact in the democracies of Western Europe'.[14]

These commendable modern elements of Condorcet's stance are juxtaposed, however, with more troubling aspects, especially a naïve faith in the triumph of science and reason, and a seemingly unbounded faith in an enlightened technocratic elite.[15] Keith Baker has referred to these aspects of Condorcet's stance as the embrace of 'a technocratic creed: the creed of men confident in their expertise, easy in the tradition of power, convinced that problems of politics are susceptible of rational answers and systematic solutions'.[16] Today, science no longer looks so benign; reason no longer appears so triumphant; experts no longer inspire such confidence. To believe otherwise is to ignore the evidence of history and to share the hubris of modern technocrats. Writing as I am (in March 2011), months after the worst oil disaster in the history of the United States, and during the frightening aftermath of an earthquake and tsunami that is threatening to engulf Japan with nuclear contamination, it is impossible to share such illusions. How many times have we received assurances from the 'experts' that it is a near statistical impossibility ('only a chance in a million') that environmental and social disasters would occur as a consequence of drilling for offshore oil or generating nuclear power? Humans have demonstrated a frightening ability to act with naïve confidence in their scientific and technological expertise.

Humans have also demonstrated that they frequently act out of selfish motives and with evil intentions. Condorcet had a more complimentary assessment, believing that rationality, collegiality and 'the moral constitution of man'[17] were strong enough components of human nature to guarantee the coordination of scientific research, the overcoming of religious factionalism and political divisions, and the ultimate triumph of equality, peace and happiness. In the final pages of his *Sketch*, he imagined a world in which rational and moral behavior had become the norm.

> I believe that I have proved the possibility, and indicated the means of resolving what is perhaps the most important problem of the human species: *that of the perfectibility of the general masses*; that is to say, to render right judgment, independent and sound reason, enlightened conscience, and habitual submission to the rules of humanity and justice, almost universal qualities; to stress that the normal state of man is guided by truth even though subject to error, subordinates his conduct to the rules of morality even though sometimes drawn into crime, nurtures gentle and pure feelings which unite him to his family, to his friends, to the unfortunate, to his country, to the whole of humanity, even though he is still susceptible of being led astray by personal passions.[18]

This is an appealing vision, but to many of us today it appears, rather, that destructive passions are inauspiciously tenacious under the thin veneer of morality. Contemporary history is unfortunately replete with examples of the disastrous consequences of less than generous passions tearing through the flimsy covering of 'civilization'. Human nature, in short, is the ineluctable serpent in our garden and, more than Condorcet and other optimists have been willing to recognize, its darker side shapes the world we live in to the detriment of the one we wish for. While rational utopias offer us a hope and a goal, they too frequently do so by ignoring historical evidence of the less attractive aspects of our natures.

15

Women's Rights and Women's Liberation in Charles Fourier's Early Writings

Jonathan Beecher

*Is not a young woman a piece of merchandise put up for sale
to the highest bidder? Is not the consent that she gives to marriage
derisory and forced on her by the lifelong tyranny of prejudice?
People try to persuade her that she is only bound by chains of flowers.
But can she really doubt her degradation, even in nations that are
puffed up with philosophy like England? ... On this point we
have hardly made any progress since that crude era when the
Council of Macon, a true council of vandals, debated whether
or not women had a soul and decided in the affirmative by a
majority of just three votes ... It is known that the best nations
have always been those which concede the greatest amount
of liberty to women. This is true of the barbarians and the
savages as well as of the civilized ... As a general proposition:
Social progress and changes of period are brought about by
virtue of the progress of women toward liberty, and social
retrogression occurs as a result of a diminution in the liberty
of women. Other events influence these political changes; but
there is no cause which produces social progress or decline
as rapidly as a change in the condition of women. I have
already said that the simple adoption of closed harems would
speedily turn us into barbarians, and the mere opening of the
harems would enable the barbarians to advance to civilization.
In summary, the extension of the privileges of women is the
fundamental cause of all social progress.*[1]

When Charles Fourier delivered the manuscript of his first book, the *Théorie des quatre mouvements et des destinées générales* (1808), the publisher expressed stupefaction. 'This title seems strange to you,' said Fourier. 'It has to be. Some day you will know why.' Upon encountering a similar reaction from his bookseller in Paris, Fourier replied only that the book's title, like its contents, was a 'riddle' that he would explain later.[2] A riddle: so the book must surely have seemed to its few contemporary readers, and so it has seemed to subsequent generations of readers. The riddle of *Théorie des quatre mouvements* begins with its title page. The author's name is not given; the place of publication (which we know to be Lyon) is identified as Leipzig; and the book is identified in its subtitle as the 'prospectus and announcement' of an unidentified 'discovery'. Things get even more confusing when one opens the book and starts to read. The 'four movements' of the title are not helpfully defined. And the book itself is an outlandish mixture of preambles, notes and epilogues in which shrewd criticism of contemporary commercial practices, of marriage and the family system, and of the French Revolution, appear side by side with speculations on the copulation of the planets and the imminent transformation of sea-water into 'a sort of lemonade'. Fourier later wrote that the strangeness of the book was calculated: it was an intentional travesty, a work of 'studied bizarreness'. His purpose in publishing so strange a book had been, he explained, to confuse potential plagiarists and, at the same time, to test the reactions of the public – to note which of his ideas were scoffed at and which taken seriously.[3]

In 1808, Charles Fourier was thirty-six years old. For the previous decade he had been living a double life. Employed as a travelling salesperson and clerk for silk merchants at Lyon, he saw himself as an 'inventor' who had improved upon the work of Isaac Newton. Newton had determined the laws of gravitational attraction, but it had been left to Fourier, 'a scientific pariah ... an almost illiterate shop clerk', to discover the means to gratify and harmonize all the human passions. His law of 'passionate attraction' completed Newton's work and was destined to 'conduct the human race to opulence, sensual pleasures, and global unity'.[4] His book was indeed the prospectus to this great discovery and he hoped to follow it with a complete treatise in six volumes. This would include, among many other things, a detailed plan for the organization of a community made up of small 'passional' groups whose members would be inspired to work at socially useful tasks by 'rivalry, self-esteem, and other stimuli compatible with self-interest'.[5]

Not surprisingly, Fourier's book sold poorly. In January 1809 his Paris agent wrote to inform him that exactly nine copies had been purchased. In the end most of the copies were destroyed – or simply lost – after gathering dust for decades in booksellers' basements. Only much later was the book recognized as a pioneering exploration of the social question and a founding document of both socialist and feminist thought.

What makes *Théorie des quatre mouvements* so interesting in retrospect is that it can be seen as one of the first great utopian socialist writings. Not only did it announce a remarkable utopian vision, a utopia in which the full and free expression of the passions would serve to promote concord and social unity, it was also one of the first major works to define both 'the social question' and 'the woman question' as the nineteenth century came to conceive of them. The fraud, duplicity and 'industrial anarchy' promoted by the system of free competition; the endemic poverty of the most advanced 'civilized' societies; the irrelevance of the rights of man without the right to work – these issues, which were the stuff of subsequent discussions of the social question, were all forcefully raised in *Quatre mouvements*. So were issues that only later became central to feminist social criticism: the flourishing of prostitution and 'conjugal slavery' in a world made by and for men; the deception and hypocrisy that were the underside of modern marriage; and the repression of the instincts of women not inclined by nature to child-rearing and domesticity.[6]

Théorie des quatre mouvements also offered 'glimpses' of a better world – a world organized according to the 'dictates' of the passions. This was a world of abundance, in which all work would be gratifying, even the humblest individual would eat sumptuous meals in agreeable company, and the poorest village in the Alps or the Pyrenees would have an opera 'similar to that of Paris'. In such a society, imagined Fourier, women would enjoy social, economic and sensual opportunities unthinkable in the male-dominated world to which he referred derisively as 'civilization'.

In unfolding his vision of a free and wholly non-repressive society, Fourier began with a critique of marriage and the family system. If poverty was the prime source of physical suffering in civilization, Fourier wrote, the most intolerable psychic constraints of civilized society were those imposed by the institutions of marriage and family life. Thus, he attacked these institutions on all fronts and with all the weapons at his disposal. His critique ranged from tirades against the moral vices inherent in the family system to satirical invocations of the 'joys' of domestic life, from dry commentaries on the defects of the family as an economic unit and as an instrument of childrearing to pseudoscientific enumerations of the drawbacks of marriage for both partners and a taxonomy of types of cuckoldom. However, through all of this ran a recurrent theme: civilization was an order built on the repression of instinct, and its cornerstone was the institution of monogamous marriage.

Since the institution of marriage symbolized the failure of civilized man to devise institutions capable of satisfying the most basic human needs, Fourier never tired of pointing out its drawbacks. Sometimes, as in his 'Hierarchy of Cuckoldom', he focused on the plight of husbands. But he insisted that the principal victims of marriage were women. He described marriage as a 'mercantile calculation' in which the woman was no more than 'a piece of merchandise offered to the highest bidder'.[7] Once the transaction was concluded, she became in the eyes of the law her husband's exclusive property. Until that time, civilized society obliged her to remain chaste. If her dowry or her looks failed to attract a suitable purchaser, she was left to wither on the vine. 'Just what are the means of subsistence of impoverished women?' asked Fourier. 'Prostitution, more or less prettied up, is their sole means of support, and philosophy even begrudges them that. This is the state to which they have been reduced by civilization with its conjugal slavery.'[8]

Fourier's discussion of 'the woman question', which was most fully developed in this, his first work, is one of the aspects of his thought for which he was and is best known. He was the first of the early European socialists to put a thoughtful and rigorous analysis of the situation of women at the centre of a comprehensive critique of his society. His writings on 'the woman question' were greatly admired by Flora Tristán and Désirée Véret (both of whom knew Fourier in his old age), and other pioneer French feminists; and his disciples did much to give currency within the socialist movement to the idea of the emancipation of women.[9] This being the case, it is worth emphasizing one distinction. Unlike the socialists of the 1840s, who argued for women's emancipation on moral grounds, Fourier's argument was utilitarian. He saw the servitude of women as a 'blunder' that victimized society as a whole and retarded its development, most conspicuously in the economic sphere.[10] Thus he concluded his analysis of 'the debasement of women in civilization' by asserting that there could be no real social progress until women were emancipated, both in their private lives and in the workplace.

Social progress and changes of historical period take place in proportion to the advance of women toward liberty, and social decline occurs as a result of the diminution of the liberty of women ... The extension of the privileges of women is the fundamental cause of all social progress.[11]

Fourier went on to argue that 'there is in every historical period a trait that forms the PIVOT OF THE MECHANISM and whose absence or presence determines changes of period. This trait is always drawn from love.'[12] Thus in the period of barbarism, immediately preceding civilization, the essential trait was 'the absolute servitude of women' in the harem; in civilization the key institution was 'exclusive marriage'. The main cause for the transition from barbarous to civilized societies was the breakup of the harem and the shift from the 'absolute servitude of women' to the granting of some civil rights to women under the system of monogamous marriage. Had the French revolutionaries seriously attacked the institution of marriage, further progress would have been made.

There was very little that prevented the vandalism of 1793 from suddenly producing a second revolution as marvelous as the first was horrible. The whole human race was approaching its release; the civilized, barbarian and savage order would have disappeared forever if the Convention, which trampled down all prejudices, had not bowed down before the only one that had to be destroyed, the institution of marriage ... This is the final blow that the French Convention failed to deliver because of its timidity. How could an Assembly that was so strongly hostile to half-measures have limited itself to a half-measure like divorce?[13]

Looking towards the future, Fourier suggested various proposals for the gradual emancipation of women that could open the way for the transition from civilization to the ideal society that he called Harmony. Women might simply be granted full sexual liberty at the age of eighteen; groups of eighty to 100 men and women might live together in 'progressive households' in which members of both sexes would benefit from flexible arrangements concerning lovemaking and the performance of domestic chores. The point in any case was that women should enjoy rights and privileges comparable to those of men – equal educational opportunities, freedom from the tedium of housework, freedom in the choice of sexual partners. Only when these rights were granted, and when the long struggle for women's emancipation was complete, could both sexes finally enter the new amorous world.[14]

The publication of *Théorie des quatre mouvements* apparently won Fourier a moment of local celebrity. In May 1808, a friend wrote to him 'with pleasure that women are encouraged by your work. I hear that the ladies of Lyon are wild about it.'[15] But if the women of Lyon were enthusiastic about *Quatre mouvements*, their husbands ignored its existence. It was not reviewed in the local press, mentioned in the annals of any of Lyon's numerous learned societies, or even included among the acquisitions of the public library. In Paris a few reviews eventually appeared, but they simply ridiculed Fourier's 'absurdities' and raised questions about his sanity.

During the years that followed, Fourier was to be haunted by the rejection of *Quatre mouvements* by 'the Parisians'. When he sat down to write, it was only to catalogue the 'litany of jeers' which had greeted his book, to inveigh against the spirit of sarcasm and raillery dominant in France, and to console himself with fantasies of revenge and ultimate triumph. For six years he abandoned serious intellectual work and remained at Lyon, eking out a modest living in 'the jailhouse of commerce'. In 1815, however, he was able to retire to the countryside to devote all his efforts to the composition of the great treatise heralded by *Quatre mouvements*.

The five years that Fourier spent in the countryside – in the village of Belley, to the east of Lyon – marked the most fruitful period of his entire intellectual life. He at last found the time and energy to set down on paper a comprehensive exposition of his doctrine. Its rudiments had been clear in his mind since his initial 'discovery', but what Fourier managed to do at Belley was refine his earlier speculations and explore new branches of the doctrine. He devoted particular attention to problems relating to love and sexuality. In five thick notebooks, collectively entitled *Le Nouveau monde amoureux*, he elaborated the vision of sexual harmony hinted at in *Quatre mouvements*. Here Fourier described in detail the institutions and activities of a totally non-repressive society, a society which would ensure for all men and women an emotional and erotic life immeasurably freer and richer than a repressive civilization could ever provide. In such a society, Fourier argued, human relations would take on a new character, and the passion of love would necessarily undergo an extraordinary metamorphosis. No longer a diversion or a private affair, love would instead become an essential part of the collective life, a force for social harmony whose binding power would be felt throughout the ideal community.[16]

Fourier stipulated three conditions for the realization of his amorous utopia. The first condition was the full emancipation of women, on which he had nothing to add to the arguments made in *Quatre mouvements*. The second condition was the recognition of the sheer diversity of human sexual inclinations. According to Fourier, the failure of civilization to devise a tolerable 'amorous regime' resulted in large part from the belief that all men and women were essentially the same in their sexual wants. This belief, which Fourier described as 'erotic Jacobinism', was generally accompanied by the claim that the 'natural' form of sexual grouping was the heterosexual couple. But Fourier insisted that to force everyone into a single mould could only result in pain and frustration. In devising an erotic hierarchy for his new amorous world, he maintained that the highest ranks would be open only to individuals with a passionate attraction to members of both sexes.

The third condition for the realization of Fourier's amorous utopia was the granting of a 'sexual minimum'. In Harmony, he wrote, every mature man and woman must be guaranteed a satisfying minimum of sexual pleasure. Whatever his or her age, and no matter how bizarre their desires, no one would go unsatisfied. Fourier maintained that this sexual minimum would play a role in the amorous world similar to that played by his 'social minimum' in the world of work. Labour could become an instrument of human freedom and self-expression only when people were freed from the obligation to work by a guaranteed income. Similarly, love could become the liberating and binding force that it was meant to be only when its expression had been purged of every tinge of coercion and constraint. For Fourier the important thing about the sexual minimum was that it removed the fear of sexual deprivation that corrupted and falsified amorous relations in civilization.[17]

Fourier never tried to publish *Le Nouveau monde amoureux* in anything like its complete form. Partly owing to financial difficulties, partly because of new discoveries, and primarily out of fear of alarming his readers by too full a revelation of his sexual utopia, he decided to issue an abridged and expurgated treatise in two volumes instead of the projected six. Fourier's shortened version of the theory appeared in 1822 in two 700-page volumes under the intentionally modest title, *Traité de l'association domestique-agricole*. Nowhere in this volume, nor in his subsequent works, did Fourier publish any detailed account of the radical transformations that amorous relations would undergo in his ideal community. And in all of this later work Fourier simply elided the view of history premised on the assumption that improvements in the status of women are the key to all social progress. Instead, he argued in his later work for the priority of economic relations as catalysts of historical change. Did this reflect a change in Fourier's thinking? Probably not. It is more likely that Fourier withheld his reflections on the historical importance of the liberty of women because of the same fear that kept him from publishing *Le Nouveau monde amoureux*: the fear that he could never find a financial backer if he presented himself too explicitly as a prophet of sexual liberation.

Only in 1967 – 150 years after its composition – was *Le Nouveau monde amoureux* finally published.[18] But Fourier's reflections on 'the woman question' – and especially his critique of the position of women in civilization – had been richly developed in his very first work. Not surprisingly, some of his first followers were women who had been drawn to Fourier by his understanding of and sympathy for the plight of women in contemporary society. Oddly, some of these first female Fourierists – notably Clarisse Vigoureux and Zoé Gatti de Gamond – were women of conventionally puritanical moral standards who would have been shocked by the baroque sexual fantasies of *Le Nouveau monde amoureux*.[19] But they were excited by Fourier's assertion that 'the extension of the privileges of women is the fundamental cause of all social progress'. And this declaration was taken up by more radical feminists and socialists in the 1840s. It remained for later generations to recognize the full extent of Fourier's commitment to an ideal of sexual liberation, one which had only been hinted at in the *Théorie des quatre mouvements*.

16

A Tale of Two Cities: Robert Owen and the Search for Utopia, 1815–17

Gregory Claeys

*Every society which exists at present, as well as every society
which history records, has been formed and governed on a belief
in the following notions, assumed as first principles:
1st. That it is in the power of every individual to form
his own character.
Hence the various systems called by the name of religion,
codes of law, and punishments. Hence also the angry passions
entertained by individuals and nations towards each other.
2nd. That the affections are at the command of the individual.
Hence insincerity and degradation of character. Hence the miseries
of domestic life, and more than one half of all the crimes of
mankind.
3rd. That it is necessary that a large portion of mankind should
exist in ignorance and poverty, in order to secure to the
remaining part such a degree of happiness as they now enjoy.
Hence a system of counteraction in the pursuits of men,
a general opposition among individuals to the interests of
each other, and the necessary effects of such a system – ignorance,
poverty, and vice.
Facts prove, however,
1st. That character is universally formed for and not by, the individual.
2nd. That any habits and sentiments may be given to mankind.
3rd. That the affections are not under the control of the individual.
4th. That every individual may be trained to produce far more than
he can consume, while there is a sufficiency of soil left for him to
cultivate.
5th. That nature has provided means by which population
may be at all times maintained in the proper state to give the
greatest happiness to every individual, without one check
of vice or misery.
6th. That any community may be arranged, on a due
combination of the foregoing principles, in such a manner,*

as not only to withdraw vice, poverty, and, in a great degree,
misery, from the world, but also to place every individual
under circumstances in which he shall enjoy more
permanent happiness than can be given to any individual under
the principles which have hitherto regulated society.
7th. That all the assumed fundamental principles on which
society has hitherto been founded are erroneous, and may be
demonstrated to be contrary to fact. And
8th. That the change which would follow the abandonment of
those erroneous maxims which bring misery into the world,
and the adoption of principles of truth, unfolding a system
which shall remove and for ever exclude that misery, may be effected
without the slightest injury to any human being.[1]

Students of early socialism, and of Robert Owen in particular, will be familiar with the 'two Owen' problem. After he assumed management of the New Lanark mills in early 1800 Owen became an enormously successful and wealthy manufacturer. He was a kind rather than a ruthless manager, but there was little indication that around 1815–17 he would shift from paternalistic management to proposing 'villages of co-operation' in which property would be shared in common – an enterprise to which he would devote the rest of his life. How should we account for this alteration, and Owen's invention of 'the social system', as it was first termed, shortly, by the mid-1820s, to become 'socialism'? The question of Owen's motive for this momentous shift in opinion has never been adequately explained. We know, of course, that his outlook from the mid-1790s onwards was dominated by the doctrine that circumstances determined character; that he believed that producing a more charitable type of personality was possible; and that the industrial working classes provided, at least in the setting of New Lanark, the prospect of performing such an experiment. That an obsession with competition and private property generally generated the opposite type of character to that Owen sought to instil he had clearly believed for some years. Yet Owen could easily have rested with the paternalist system introduced at New Lanark, where food was secured at nearly cost price, morals and cleanliness were policed, and education provided for children, without embracing the communist system. Such was his starting-point in public life, as announced in *A New View of Society; Or, Essays on the Principle of the Formation of the Human Character* (1813–16). Here he placed himself beside Elizabeth Fry, William Wilberforce and other great philanthropists of the age – none of whom would embrace the social system. Why then did Owen shift his position so dramatically?

There are at least four, to some degree interrelated, ways of explaining this change. The first is that Owen's system of education, as epitomized in the founding of the Institute for the Formation of Character in 1815–16, persuaded him that the optimal character he sought to produce – epitomized by the word 'charity' – could only be created where private property had been largely eradicated.[2] To crave property engendered selfishness, which undermined all genuine charity. Since forming his new partnership in 1813 Owen had had more complete control over the educational process than previously. He genuinely believed – and there is enough auxiliary evidence to lend confidence to his view – that his educational system and other reforms had done much to improve the behaviour of the inhabitants of New Lanark. His grand conclusion from the experiment may have been that even greater benefits would be derived from sharing the rewards of labour much more equally.

A second, and related, hypothesis might be termed 'creeping socialism'. Owen had begun his experiment at New Lanark with a limited degree of collective activity, but gradually expanded the public sphere, eventually opening a public kitchen and dining room in 1819 in order to reduce cooking costs by some £4,000 to £5,000 per year. The social system might be understood as gradually evolving out of the New Lanark model of 1800. Owen had created a manufacturing village in which 'order, good government, tranquillity and rational happiness' prevailed more than anywhere else, according to one American visitor, Mr Griscom. If these had been achieved by marginal collectivization, an extension of the principle on a grander scale might attain even more wondrous results.

A third hypothesis might be termed 'ideological conversion'. Although Toryish in his practical politics in the 1790s, Owen had been exposed from at least 1813, through his connections with the most important radical philosopher writing in the 1790s, William Godwin, to collectivist proposals like the famous 'pantisocracy' ideal of settlement in the United States contemplated for a time by Robert Lovell, Samuel Taylor Coleridge and Robert Southey.[3] He knew of the land nationalization proposals of Thomas Spence, with whom he was once famously confused.[4] He was aware in addition of many strands of Christian communalism, including that associated with Thomas More, with whom Southey would later compare him at great length.[5] In addition he became familiar with the more practically driven communal schemes for organizing the poor, such as John Bellers' 'Colleges of Industry' proposals, which he reprinted in 1818 with the help of Francis Place (who also opposed community of goods in principle).[6] He gradually became acquainted with successful communal experiments in Britain, in continental Europe, and in the new world. Certainly Melish's description of the Rappite community in Pennsylvania was a source of this enthusiasm as early as 1815; Podmore was 'tolerably certain' that Owen had read the review in the *Philanthropist* if not the book itself.[7] In 1824 he would acquire George Rapp's Harmony community in Indiana, renaming it New Harmony. The attractions of one or several of these schemes may have persuaded Owen that only full-scale communalism would produce a genuinely 'social' humanity.

Finally, we may consider that Owen underwent something like a religious conversion in the years preceding 1820, driven perhaps in part by the enormous exasperation of advocating his plans *ad infinitum* to hundreds of possible supporters, and failing to achieve a substantial measure of factory reform, which was a key initial goal in widening the successes of New Lanark.[8] Owen would of course both attack established religions, most publicly in August 1817, and advocate his own alternative 'New Religion' based upon the charitable ideal.[9] By 1816 he spoke of hoping to see 'universal love prevail'. His language in 1817 in particular, and most notably at the City of London Tavern meeting of 21 August, became stridently millenarian, as has often been noticed.[10] Indebtedness to Quakerism in many aspects of his thought is undoubted. This would help to account for the fact that the communal property proposals he now advocated had historically been associated with religious orders in particular, if not indeed Christ's own apostles. But many believed that they were practicable on a wider scale, if at all, only in the City of God, not in the fallen City of Man.

It is fairly evident that Owen's decision to embrace the 'social system' doubtless stemmed from some complex combination of these factors. Let us now look chronologically at Owen's development to see what evidence exists for prioritizing these hypotheses.

Owen's espousal of socialism – although the term itself of course was not yet in use – has traditionally been dated from 1817.[11] It was at this time that Owen, reporting to the Committee on the Poor Laws, attributed the great increase in pauperism to the effects of machinery. Large-scale unemployment could be solved only be employing the poor on the land, on farms of 1,000 to 1,500 acres suitable for about 1,200 people, set up by local authorities. The parallelogram model was introduced at this time, with proposals for children to be housed in dormitories in order to train them more effectively. Meals would be taken in common, and all would share equally in the profits of the enterprise. Competition and selfishness would be replaced by association. Shortly afterwards, Owen proposed that such plans might eventually be extended to the entire society. Communities might, he supposed, be subdivided according to wealth, religion and political outlook, in order to enhance their attractiveness, the wealthy bringing capital to employ the poorer. But the ultimately communistical bent of the whole scheme was quite evident. Some supporters, led by the Duke of Kent and David Ricardo, tried in 1819 to insist that community of goods was not crucial to the success of Owen's plans. But he was evidently wedded to the ideal, and Owen was a man unlikely to retreat once his mind was made up. Instead, in *Report to the County of Lanark*, of 1820, he announced his embracing of a labour standard of value, and his wish to supplant the system of competition entirely. There was no turning back after this point.

A focus on these proposals and Owen's millenarian language in 1817 must be balanced by evidence of the drift of Owen's ideas in the several preceding years. His lament in 1815 that the progress of the manufacturing system had introduced 'a fondness for essentially injurious luxuries among a numerous class of individuals who formerly never thought of them', and had 'generated a disposition which strongly impels its possessors to sacrifice the best feelings of human nature to this love of accumulation' indicates, that the loss of the 'comparatively happy simplicity of the agricultural peasant' weighed heavily upon him.[12] This shows that Owen had already embraced a *systematic* rejection of competition and heavy factory labour. However, there is some evidence to suggest that Owen had already embraced some form of collectivist ideal. At the time that William Hazlitt was caricaturing Owen as a pale shadow of Godwin, preaching a doctrine 'as old as society itself', in August 1816,[13] Owen visited Robert Southey, who shared his worries about the manufacturing system and described his judgement and feelings as 'entirely with him'.[14] Southey was surprised to find during an hour-long conversation that Owen was 'neither more or less than such a Pantisocrat as I was in the days of my youth. He is as ardent now as I was then, & will soon be cried down as a visionary.' He described Owen's plans as including wanting the poor and unemployed to 'live in community', but warned that the plan for employing paupers in agriculture 'ought not to be confounded with his metaphysics'.[15] When he visited New Lanark in 1819, however, he worried that Owen had not contemplated the difficulties of a system that 'took for its foundation the principle of a community of goods', which he feared could only be maintained 'by absolute power' – indeed he likened New Lanark to a plantation.[16] The real, long-term division between them was that Owen, Southey thought, did not appreciate that building on any foundation other than religion, is 'building upon sand'.[17] He would elaborate on this theme at length some ten years later, still noting that 'Owen's views tend to an entire community of goods' – a scheme he rejected on the basis of both 'theory and experience'.[18]

The Owen–Southey encounter sheds light on various aspects of our key question here. First, it is clear that Owen had embraced a communitarian ideal before 1817. Whatever Southey may have remembered by the term 'pantisocracy', it certainly implied an emphasis upon voluntary communal living and shared property.[19] Second, it is entirely possible that Southey's insistence (among others) upon a religious basis for any such practice led Owen to concoct his 'new religion' of charity, upon which he lectured extensively in 1830, but which was chiefly a restatement of his original necessitarian principles.[20] This does not assist us in ascertaining the source of Owen's communitarianism, except to discount a religious conversion in 1817 as such. We can, however, probably exclude Thomas Spence as a source here, for Spence's schemes were not communitarian as such. Yet neither, on the scale proposed by Owen, were William Godwin's ideas, the source of Southey's own pantisocratic enthusiasms. As is well known, Owen met Godwin at least thirty times in 1813, eight times in 1814, seven times in 1816, five times in 1817, and less often thereafter. Doubtless Godwin helped clarify Owen's philosophical necessitarianism, particularly the doctrine that 'the characters of men originate in their external circumstances'. But he is an unlikely source for the pauper relief schemes of 1816–17; the thrust of Southey's objections about the eradication of individuality in such communities would have been Godwin's first line of objection as well. More likely models, as Podmore has indicated, were Bellers' schemes, and reports of the Shaker communities in the United States. Bellers deserves priority here, as Owen would claim in 1817 that the 'combinations of these principles' had first been proposed by him in 1696.[21] Yet Owen added that 'on discovering it, I had it reprinted'; the reprint was in September 1817. It would seem, then, that Bellers proved a point Owen wished to enforce, but he was not the source of Owen's communitarianism as such, even if, as Podmore suggests, Owen was indeed led to 'still further develop his Plan upon the lines laid down by Bellers'.[22]

Given the paucity of correspondence and other evidence about Owen's opinions before 1817, and his own extraordinary coyness about the origins of some of his views, we cannot ascertain with any degree of certainty when his co-operative and communitarian ideals originated, and what their precise source was, indeed if there was one. There is no reason to doubt Owen's own view that the cumulative experience of his management of factories in Manchester and at New Lanark had led him to believe that he knew how 'ultimately to make the human race good, wise and happy'.[23] But it is equally beyond dispute that New Lanark was not conducted upon 'pantisocratic' principles – that it was not a profit-sharing enterprise based upon community of goods. Yet we also have no reason to doubt Southey's description of Owen's sympathy for such a scheme in 1816, even if the details of what he proposed did not become clear until 1817–18.

So there remains a mystery respecting Owen's 'pantisocratic' opinions, for Owen was doubtless well aware of the distance between New Lanark and utopia (a term Southey used with reference to Owen's plans). Podmore may have been right in supposing that New Lanark was for Owen 'the microcosm in which the discerning eye might trace the outlines of the larger cosmos',[24] but New Lanark was not Paraguay, not Harmony, not Sparta nor indeed Utopia. In New Lanark, profits were not shared, and it was not governed democratically by a committee of those of a certain age, as Owen would propose by 1817. It was, to all intents and purposes, Owen's personal fiefdom, less perhaps the City of Man than the kingdom of one man; and the fact that he governed it so benevolently was of course greatly to his credit. But all his achievements there paled beside the 'Plan', as it was usually termed around 1817. Self-educated, sometimes insufferably self-confident, Owen was nonetheless no fool, and knew what the communistical ideal stood for. The City of God was that of communal sharing; the City of Man stood for selfishness and private property. So had the Christian dualism run since time immemorial; yet there were many instances where the City of God had been transformed on earth. Well might Owen in 1817 trumpet salvation by introduction of the language of the millennium. This reflected his acknowledgement that the 'Plan' had a sacred pedigree he had not formerly wished to associate with his proposals. The language of 1817, then, did not reflect Owen's 'conversion' to a millenarian outlook, but the recognition that the 'Plan' formed at least by 1815 was ideologically closer to the tradition of utopian communitarianism than the experimental developments at New Lanark had been. Owen now acknowledged that 'pantisocratic' opinions were not like piecemeal social engineering. Socialism lay closer to Utopia than to New Lanark by far, but a long journey lay ahead for Owen before the final shipwreck of the great Queenwood community in 1844 finally put paid to his most cherished ideals.

17

How to Change the World: Claude-Henri de Rouvroy, comte de Saint-Simon

Neil McWilliam

European society is no longer made up of children whose interests require that they be subject to strong and active supervision; it is composed of men whose education has been completed, and who seek only instruction. Politics should no longer be anything other than the science of obtaining for the masses the greatest possible quantity of material goods and moral benefits [jouissances]. Leaders, though dominated by old prejudices and subject to the empire of illusions, by their conduct nonetheless pay homage to the power of opinion; they are beginning to show, if not by their acts, at least by the form in which they couch them, that they no longer hide from themselves that they are dealing with reasonable men, who do not wish to live to be governed, but who consent to be governed in order to live better. They favour, I know (insofar as they can in the present state of things), the arts, the sciences and industry; but why do these three great classes [capacités], who could survive unaided, and without whom nothing could survive, need to be favoured? Could they not say to the leaders: 'What is there in common between us and you? Why is it that we are at your mercy? To whom does the nation owe its wellbeing? Who upholds the throne, us or you? It is in our breasts, from the depths of our studies, our workshops, our factories, and not from your offices and dining rooms, that everything useful to society emerges. If we imagine a project useful to the common good, we are obliged to request that you take it into account. Since your talents [capacités] are inferior to ours, since the only talent you possess is for surveillance and policing, which must every day become less important, how is it that you are placed so much above us, that you wish to reduce us to your passive instruments – we, without whom you would find it impossible to accomplish the slightest act? Isn't your arrogance as inappropriate, as ridiculous as that of a coachman whose pride in being seated high on his box leads him to imagine he is above his master, who pays him and feeds his horses?'
Just imagine if one of us made such a speech to a leader, his response would be quite simple: 'I have nothing to say to you', he would reply. 'You are divided; we are united.'

*This reproach, gentlemen, would be justified. Unity, which is a virtue
and safeguard of the weak, is also one of the duties of the strong.
Yet far from harmony reigning amongst us, there is, between scientists,
industrialists and artists, a sort of permanent hostility. I would not claim
that the fault lies with one party; it is reciprocal.*[1]

The words are those of an artist, opening up a vigorous dialogue with two other protagonists who, like him, are defined simply in terms of their occupations: a *savant* represents the scientific community, while an *industriel* speaks on behalf of the manufacturing interest. All, in turn, expound ideas that are rooted not only in their individual activities, but also in the personalities and preconceptions that ostensibly accord with their respective social roles. All three, and the artist above all, are animated by an impatience with the shortcomings of the post-Restoration (1815–30) political order; all three call for its replacement with a system of governance attuned to the needs of society at large and administered by individuals possessing real skills rather than inherited titles or honorific positions. The result, they agree, would be a world in which peace and progress flourish, and the material well-being of the masses enjoys unprecedented priority.

The *Dialogue* was published in December 1824 as the 'Conclusion' to a collection of essays ranging over questions of philosophy, physiology and social and industrial organization produced by Claude-Henri de Rouvroy, comte de Saint-Simon (1760–1825) and a group of young followers dedicated to promoting his ideas. The *Dialogue*'s authorship is subject to dispute:[2] although commonly attributed to Saint-Simon himself, working with his assistant Léon Halévy, it may be the work of another disciple, the mathematician and banker Olinde Rodrigues, an influential defender of the master's doctrine in the turbulent years following his death. Whoever actually composed the text, it seems entirely consistent with the overall tenor of Saint-Simon's thought on the eve of his death, and represents an important moment in the evolution of the doctrine for a number of reasons. As Saint-Simon's ideas had developed since his emergence as a political thinker during the Empire, so his early commitment to guaranteeing social stability through intellectual reform had been eclipsed by an increasing interest in industry and particularly its capacity to advance popular well-being. With his last major work, *Le Nouveau Christianisme*, left incomplete at the time of his death, Saint-Simon sought to devise mechanisms for overcoming social division and the individualism that nurtured it, and for laying the foundations of a world in which brotherly love would promote altruism and mutuality. Religion, he believed, provided an effective means of strengthening the bonds between individuals and social classes by appealing not to rational interests in a dry, expository fashion, but to something more visceral that could be mobilized through an appeal to feeling and imagination. The belief that emotion and not reason held the key to fostering a desire for change amongst people underlies the artist's promotion as a sort of secular equivalent to the priest in the *Dialogue*. It is he who takes the lead in addressing representatives of the two other productive classes, and it is he who most fully expounds the nature of far-reaching social reform and the means of achieving it.

The artist's remarks echo Saint-Simon's belief that a central goal of political change was to 'replace the government of men by the administration of things' – future societies, in other words, would consist of self-regulating groups of individuals united around a common goal of industrial production. As such, current notions of government as an essentially coercive directing body would become redundant, since individuals' commitment to collective well-being would eradicate the need for control. For the artist, a crucial distinction is to be drawn between an anachronistic ruling class of politicians, aristocrats and churchmen, whom he likens to prefects in a school charged with maintaining order, and the three classes who participate in the *Dialogue*. All bring to bear a skill essential for the prosperity of society and as such, he argues, are as vital to its effective functioning as teachers are to the operation of a school. Yet, as he concludes, divisions amongst this group have prevented them from assuming their pivotal role and ushering in a new era of equity and prosperity.

These divisions relate to Saint-Simon's understanding of the relationship between social groupings (*capacités*) and psycho-physiological difference. From his earliest published writings, Saint-Simon revealed a particular interest in physiological theory – indeed, his early work is predicated on a belief that once physiology matured into a positivist science, it would provide the epistemological foundations for a scientifically objective understanding of social phenomena. Saint-Simon followed contemporary medical theorists such as P.J.G. Cabanis and Xavier Bichat in emphasizing innate individual difference – a break with Enlightenment ideas, which had followed Locke in arguing that most of what rendered individuals distinct one from another could be attributed to the impact of sensory experience accumulated over the course of a lifetime. Cabanis, in his lectures to the Institut, broke with this dominant model, and in so doing stimulated considerable interest among liberal thinkers associated with the Idéologue group.[3] His ideas were expanded with the publication in 1800 of Bichat's *Recherches physiologiques sur la vie et sur la mort*, which argued that humans could be differentiated into three broad groups: 'sensory', 'cerebral' and 'motor'. It was this division that provided the basis for Saint-Simon's own tripartite division between artists, scientists and *industriels*.

Because of his reading of contemporary political theory, as well as through his understanding of physiology and his observations of post-Revolutionary France, Saint-Simon was acutely aware of the threat that individualism posed to social cohesion. His hostility to contemporary liberal theorists, and his disdain for *oisifs* – wealthy idlers who exploited society for personal gain – led to increasing frustration at the obstacle that individual interest posed to social reform. As he argued in 1821: 'The decadence of old general doctrines has allowed the development of egotism, which invades society every day and is firmly opposed to the formation of new doctrines.'[4] The only solution, he maintained, was to oppose individualism with philanthropic altruism. And, as he quickly came to realize, the most effective means of achieving such change was by an appeal to the imagination, which would overcome the obstacle of self-interest erected by reason, and carry society forward on a wave of enthusiasm. Hence, later in the *Dialogue*, the artist famously (and controversially) proclaims:

> It is we artists who will serve as your vanguard [avant-garde] since art's power has greater immediacy and rapidity … Since we speak to man's imagination and sentiments, we must always exert the strongest and most decisive effect. If today we seem to have no role, or only a very minor one, this is because the arts lack what they must need for their energy and success: a common impulse and a ruling idea.[5] (341)

The artist's diagnosis of art's failure to realize its social potential brings us back full circle. Its current impotence is itself the consequence of individualism: in his opening remarks, the artist recognizes that he and his kind have been too inclined to disdain reality and isolate themselves in an 'ideal world … that offers us the sweetest pleasures and the purest consolation' (339). His confession encourages his interlocutors to engage in similar self-criticism: the scientist acknowledges that he too cuts himself off from society in 'solitary meditation', while the *industriel* recognizes that his class's 'love of money' overcomes more general interests (371, 383). Each, then, suffers from a form of individualism that is intrinsic to the physiological types that they embody; their inclination is thus to isolate themselves in ways that their innate characteristics actively promote. It is for this reason that the artist observes the need for an act of will to bring them together in an alliance that will overcome their present isolation and the sense of frustration that it promotes (322).[6] Such an alliance is thus conceived as advancing art, science and industry at the same time as it promises a radical re-ordering of society.

Divisions within the three *capacités* are symptomatic of a more pervasive individualism that the proposed alliance between the artist, the scientist and the *industriel* is intended to rectify. The objective is to institute a social system in which industrial production offers the means for promoting a more equitable distribution of wealth in a society which nonetheless remains hierarchized and, as the artist emphasizes, 'is hostile only to idleness, and is essentially favourable to royalty, to religion, to the sciences, arts and industry – in a word, to everything that is useful to men' (361). Despite these apparent concessions to the status quo, the three interlocutors regard their union as effecting a fundamental change of values as science and the arts effectively become the new spiritual power and industry acquires supreme temporal authority (366).[7] Thus, the scientist proposes that future responsibility for public education should be shared between his class and that of the artist in order to promote popular sympathy for industry and for peace. Such an educational alliance, he suggests, will enhance not only the popular intellect but also encourage the development of 'social feeling [*sentiments sociaux*]' (374) – altruistic impulses that foster cohesion and to which the artist is supremely able to appeal.

Achieving such a change had long seemed particularly challenging to Saint-Simon. Although he had taken a sympathetic stance towards the revolutionary upheaval of the 1790s, in many ways his early work was inspired by a desire to forestall any recurrence of civil unrest. As he became increasingly committed to fundamental social and political reform, he was confronted by the question of how best to effect radical change while avoiding internecine violence – a problem that had proved sufficiently intractable for him to propose a mass petition to the king in order to persuade the authorities to take up his ideas. Announcing in the *Dialogue*, with greater optimism than accuracy, that '[h]enceforth, insurrection is impossible in France' (364), the artist offers to direct his talents towards this process of mass conversion. The power of imagination, he claims, will usher in far-reaching social transformation in a peaceful and comprehensive manner. According to the artist, past failure to appreciate the masses' limited responsiveness to reasoned argument has handicapped the ability of innovators to win popular enthusiasm for their ideas. As he points out to the scientist: 'reasoning merely convinces, whilst feelings [*les sensations*] persuade and excite' (337–8). The artist himself is described, in a footnote at the beginning of the *Dialogue*, as 'a man of imagination', whose field of action covers 'everything that has sensation as its object' (331, note). In a way that sets the tone for subsequent Saint-Simonian discourse, the artist is thus identified not with a specific medium but with a particular means of address, an ability to transcend reason and appeal to more instinctual aspects of human response. Yet the artist qualifies his claim to appeal to this impulsive, visceral and potentially wayward side of the personality by arguing that in the future his creative talents will be directed to useful ends, as opposed to 'retrograde' work that appeals to 'imagination without an object' (343).

Saint-Simon's rehabilitation of imagination as a transformative social force finds its roots in the eighteenth century, when theorists such as Diderot emphasized the value of emotion both as a source of aesthetic pleasure and as a powerful moral catalyst.[8] The revolutionary era's recourse to popular festivals drew upon an analogous sense of the arts' capacity to enthuse spectators who would otherwise be resistant to the reasoned exposition of civic virtues that dramatic spectacle was able vividly to bring to life.[9] Such initiatives offered a recent precedent for the way in which, in the *Dialogue*, the artist presents imagination as an infallible spur, propelling society towards a glorious future of concord and solidarity. Yet, for all his inspiring words, the *Dialogue* ends on a rather anti-climactic note. As the three protagonists agree on the need to join forces to relieve society of its currently dysfunctional form of government, the only proposal that the artist can come up with is the production of an encyclopaedia, drawing on the celebrated eighteenth-century example that he argues precipitated the 1789 revolution, and a journal, in which the three *capacités* will set out their ideas for change (386).[10] Such modest ambitions suggest the extent to which, at this point, Saint-Simon and his circle remain tied to a predominantly rationalist perspective and have only a limited sense of how the imagination's potential as a transformational force might actually be mobilized.

The artist's proposal is inspired by his contention that society itself is on the brink of an epochal change: 'the great work of Christianity is coming to fruition [*s'accomplit*]', 'fraternity reigns amongst men and nations', 'society is becoming increasingly positivist' (342). No evidence is offered to support these assertions, and it is clear that Saint-Simon was unsure as to how to promote his ideas for social reform in a climate that, in actuality, showed only limited potential for change. For many post-Revolutionary commentators, including Saint-Simon himself, one of the most conspicuous features of national life was a pervasive sense of uncertainty, articulated in 1825 in Théodore Jouffroy's assertion that '[a] new generation is growing up, born in the midst of scepticism'[11]. It was in response to this sense of doubt and drift that a band of young intellectuals, many of whom had been trained in the elite Parisian engineering school, the *Ecole polytechnique*, congregated around Saint-Simon in his later years, and developed his legacy in the school that they established in France before leaving on mission to Egypt in 1833.

With the emergence of Prosper Enfantin as the dominant force within the group in the late 1820s, the positivist element of Saint-Simonian doctrine was steadily overshadowed by the emphasis on religiosity that Saint-Simon himself had begun to sketch out in his later writings. The emergence of a *Religion saint-simonienne* in 1828 and the adoption of a quasi-monastic group existence in the Parisian suburb of Ménilmontant in 1832,[12] indicate a growing commitment to sentiment, as opposed to reason, as the bedrock of the new doctrine. Yet, just as the *Dialogue*'s artist remained hidebound by the authority of the written text in his allegiance to the journal and the encyclopaedia, so the Saint-Simonians of the July Monarchy tended to favour purely discursive means of propaganda that privileged the cognitive power of the word. The group's celebrated *prédications* – doctrinal lectures that seem to have relied on verbal histrionics to underscore their effect – and quasi-liturgical ceremonies during the Ménilmontant retreat seem relatively timid in their recourse to traditional discursive formats. Yet, behind closed doors, the group allowed their imaginations to run riot in ways that the *Dialogue*'s artist could scarcely imagine. As the figure of the priest increasingly usurped the artist's role as principal minister to the popular imagination, so members of the group confected a new gospel, *Le Livre nouveau*, in which they speculated about the affective power of language, sound and colour, and envisioned a cathedral of the future which would enthral the faithful through a panoply of sensual effects.[13] Although social solidarity and industrial progress remain central to these speculative excursions, under Enfantin emotion takes on an ecstatic force that, rather than surpassing the power of reason, seems altogether to suppress its restraining power in the interests of spontaneous allegiance. As Enfantin remarks in 1831, in a chilling echo of future totalitarian sloganeering: 'Man is FREE when he loves what he MUST DO'.[14]

If such an assertion compromises the value of sentiment by envisaging its implicit regulation, it points to an authoritarian current in Saint-Simonian thought that seems to contrast most markedly with the ostensibly libertarian perspective of the Saint-Simonians' main rival, Charles Fourier. Fourier's indictment of modern *civilisation* for repressing the free-play of sentiment, and thus bringing about crime, deviation and misery, envisions a *nouveau monde industriel et sociétaire* in which individual feeling would be in perfect harmony with collective interest. Here again, however, freedom is more apparent than real, as Fourier's obsessively detailed, baroque vision of future happiness gradually expels any sense of spontaneity or idiosyncrasy from a world where even the most eccentric impulse has been anticipated, and catered for, by a social vision of suffocating inclusiveness. In common with the communist paradise sketched out during the same years in Etienne Cabet's *Voyage en Icarie* of 1842, the utopian vision of these early nineteenth-century theorists is ultimately rooted in a highly qualified understanding of individual liberty.

18

The Utopian Organization of Work in Icaria

David Leopold

*I went back to join Valmor, who was meeting me in the clock-making
workshop where one of his cousins worked …
How amazing it was! Everything is together there, from the raw materials
lined up in the first storehouse to the clocks, pendulums, watches,
and devices of all sorts set out in a final warehouse that resembles a
brilliant museum. The special clock-making workshop is a three-storied
building of a thousand square feet, held up by iron columns instead
of thick walls, which make each floor into one big room, perfectly
illuminated by a very simple system of light diffusion. On the bottom
floor are enormous, heavy machines for cutting the metals and roughing
out the pieces. On the top floor are the workers, divided into as many
groups as there are different pieces to make; each one always makes
the same piece. You would think you were seeing an army regiment;
such is the high degree of order and discipline there.*[1]

The life and work of Étienne Cabet (1788–1856) challenges the familiar
but lazy contrast often drawn between utopian 'dreamer' and effective
political actor. Cabet was both the author of a classic literary utopia – in which
a visitor from the author's own world discovers a superior civilization in a
(geographically) distant location – and an effective political organizer who
played a significant role in the nascent workers' movement in France.

Born into a republican and artisan family in Dijon, Cabet subsequently
pursued a legal and political career in Paris. He joined the *charbonnerie* (a secret
society based on freemasonry) in the 1820s, and was elected to the National
Assembly following the 1830 Revolution. Cabet also launched *Le Populaire*,
a hugely successful republican newspaper, with an artisan readership (but
cross-class ambitions), which sold 12,000 copies per issue in Paris alone, in
1833.[2] Indicted for publishing seditious articles, he took the legal option of
exile for five years to avoid being imprisoned for two years in France.

Exiled in London, Cabet wrote prolifically, kept radical company, and added
a commitment to 'community of goods' to his republicanism. Cabet would
later claim that the idea for *Voyage en Icarie* had come to him whilst perusing

More's *Utopia* (1516) in the British Museum. Other influences on the work are much contested, but include: an early exposure to Fénelon's *Telemachus* (1699); the egalitarianism (but not the violence or secrecy) of Babouvism; and the gradualism and communitarianism of Robert Owen.[3]

Cabet returned to France in 1839, resurrecting *Le Populaire* as a monthly advocating 'Icarian communism' alongside descriptive accounts of contemporary social and economic conditions. The Icarian movement developed strong provincial support, especially in Reims, Lyon, Nantes, Périgueux, Toulouse and Toulon.[4] However, after 1845, the movement took on some of the characteristics of a sect; Cabet increasingly portrayed communism as 'true' Christianity, and in 1846 announced his ambition to found a communitarian settlement in America.[5] This move fractured the Icarian movement and damaged *Le Populaire*, since many supporters neither wanted, nor could afford, to 'abandon' France.[6]

Having failed to sustain his initial impact on the revolutionary events of 1848, Cabet joined the supporters he had encouraged to migrate. (He returned to France, from May 1851 to July 1852, to answer legal charges concerning the emigration, but otherwise spent the rest of his life in America.) After a series of difficulties and a false start in Texas, the Icarians took over a Mormon settlement at Nauvoo in Illinois. In 1856, a long-germinating schism saw Cabet expelled by a (small but stable) majority unhappy with his financial (mis)management, divisive policies and growing authoritarianism. Cabet took 124 adult loyalists with him, but died before they reached the site of their new settlement (Cheltenham, Missouri).[7]

Voyage en Icarie was first published (pseudonymously) in 1840, although it was the second (1842) edition which adopted that now familiar title and abandoned the conceit that it had been written by the fictitious English nobleman who was its central protagonist. Part One provides an account of the main political and social institutions of Icaria. Part Two provides an imagined history of Icaria, a reply to certain objections, and an appeal to a bewildering selection of (often unlikely) authorities on equality and community (running from Apollonius to Zoroaster). Part Three rehearses the 'Doctrine Communitaire' of its author, and emphasizes the importance of transitional arrangements.

Voyage en Icarie could not be called a literary masterpiece. Its programmatic and romantic threads – the pill and its sugar coating – barely hold together. (The visible join is reproduced in miniature within Cabet's book, when Lord Carisdall reads an overly didactic novel elucidating Icarian marriage arrangements (139/114).) Nor is the sugar coating well made; most characters can barely muster one dimension, and the melodramatic romance is contrived and dated.[8] However, the literary form might have had some protective function – complicating Cabet's liability under increasingly strict press laws in France.

Voyage en Icarie has some interesting formal features. Not least, it contains an account of the historical emergence of Icaria – a narrative involving revolutionary origins, a benevolent 'dictator' and a lengthy period of transition to communism – confounding those who (mistakenly) claim that utopias never explain their own origins.[9] However, I focus here on its social and political content, and especially the discussion of work.

Cabet holds that all of the evils familiar from human history (war, disorder, torture, crime and more) are the result of poor social organization, and especially the result of inequality. Consequently, we should not hesitate to re-organize society in order to eradicate them, and Icaria, he suggests, can give us 'an example' (to be modified and perfected by others) of how that might be done.[10]

The central values of Icarian society are equality and community; the 'duties and benefits' of association are shared equally, and ties of 'fraternity' turn society into a single 'family' (35/31). These central values find institutional embodiment (economically) in the community of property, and (politically) in a democratic republic. 'Democracy' is identified with popular sovereignty and a high degree of participation (there are no political parties and only a single national newspaper). Icaria is a rule-governed and non-liberal society; the legislature, for example, regulates 'everything pertaining to their persons, actions, goods, food, clothing, lodging, education, their work, and even their amusements' (37/33). Yet this highly regulated egalitarian communism still constitutes something of a 'half-change' (to borrow an expression from William Morris). For example, family structures and gender roles are modified rather than transformed; women, for instance, appear to be excluded from political decision-making yet retain a monopoly on housework. Moreover, whilst there are huge republican festivals (worthy of the imagination of Rousseau), the Icarians mainly spend their leisure time in gentle bourgeois pursuits – concert-going, promenades, horseback riding, the theatre and picnics.

As for productive activity, Icaria is not Cockaygne (the mythical land of plenty where ready-roasted pigeons fly onto your plate). Work remains necessary, and the moderate abundance is hard won. Icarian productivity is portrayed as the result of the eradication of idlers, the absence of unproductive occupations, the extensive use of machinery, the application of a detailed technical division of labour, and widespread technological innovation.

First, in Icaria everyone 'is a national worker and works for the republic' (100–1/82). In particular, there are no idle rich. Dukes, marquises and barons have become locksmiths, printers and architects; although a stray 'us' and 'them' in the mouth of one such Icarian suggests that the historical memory of class origins has not yet entirely waned (28/25). Women are also now part of the republican workforce, although Cabet's imagination limits them to certain kinds of gendered (and segregated) production.[11] The women's workshop visited by Carisdall is devoted to millinery, and overflows with 'brightly colored silks and velvets, laces and ribbons, flowers and feathers' (136/112). Other women's workshops are said to involve 'the seamstresses, the florists, the makers of undergarments, the laundresses, and so forth' (138/113).

Second, certain 'unproductive' occupations have disappeared. Gun and dagger manufacturers, notaries and stockbrokers, for example, have gone the way of the nobility. Most importantly, we are told, the 'curse of domestic service' has been eradicated (except, the sceptic will suggest, for women) (28/25). In one revealing case, the occupational role survives but is no longer occupied exclusively; Valmor (Carisdall's host) dismisses the suggestion that the role of the police force has disappeared, remarking that 'nowhere on earth' are there more police officers, since 'all our citizens' are required to enforce the law, and pursue miscreants (132/108).

Third, much human labour has been replaced by machinery. Non-agricultural production mainly occurs in huge, heavily mechanized, communal workshops devoted to particular branches of industry. In one print shop, for example, a variety of machines do 'almost everything themselves', replacing 'almost fifty thousand workers' (32/29). And in the republican bakery, 'ingenious machines knead the dough, cut it, and carry it to the ovens' (48/42). Initially, machinery was adopted to perform 'all the dangerous, tiring, unhealthy, dirty, or disgusting work' (101/83). However, mechanization has clearly progressed much further; at a wedding, for example, we discover a 'mechanical orchestra' without 'a single musician' (205/167).

Fourth, in the work that remains, a detailed technical division of labour is applied. In the women's millinery workshop, for example, 'each worker is used to doing the same operation all the time, and this repetition doubles yet again the speed of the work, while making it perfect' (137/112). In a letter home, one of the visitors confirms the savings and perfection resulting from 'machines or workers' performing the same operation (60/50). It is a revealing elision; reduced to simple repetitive tasks, human and mechanical labour look to be largely interchangeable.

Lastly, Icaria is an innovative society, with constantly advancing technology. We are shown a dazzling array of new products: smokeless fuels; submarines; dust-resistant furniture; odourless gas lighting; steerable air balloons; and so on. More entertaining breakthroughs include adumbrations of astro-turf – 'a sort of wetted mastic that turns neither to mud nor to dust' covers an arena – and of muzak – 'soft music produced by an invisible machine' plays in a hospital (112/92, 256/211).

Many questions remain. Not least, one might wonder how the decisions to produce are made in the absence of markets. Predictably, it is the republic which decides what will be made (providing the necessary resources and gathering up the resulting product) (100/82). The same is true of foreign trade decisions, since Icaria is not autarchic and imports materials and products where it is efficient to do so (164/134). Domestic production follows a deceptively simple (and never fully elucidated) priority rule, making: first, those things that are 'necessary' (for survival); second, those things that are 'useful'; and last, those things that are 'pleasing' (100/82). (Where feasible, all three categories of product are made.) The resulting output is distributed equally, and time-rationed if it cannot be given to everyone outright (subject to everyone being able to enjoy it alike). Thus, since there are only enough horses for a tenth of the population, each family gets to go riding on every tenth day (221/180). Much here depends on the statistical and information-gathering expertise of the republic, and those cognisant of the informational function of market mechanisms are likely to remain sceptical.

Readers might also wonder about the Icarian work ethic. It is one thing to recognize that society requires production, but quite another to understand what motivates the individual workers to turn up for their shift and pull their weight. This concern is magnified by the distributive principle emblazoned on the frontispiece of *Voyage en Icarie* in its 1845 edition: '*A chacun suivant ses besoins. De chacun suivant ses forces* [To each according to their needs. From each according to their powers].' (The anticipation of Karl Marx's so-called 'needs principle' will be apparent.) Crucially, this principle breaks the link between the size of an individual's contribution to social production and the size of their material reward. Icarians, we learn, instead receive goods according to 'sex, age, and a few other circumstances provided by law' (36/32). Moreover, whilst coercion is not ruled out, it is seemingly not needed in order to elicit the required contribution. The necessary productive effort is generated in two steps: by lightening the burden of work, and increasing the moral motivation to bear that lightened load.

The burden of productive activity is reduced by its being made shorter, safer, cleaner, physically undemanding and pleasurable. The working day begins at 6 a.m. and lasts for only six or seven hours depending on the season (the shortness here would be more striking to Cabet's contemporaries). Workplaces are subject to the Icarian preoccupation with safety: protective barriers are widespread (by riversides, for instance), the air is purified, large wild animals have been eradicated, and so on. Cleanliness is also an obsession; in the stone mason's workshop, for instance, every precaution is made to avoid dirt, and even the workers' clothes are free of dust and mud (104/85). Work is physically undemanding; thus masons never have to carry a load, but simply direct the machinery that replaces human physical force (104/85, 154/126). Finally, work is made pleasurable. However, it is clear that Cabet views work as an intrinsically burdensome activity, and the pleasures here are external to productive activity as such. In particular, Icarian workers are seemingly invigorated and entertained by engaging in, and listening to, periods of communal song (interspersed with periods of silence and periods of conversation). Readers might be doubtful, but Carisdall trembles when, in the women's workshop, 'those 2,500 pretty mouths opened to sing a magnificent hymn, far too short, in honor of good Icar' (the founding father of the republic) (137/113). As a cumulative result of these arrangements, work has become 'so untiring, and even pleasant' that many Icarians ignore the nominal retirement ages (of fifty for women and sixty-five for men) (101/82).

The lightened burden of productive activity still needs to be carried, and in the absence of either material incentives or coercion, Icaria utilizes what might be called moral motivations. Negatively, 'laziness and idleness' are 'stigmatised' at least as fiercely as theft and robbery are condemned elsewhere (102/84). Positively, 'the honour with which all forms of work are treated by public opinion' plays a crucial motivational role. From an early age, Icarians are taught to 'love and value' their work as a form of public service owed to the community as a whole (101/83). Moreover, Icarians happily discharge this civic duty out of 'republican passion and feeling' (270/222).

The satisfactions of public service may be sufficient, but there are additional honorific incentives to encourage even greater technological innovation. Citizens are encouraged from an early age to make themselves 'even more useful to society' by making a discovery or invention, and those who succeed earn 'special esteem, public recognition, or even national honours' (102/84). Icaria is littered with material tributes to those who have made discoveries or won competitions (such as that to design the model city of Icara). Perhaps the most ubiquitous is the charming little statue found above the toilet door in every Icarian home, immortalizing the woman who invented a procedure for expelling 'les odeurs fétides' (89/73, 66/55).

Work also plays a symbolic role in Voyage en Icarie, representing the identity and character of Icarian citizens and society more generally. It is in the huge communal workshops, Valmor tells Carisdall, that the 'intelligence and reason' of the people and government really 'shine forth' (103/84). The dominant images of productive activity always involve order and discipline. Icarian work, like Icarian society, functions in precise and regimented ways, which can initially appear to leave individuality with no space to emerge (let alone develop and flourish). In the clock-making workshop, workers are said to form a 'little army', and Carisdall remarks that you 'would think you were seeing an army regiment; such is the high degree of order and discipline there' (60/51). And in the masons' workshop, Valmor uses the language of clockwork, observing that 'this ensemble forms but a single vast machine in which each cog fulfils its function without irregularity' (105/86).

Military and mechanical images might predominate but individuality does have some place. In particular, at the age of seventeen (women) and eighteen (men), Icarians get to choose the occupations they will enter. There are some constraints here; for example, the republic calculates which jobs are needed, and women are restricted to the 'industries that are particular to women' (106/87). However, given certain features of Icarian occupations – that material rewards are independent of individual performance, that all jobs are held in the same esteem, that no job is burdensome, and so on – the choices that remain would seem to reflect individual preferences and proclivities. (If a particular occupation is oversubscribed, the places are allocated by means of 'a competition, examinations, and the judgment of the competitors themselves who make up a jury' (106/86–7).) Whatever one's views about the feasibility and desirability of such arrangements, Cabet is acknowledging issues of individuality here (just as elsewhere he tries, albeit not entirely successfully, to explain how the sumptuary laws allow variety as well as uniformity) (56–9/48–50).

Cabet appears not to recognize that (some) work might (potentially) be an *intrinsically* pleasurable activity. He is unsympathetic to the idea – emphasized elsewhere in the socialist tradition – that organized in the right way, productive activity could be creative and fulfilling in itself. Given that the enthusiasts for Icarian communism were craft workers (tailors, shoemakers, weavers, cabinetmakers, hatters, locksmiths, and so on), modern readers are liable to be puzzled by their apparent willingness to abandon artisanal skills in favour of machine-tending and the mindless repetition of small mechanical tasks. Modern concerns about alienation are noticeably absent. In the present context, any explanation must remain tentative, but from the vantage-point of artisans (not proletarians) in a largely pre-industrial France, the costs of de-skilling were largely unknown, whilst the march of mechanization could easily seem inevitable, and the compensations of association overwhelming. Negatively, Icaria promised to release artisans from the grip of commercial middlemen, the dangers of downward social mobility, the threat of grinding poverty and the burden of over-work. Positively, it promised to provide them with a heady cocktail of egalitarianism, community, material plenty, bourgeois culture, compatibility with Christianity and republican virtue.

In such circumstances, it is perhaps not so surprising that parts of Cabet's audience found themselves identifying so fully with the fictitious visitors to Icaria who were 'dazzled by so much reason and so much happiness' (161/51). One of the latter concludes a long descriptive letter home, by imagining the recipients' likely reaction: 'I believe I can hear you exclaiming, along with me: Fortunate Icarians! Unfortunate Frenchmen!' (48/42).

19

The Horror of Strangeness: Edward Bellamy's *Looking Backward*

Matthew Beaumont

I think it must have been many seconds that I sat up thus in bed staring about, without being able to regain the clew to my personal identity. I was no more able to distinguish myself from pure being during those moments than we may suppose a soul in the rough to be before it has received the ear-marks, the individualizing touches which make it a person. Strange that the sense of this inability should be such anguish! but so we are constituted. There are no words for the mental torture I endured during this helpless, eyeless groping for myself in a boundless void. No other experience of the mind gives probably anything like the sense of absolute intellectual arrest from the loss of a mental fulcrum, a starting point of thought, which comes during such a momentary obscuration of the sense of one's identity. I trust I may never know what it is again.

I do not know how long this condition had lasted – it seemed an interminable time – when, like a flash, the recollection of everything came back to me. I remembered who and where I was, and how I had come here, and that these scenes as of the life of yesterday which had been passing before my mind concerned a generation long, long ago mouldered to dust. Leaping from bed, I stood in the middle of the room clasping my temples with all my might between my hands to keep them from bursting. Then I fell prone on the couch, and, burying my face in the pillow, lay without motion. The reaction which was inevitable, from the mental elation, the fever of the intellect that had been the first effect of my tremendous experience, had arrived.[1]

*L*ooking Backward 2000–1887 (1888) is of almost incalculable importance to the history of the utopian form. Edward Bellamy's socialist romance was by far the most popular and ideologically influential utopia produced in the late nineteenth century, a time when novels about the future probably appeared in greater numbers than at any other period in Western history. At the *fin de siècle*, utopian fiction suddenly seemed to be an intellectually and commercially viable medium for communicating political ideas, especially oppositional ones, on both sides of the Atlantic. Ordinary middle-class readers as well as socialists of one stripe or another were electrified by the possibilities of the form. *Looking Backward* – which was only the second novel published in the United States to sell a million copies – was chiefly responsible for this state of affairs. Everyone interested in the so-called 'social question' debated the book, 'down to the boot-blacks as they s[a]t on the curbstones'.[2]

Bellamy's utopia caused a sensation in part because of its eloquent and quietly furious indictment of capitalist society. It was published at a time of rising unemployment and deepening industrial disputes, when people throughout the industrialized nations started to lose that supreme sense of confidence in the capitalist system which had characterized the third quarter of the century. At bottom, this was because of a sustained economic crisis that had seen capitalism slide in and out of recession since the early 1870s. If capitalist society for the first time seemed disconcertingly unstable, however, its collapse did not seem imminent. The working-class movement was inspired to an unprecedented extent by visions of a post-capitalist society; but, as the century reached its end, and inter-imperial rivalries intensified, breeding conflicts that finally climaxed in 1914, these visions started to dissolve into the distance. The explosion of utopianism at the *fin de siècle* was an expression of the disappointments as well as the achievements of socialists in this epoch. On the Left, the popularity of utopian dreaming was partly the effect of a historical situation in which socialists were incapable of exploiting in practical terms the political opportunities that had opened up to them.

In this climate, *Looking Backward* became a *cause célèbre* because, in addition, its innumerable readers used it as a kind of guidebook to the possibilities of a post-capitalist society. As such, it inspired others to offer blueprints for the future. Some were openly motivated by fear of its mass appeal. Alfred Morris, for example, attacked *Looking Backward* from the Right in *Looking Ahead!* (1892), which complained, not completely inaccurately, that 'Socialist leaders, when pressed to formulate their policy, were in the habit of referring enquirers to [Bellamy's] book, as affording a complete and unanswerable solution'.[3] William Morris, for his part, attacked it from the Left in *News from Nowhere* (1891), a utopian romance that promoted the peaceful pastoral vision of a communist society formed in the aftermath of violent socialist revolution. Some contemporary readers, in contrast, were motivated to compose utopias by devoted enthusiasm for Bellamy's secular vision of the heavenly city. Others simply lifted plot devices from the book, like H.G. Wells in *When the Sleeper Wakes* (1899). Bellamy himself published a sequel, *Equality*, in 1897. According to Krishan Kumar's calculations, at least sixty-two novels directly indebted to Bellamy's utopian model were published in the United States and Europe between 1889 and 1900.[4]

The utopian tradition that commenced with Thomas More's *Utopia* (1516) had generally located the ideal society about which it dreamed in unmapped space. Bellamy's main formal contribution to the utopian tradition was instead to cement its association with unmapped time, by relocating the ideal society to a relatively far-distant future. In this respect, he built on polemical, often dystopian, narratives from the second half of the nineteenth century, like George Chesney's *The Battle of Dorking* (1871), which depicted dramatic social alternatives to the present unfolding in the immediate future. *Looking Backward* therefore conjoined the utopian genre to the so-called imaginary history. And this suited an epoch shaped both by an acute sense of historical expectation and a deepening suspicion that, under the impact of imperial expansion, the amount of unmapped space on the planet was rapidly diminishing. As Bellamy declared in the Postscript to the second edition of *Looking Backward*, the book 'was written in the belief that the Golden Age lies before us and not behind us, and is not far away' (197). The final clause of that sentence seems ambiguous, for if it denotes that the origins of the Golden Age lie in the nineteenth century rather than some far-distant future, then it connotes that it can be found in the United States rather than some far-distant island. Bellamy's protagonist, Julian West, who suffers from acute insomnia, falls into a deep sleep one night in 1887, thanks to the assistance of a professional mesmerist, and wakes up one day in the year 2000; in both epochs, then, he finds himself, or loses himself, in Boston. He is a time-traveller.

In his review of *Looking Backward*, William Morris claimed that 'it is the serious essay and not the slight envelope of romance which people have found interesting'.[5] Like a number of subsequent critics, he implied first that the utopia's essayistic and romantic elements are its sole formal components; and second that the latter can be dismissed as of merely incidental importance. More recently, Kumar has for example remarked that, of all the utopian fictions he discusses in *Utopia and Anti-Utopia in Modern Times*, 'Bellamy's is in fact the least interesting, considered as literature'.[6] Bellamy himself seems to have sanctioned this assumption, in spite of his comparative commercial success as an author of ghost stories and romances prior to the late 1880s. In an article of 1890, he observed that, in recasting the manuscript of *Looking Backward* after devising the idea of the 'industrial army', which he identified as 'the destined corner-stone of the new social order', he retained 'the form of romance' only reluctantly, including it 'with some impatience, in the hope of inducing the more to give it at least a reading'.[7] Kumar has pointed out that, in adopting this attitude, Bellamy was 'rejecting his own past as a romancer and story-teller': 'He was self-consciously taking on a new, more purposive role, as social critic and prophet,' he concludes; 'but in doing so he ensured that, once his ideas had been generally absorbed, or were no longer considered interesting, there was little to attract a later generation to the book'.[8] This is I believe a misrepresentation of *Looking Backward*, a novel that is in fact possessed of considerable psychological depth, as I hope to demonstrate through a close reading of the extract cited above. It seems to me that Bellamy's finest achievement is his portrait of the protagonist's psychology, the aspect of the book that has probably been most consistently overlooked in scholarly accounts of it. *Looking Backward*, I argue, is a kind of case history in the psychology of the utopian imagination.

In spite of Kumar's claim, Bellamy's utopia is therefore continuous rather than discontinuous with his previous fiction – novels like *Doctor Heidenhoff's Process* (1880) and *Miss Ludington's Sister* (1884), as well as several short stories – in which he speculatively explores abnormal psychological states. In *Miss Ludington's Sister*, for instance, Bellamy speculates about 'the immortality of past selves', imagining an alternative state of being in which one's 'past and future selves' are both immediately, perpetually present: 'The idea of an individual, all whose personalities are contemporaneous, may there be realized, and such an individual would be by any earthly measurements a god.'[9] *Looking Backward* is also a meditation on the idea of a personality consisting of both past and future selves; and rethinking it in these terms might help us recapture some of the excitement that it inspired in Bellamy's contemporaries. Fredric Jameson has commented on the difficulty of understanding this novel's initial impact, reflecting that 'the enigma of desire remains, and we are no longer very well placed to appreciate Bellamy's secret'.[10] In some respects, we are better placed to understand the 'enigma of desire', I suspect, than the book's first readers.

So the critical consensus about *Looking Backward*, which insists that, like most utopian fiction of the late nineteenth century, it is emotionally flat and lacking in affect, falsifies it. Bellamy's protagonist, to take the example that most interests me, does not, as most accounts of the book assume, make an untroubled transition to the society of 2000. In fact, West suffers something like a trauma in time-travelling to the future. His psychology is a disturbed one that raises fascinating questions about the stability of the human subject under the peculiar existential conditions of utopian imagining. Bellamy reinvented the utopian form in part by conceptualizing it as the psychological portrait of an individual who effectively becomes dislocated from time; from both the present he half escapes and the future to which he is half assimilated. 'That story of another world,' writes the narrator of one of Bellamy's short stories, 'has, in a word, put me out of joint with ours'.[11] Throughout his fiction, Bellamy is fascinated by the psychology of disjointedness, of divided consciousness. *Looking Backward* is a study of time out of joint, and of a subject that is out of joint too.

In an interesting article on 'The Insomnia of Julian West', Tom Towers once argued that the 'chronic insomnia' from which Bellamy's protagonist suffers in the late nineteenth century 'becomes the comprehensive symbol of the totality of Julian's sense of social and psychic disturbance'. His emphasis on the hero's damaged psyche is original, but the article makes a misleading assumption that the damage is spontaneously repaired once West has appeared in the utopian society of the twenty-first century: 'Julian seems reborn into a new selfhood, making him for the first time at peace with himself and his world.'[12] In fact, the opposite is the case: old neuroses cling to him and new ones emerge. Sleep, for example, remains a problem even after his reappearance in utopia. On his first night in 2000, it is in a state of 'dread' that he anticipates the moment at which he must be alone in the bedroom he has been allotted by the Leetes, his hosts in this socialist society, because he fears that the 'mental balance' that he has maintained in the presence of these 'friendly strangers' will collapse.

> Even then, however, in the pauses of the conversation I had had glimpses, vivid as lightning flashes, of the horror of strangeness that was waiting to be faced when I could no longer command diversion. I knew I could not sleep that night, and as for lying awake and thinking, it argues no cowardice, I am sure, to confess that I was afraid of it. (28)

West is poised above a psychological abyss, and he fears that it is when he has to confront his existential situation alone that he will plummet into it. Terrified that the 'horror of strangeness' will finally overwhelm him, he consequently defers the moment when he must go to bed, questioning Dr Leete, his chief interlocutor, until three o'clock in the morning. At that point, Leete prescribes him a 'dose' that will ensure 'a sound night's sleep without fail' (28); and West does indeed sleep deeply.

It is when he wakes up the next morning that he experiences an acute psychological crisis. At first, West lies quite contentedly in bed, because he has no recollection of the fact that he has travelled through time. But when he realizes that he is in an unfamiliar bedchamber he starts up from the couch and stares crazily about the apartment. Momentarily – though it seems to him to last 'an interminable time' – he loses completely his sense of 'personal identity', and finds himself adrift in a state of 'pure being'. He is being reborn, and this process of parturition, as he is assimilated to the conditions of this utopian society, is a laborious and painful one. West struggles to explain this in retrospect.

> There are no words for the mental torture I endured during this helpless, eyeless groping for myself in a boundless void. No other experience of the mind gives probably anything like the sense of absolute intellectual arrest from the loss of a mental fulcrum, a starting point of thought, which comes during such a momentary obscuration of one's identity. (45)

As he gropes in the 'boundless void', West is I-less as well as 'eyeless'.

But the sudden recollection that he has time-travelled to 2000, which succeeds this sense that his identity has been all but abolished, is no less devastating. In an instant, he realizes that all those he loved have been dead for almost a hundred years: he leaps from his bed, clasping his temples, and then flings himself back onto it, burying his face in the pillow. This psychic melodrama immediately precipitates him back into the boundless void he hopes instead to evade.

> The emotional crisis which had awaited the full realization of my actual position, and all that it implied, was upon me, and with set teeth and laboring chest,

gripping the bedstead with frenzied strength, I lay there and fought for my sanity. In my mind, all had broken loose, habits of feeling, associations of thought, ideas of persons and things, all had dissolved and lost coherence and were seething together in apparently irretrievable chaos. There were no rallying points, nothing was left stable. (46)

In a state of severe mental dissociation, he reflects on the likelihood that he has suffered a schizoidal split: 'The idea that I was two persons, that my identity was double, began to fascinate me with its simple solution of my experience' (46). But this solution, which is actually not an inaccurate one, offers little consolation. On the contrary, he becomes conscious that he is 'on the verge of losing [his] mental balance' (46).

In order to escape a complete psychological collapse, West quits the Leetes' apartment and races into the utopian city's empty streets. Like an agoraphobic adrift in the metropolis, he desperately scrambles about in Boston's unfamiliar quarters for some two hours. In this scene, the city itself effectively functions as an objective correlative for the boundless void. Finally, he races back to the apartment and collapses in a state of 'actual nausea', his brain apparently melting because of his sense of 'abjectness' and anguish: 'Throwing myself into a chair, I covered my burning eyeballs with my hands to shut out the horror of strangeness' (47). Again: the horror of strangeness. It is at this point that Leete's daughter reappears and coaxes West out of his psychotic state. However, the descriptive intensity of the passage I have cited above is such that, in spite of his assimilation to the Boston of the future thereafter, he never fully seems to escape the threat of some relapse.

The novel's poetic as opposed to political force depends on the idea established in this scene that West's identity is in some sense doubled; and that, as someone who is simultaneously a product of the nineteenth and the twenty-first century, he is doomed to inhabit the historical equivalent of what Bellamy once described in another context as a 'Jekyll-Hyde existence'.[13] Doubleness is indeed something like an obsession in the shorter fiction, where the past and future are often placed in unsettling tension with the present: stories like 'The Old Folks' Party' (1876) and 'A Midnight Drama' (1877), in spite of the quaintness of their romance plots, are probing, experimental investigations into what he describes in the latter as the 'odd feeling of being double'.[14] In the former, six young friends stage a fancy-dress party at which they must make themselves up as their future selves; that is, as they imagine they will look in fifty years' time. This game produces 'a singular effect': 'They began to regard every event and feeling from a double standpoint, as present and as past, as it appeared to them and as it would appear to an old person.'[15] As in *Miss Ludington's Sister*, past, present and future selves are rendered co-existent in *Looking Backward*.

Read from the perspective of these examples of Bellamy's speculative fiction, *Looking Backward* can be interpreted as an attempt to infuse the utopian form with psychological realism. It is a laboratory test of what, in 'The Old Folks' Party', he had called 'the fragile tenure of the sense of personal identity'.[16] West does not become magically adjusted to the conditions of Boston in 2000; plausibly enough, he remains maladjusted. Bellamy therefore dramatically redefines the narrator of utopian fiction, presenting him as someone almost terminally troubled by psychic uncertainty. In Bellamy's socialist romance, time-travelling to the future entails an existential struggle. In thus psychologizing the utopian imagination, or even psychopathologizing it, he decisively modernizes utopian fiction. In this respect, *Looking Backward* anticipates the concerns of twentieth-century science fiction more strikingly even than Wells's novels, which it is generally assumed inaugurate the genre; for, as Jameson has observed, it is 'one of the grand and dramatic merits of SF as a form that it can thus win back from the sheerly psychological or subjective such expressive powers of pathology – depression, melancholy, morbid passion – and place this material in the service of collective drama'.[17]

20

'The Incompatibility I Could Not Resolve': Ambivalence in H.G. Wells's *A Modern Utopia*

Richard Nate

The Utopia of a modern dreamer must needs differ in one fundamental aspect from the Nowheres and Utopias men planned before Darwin quickened the thought of the world. Those were all perfect and static States, a balance of happiness won forever against the forces of unrest and disorder that inhere in things. One beheld a healthy and simple generation enjoying the fruits of the earth in an atmosphere of virtue and happiness, to be followed by other virtuous, happy, and entirely similar generations, until the Gods grew weary. Change and development were dammed back by invincible dams forever. But the Modern Utopia must be not static but kinetic, must shape not as a permanent state but as a hopeful stage leading to a long ascent of stages. [...] That is the first, most generalised difference between a Utopia based upon modern conceptions and all the Utopias that were written in the former time.[1]

When H.G. Wells published *A Modern Utopia* in 1905, the book's very title indicated its ambivalent nature. Since it described an ideal community, it could be viewed as a part of the utopian tradition that had begun with Plato's *Republic* in the fifth century BC. At the same time, however, the epithet 'modern' signalled that it was also intended as a departure from this tradition. In contrast to the ideal communities described so far, Wells's utopia was not set on some remote island but rather represented a political structure of a global nature. In order to understand this change, one has to take into account the context of the late nineteenth century when European expansion had reached its final stage and a *terra incognita* to be populated with an imaginary community no longer existed. 'Time was when a mountain valley of an island seemed to promise sufficient isolation for a polity to maintain itself from outward force', Wells declared in the first chapter of his book, concluding that a world state was the only model which now remained for outlining an ideal society (8). In addition, the philosophical basis of his utopia also meant a break with tradition. In contrast to the timeless character that had still defined William Morris's *News from Nowhere* (1891), the 'kinetic' world state was conceived of as a transitory state within a never-ending process of change. After the idea of a God-given 'chain of being' had been challenged by Darwin's theory of evolution, the static vision of traditional utopias seemed no longer acceptable. What was needed was a new model of society that respected the dynamism inherent in the new biological outlook.

In order to get an idea of the nature of Wells's utopia, however, it is important to realize that his subscription to evolutionary theory also had an impact on the mode of textual presentation. The emphasis on the transitory quality of all natural phenomena had two implications. On the one hand, it implied a rejection of the creationist view of nature; on the other it pointed to the limitations of the utopian vision itself. Rather than creating a coherent utopian model, Wells aimed at testing the potentials of the utopian imagination under the constraints of a Darwinian view of the universe. On the textual level, this resulted in a degree of openness that perfectly corresponded to the author's enthusiasm for all kinds of experimentalism.[2] Adopting the experimental method in utopian writing meant that the vision of an ideal state functioned as a hypothesis open to both verification and falsification. In the case of the *Modern Utopia*, the outcome was a critical reflection on the status of utopian writing rather than a blueprint for an ideal society.[3]

If Wells intended his work as an experiment on utopian writing, he had to make sure that his readers were not carried away by the charms of his fiction. In a 'Note to the Reader', he explained that he had spent a considerable amount of time on the question of how to construct his text. Rejecting the form of an 'argumentative essay' as well as that of a 'straightforward story', he had finally decided on a 'sort of shot-silk texture', that is a combination of both forms of presentation (xlvii).

What distinguishes *A Modern Utopia* from Wells's earlier scientific romances is the fact that the reader is continually made aware of its status as a literary artefact.[4] Instead of lulling his audience into pleasant visions of an ideal society, Wells employed strategies of defamiliarization which bore a conspicuous resemblance to modernist modes of writing.[5] There are various elements which are likely to irritate the reader rather than satisfy their curiosity. Not only does Wells add a frame text in which he distances himself from the 'owner of the voice' whom he mockingly describes as a 'rather too plump little man ... laboriously enunciating propositions' (4), but he also allows his narrator to make remarks which are liable to qualify the entire utopian project. When the utopian 'voice' refers to his model as the 'monster state my Frankenstein of reasoning has made' (140), for instance, he not only professes his higher education by simultaneously alluding to Thomas Hobbes' *Leviathan* (1651) and Mary Shelley's *Frankenstein* (1818), but he also hints at the possibility that his vision may even contain some dystopian elements. A qualifying effect is also achieved through the introduction of a character who acts as the voice's antagonist. The 'botanist', as he is called, turns out to be a representative of the pre-Darwinian biology that Wells rejected. Like his eighteenth-century precursor Carl Linnaeus, the botanist is convinced of the timeless quality of classificatory models. Significantly, it is his conservative outlook which produces the collapse of the voice's utopian vision at the end of the narrative. Caught in the web of a philosophical determinism in which the 'scars of the past' make any attempt at creating a new social reality appear like a waste of time, he finally forces the narrator to redirect his attention to the bleak reality of contemporary London. As the latter finds himself disillusioned by the botanist's fatalist attitude, the only thing that is left for him is his confidence in the utopian imagination itself. 'There will be many utopias', he concludes, and adds rather vaguely: 'Each Generation will have its new version of Utopia, a little more certain and complete and real, with its problems lying close and closer to the problems of the Thing in Being' (220).

The negative depiction of the botanist cannot be understood without taking into account Wells's profound distrust in the reliability of classificatory models. On the one hand, this distrust had its roots in Darwin's refutation of the stable categories of creationism; on the other, it sprang from an epistemological scepticism the author had expressed early on. When Wells prepared the Atlantic Edition of his works in the 1920s, he took care that his epistemological essay 'Scepticism of the Instrument' was appended to A Modern Utopia.[6] Given the author's nominalist standpoint, it is not surprising to find the utopian narrator also regarding all classificatory models with suspicion and insisting on the primacy of the individual. 'Until you bring in individualities, nothing comes into being', he declares in the first chapter, and for this reason he also rejects the utopian models of Plato and Thomas More. Instead of paying respect to the 'blood and warmth and reality of life', these authors had merely presented 'generalised people' (7). With regard to his own textual experiment, it is noteworthy that the voice rejects generalizations for aesthetic as well as political reasons. Aesthetically, they make a presentation appear 'jejune'; politically, they prove dangerous by not taking into account the complexities of social life. The narrator's concern for personal liberties shows that he is well aware of the dangers which can result from placing the demands of the community above those of the individual. In a chapter which harshly criticizes the typologies used in contemporary racial anthropology, he even characterizes 'crude classifications and false generalisations' as the 'curse of all organised human life' (191).

Set against the typological schemes employed in the social discourse of Wells's time, the narrator's arguments appear like an exercise in deconstruction. Although he is ready to acknowledge that every human being is naturally inclined to generalize from his or her singular experiences, he points to the dangers inherent in this approach. As far as social phenomena are concerned, the complementary processes of inclusion and exclusion which often accompany the process of generalizing are seen as a major problem. 'The natural man does not feel he is aggregating at all, unless he aggregates *against* something', the narrator states in a chapter on 'Race in Utopia' and explains that general categories are often based on binary distinctions in which one element is preferred to the other: 'The Anti-idea, it would seem, is inseparable from the aggregatory idea; it is a necessity of the human mind. When we think of the class A as desirable, we think of Not-A as undesirable' (189). Significantly, the narrator points to the botanist to illustrate how the human drive to generalize can produce prejudices which lack any rational basis. As he explains, the botanist

> has a strong feeling for systematic botanists as against plant physiologists ... but he has a strong feeling for all ... biologists, as against physicists and those who profess the exact sciences ... but he has a strong feeling for all who profess what is called Science as against psychologists, sociologists, philosophers, and literary men ... but he has a strong feeling for all educated men as against the working man ... but so soon as the working man is comprehended together with those others as Englishmen ... he holds them superior to all other sorts of European. (190)

Remarks such as these prove that Wells was very sensitive towards the ways in which classificatory models could be employed to petrify existing social prejudices. What disturbed him most were the typological schemes used by nationalists and racial anthropologists. Using the narrator as his voice, he warned that national and racial prejudices could be 'responsible for a large proportion of the wars, hardships, and cruelties the immediate future holds in store for our earth' (194). As we know today, it was a warning which would become prophetic within less than a decade.

What proved difficult, however, was the attempt to harmonize the critique of generalizations with the plan of sketching an ideal society. The problem lay in the fact that, by definition, utopian writing had to deal with social categories. As Justin Busch has remarked recently: '[U]topian thought is, of necessity, thought which deals in political generalities, however important the individuals as individuals may be seen as being within the final structure.'[7] Accordingly, Wells's narrator finds himself caught between his distrust of classificatory models and his simultaneous desire to outline the general characteristics of his ideal society. If one compares those passages which outline his epistemological scepticism with those which describe the social structure of the utopian society, his dilemma becomes obvious. Trying to avoid the pitfalls of a naïve essentialism, the narrator argues that his social classes are based on pragmatic rather than philosophical principles. 'It is not a classification for Truth, but a classification to an end', he explains in the hope of not violating his own philosophical premises (160). What comes out of this can only be called a rhetorical manoeuvre. While on the one hand he professes a regard for 'humanity as a multitude of unique individuals in mass', on the other, he suggests that 'one may, for practical purposes, deal with it far more conveniently by disregarding its uniqueness and its mixed cases altogether' (160). The ensuing 'pragmatic' classification is a rigid one, consisting of just four temperaments – the 'poietic', the 'kinetic', the 'dull' and the 'base' (157). The first group consists of highly talented individuals who also make up the 'Order of the Samurai' – an intellectual and moral elite which calls to mind Plato's 'guardians' as well as contemporary concepts of a 'new aristocracy'.[8] The second comprises administrators who carry out the plans of the 'poietic'. While the first two groups meet the requirements of the utopian society, the third and the fourth fall short of its demands. The 'dull' lack sufficient intellectual capacities; the 'base' are characterized by their criminal energy and anti-social behaviour. Although the narrator maintains that the four temperaments are not hereditarily determined but of such a nature that people 'drift' to them 'of their own accord' (157), it is difficult to see how his classification could ever be brought in line with his belief in the primacy of the individual. Even more disturbing, the narrator's definition of four social classes betrays the very characteristic which, on another occasion, leads him to 'regard all generalisations with suspicion', namely their function to separate a desirable class 'A' – the 'poietic' and 'kinetic' – from an undesirable class 'Not-A' – the 'dull' and the 'base'.

That the narrator's classification of social types is based on strategies of inclusion and exclusion becomes clear by looking at another chapter entitled 'Failure in a Modern Utopia'. Here, the voice argues in favour of 'a kind of social surgery' to ensure that the number of undesirable individuals be held in check (84). The reader is informed that the utopian state is active in preventing the 'dull' from propagating, thus adhering to a kind of negative eugenics. The 'base' are segregated from the rest of society by being deported to remote islands which lie 'apart from the highways of the sea' (85). If such policies offend the modern reader, they are still fairly moderate if compared to Wells's earlier writings. In contrast to the grim forecasts he had made in his *Anticipations* (1901), the setting up of 'lethal chambers' is now explicitly dismissed.[9] Still, the narrator's 'social surgery' included practices which clearly violated the principle of human rights that Wells would defend in his later years. Although the narrator professes that 'even for murder Utopia will not ... kill', he explicitly excludes from this practice 'deformed and monstrous and evilly diseased births' who still receive as little mercy as they did in Plato's *Republic* (84).

Given its rigid social policies, it is hardly surprising that the *Modern Utopia* has met with some negative criticism.[10] It must be noted, however, that those readers who have taken Wells's book as a blueprint for a perfect society have failed to acknowledge its status as a textual experiment. A closer look at the text reveals the outcome of this experiment is anything but clear. Interestingly, it is the increasing complexity of the narrator's vision – a complexity which results from his intention to 'bring in individualities' – which is responsible for the fact that his imagination finally fails him. Towards the end of his narrative, he has to admit that 'a Utopia is a thing of the imagination that becomes more fragile with every added circumstance, that, like a soap-bubble, it is most brilliantly and variously coloured at the very instant of its dissolution' (209). In the final chapter, the botanist's unwillingness to shake off the past turns out to be the decisive factor in making the utopian 'bubble' burst. After the experiment has failed, the narrator falls silent and Wells himself takes over. Reflecting on the tensions which result from the divergent tasks of drafting a social scheme and accepting the unique character of every single item, he confesses: 'In that incongruity between great and individual inheres the incompatibility I could not resolve, and which, therefore, I have had to present in this conflicting form' (222).

Indeed, what remains of the utopian vision is little more than this 'conflicting form' which only corroborates the Darwinian outlook the author has subscribed to from the beginning. If the ending betrays a loss of confidence in the concrete utopian model, this does not diminish the value of the utopian imagination. When the narrator concludes that 'each generation will have its new version of Utopia' (19), this statement can be interpreted as an acknowledgment of both the futility of any utopian programme and also as an expression of his unbroken belief in the 'principle of hope' which Ernst Bloch declared to be the driving force behind all utopian thought.[11] Wells's future career as a writer suggests that the latter reading is the more appropriate one. If there is a common characteristic detectable in all his works, it is his readiness to permanently reshape his political visions and to adapt them to the changing conditions of the twentieth century. Although it seems that he was not always aware of the problematic implications of some of his proposals, his readiness to revise his schemes clearly distinguished him from those contemporaries who succumbed to the charms of totalitarian ideologies. If viewed in this way, the bursting of the narrator's 'bubble' does not necessarily signify a failure of the experiment; it could equally be viewed as indicative of the author's awareness that the only utopia which made sense in the modern world was one which was sufficiently flexible to question and able to adapt itself.

21

Utopian Journeying: Ursula K. Le Guin's *The Dispossessed*

Laurence Davis and Peter G. Stillman

True Journey is return[1]

One of the most persistent criticisms of the literary utopia is that it is radically anti-historical, in the sense that it depicts distant times or places qualitatively different and cut off from the useless burdens of the present and past. From this perspective, the spirit of the utopian is in essence Platonic rather than Heraclitian, because it denies the essential flux inherent in all being. Whereas Heraclitus famously believed that you cannot step twice into the same river, because both you and the river waters flow in continual change, Plato's *Republic* inaugurated a tradition of ideal societies based on timeless and absolute standards occupying a fixed space outside of history. As a result, so the argument goes, literary utopias are either politically irrelevant fantasies or potentially dangerous expressions of a despotic desire to re-shape reality according to an impossible ideal.

To some extent, these criticisms of utopia have merit. Many early modern European utopian writers from More to Bacon and Campanella did indeed imagine qualitatively different futures bereft of historical roots and devoid of processes tending to upset them or change their design. Although the formation of utopian expectations, values and norms was historically embedded in the background of utopian thinking, history as a continuing concern for the past was rejected because of a belief that the new ideal world had to emanate from reason, nature or morality.[2]

Influenced no doubt by ever-accelerating processes of capitalist globalization, the dominant trend of subsequent Enlightenment and Industrial era utopian thinking has been to postulate a break between the dynamic present of modernity and its comparatively 'primitive' static past. One thinks, for example, of the many so-called 'progressive' or 'dynamic' utopias of the nineteenth century, which acknowledge the extent to which utopian ideals are bound up with time and history, but only insofar as history is conceived in linear, law-like and necessarily progressive terms as a set of fixed and hierarchical stages leading ultimately to a future perfection.

Ursula K. Le Guin discusses her departure from this dominant trend of anti-historical utopia in an exceptionally thought-provoking paper on literary utopias that she delivered at the University of California in 1982, eight years after the publication of her first utopian novel *The Dispossessed* and three years prior to the publication of her second utopian novel, *Always Coming Home*. Le Guin signalled that her chief focus was the theme of 'returning'.[3] While this may seem an unusual theme for an essay on utopias, its rationale becomes clear once Le Guin identifies the primary target of the essay's critical commentary: namely, what she refers to as the 'Euclidean' or rationalist utopia.

According to Le Guin, it is the very essence of this utopia that it is, as More said in naming it, nowhere. A reaction of will and reason against, away from, the here and now and the fetters of the past, the Euclidean utopia is pure model and goal. Like capitalism and industrialism and colonial 'development', it is able to speak only in the future tense, the language of progress, and is thus inherently uninhabitable. Like them as well, it is also potentially highly destructive of what is, insofar as it blinds us to the infinite meaning and beauty hidden in the every day, and propels us forward in an ever more breathless and desperate pursuit of the unattainable. It aims for a goal of static perfection, in which the variegated diversity of life is regulated by principles of reason that are embodied in structures.

The focus of the non-Euclidean utopia, by contrast, is on the temporally extended present, the 'right here, right now' inhabited by living, breathing human beings. Paradoxically, it is such that if it is to come, it must exist already. Indeed, according to Le Guin, it has existed already, as a feature of many of the so-called 'primitive' societies crushed under the wheels of technological 'progress'. It has also flourished in literary form in a relatively small number of utopian works, such as Robert Nichols's four-volume *Daily Lives in Nghsi-Altai* (1977–9) and Austin Tappan Wright's *Islandia* (1942), which explicitly rejected the dominant ideology of endless material progress. Clearly associating herself with this tradition, Le Guin urges her listeners and readers to pay heed to the Taoist advice to return to roots, and the Cree counsel to emulate the porcupine in going backwards while looking forward. Again recalling Native American lore, she recalls that Coyote country was not mapped, and suggests that perhaps the utopist would do well to 'lose the plan, throw away the map',[4] and pay far greater attention to the *communitas* implicit in the landscape of the present.

In *The Dispossessed*, Le Guin breaks radically from this rootless utopian tradition and explores the characteristics of the non-Euclidean utopia. Her novel begins and ends with the chief protagonist Shevek travelling between the worlds of Urras and Anarres, a neighbouring planet or moon settled some 170 years prior to the start of the story by anarchist syndicalist revolutionaries from Urras. A brilliant physicist working on a unified theory of time, Shevek grows up on Anarres and gradually becomes aware of its shortcomings; he journeys to Urras, witnesses first hand its inequalities and injustices, supports a revolutionary movement there that is violently repressed, and returns home to Anarres.

One of the most distinctive features of Le Guin's utopian narrative is that it is grounded[5] in a rich landscape of time and place that is the antithesis of ideologies of perpetual progress and human perfectibility. Early in the novel Shevek reflects that 'you shall not go down twice to the same river, nor can you go home again' (54). But from this acceptance of transience he also develops a sophisticated theory of time wherein what is most changeable is the fullest of eternity, and in word and deed he demonstrates that 'you *can* go home again ... so long as you understand that home is a place where you have never been' (55).

In this chapter we elaborate on Le Guin's creative development of the utopian tradition by exploring ways in which she narrates utopia without assuming unchanging utopian frameworks, linear progress, or human perfectibility. Specifically, we focus on the themes of change, freedom and initiative, promises, and utopian journeying.

Unlike utopias of perfectibility and stasis, Le Guin's utopia foregrounds change at both a societal and an individual level. The anarchist utopian society on Anarres originates in revolutionary change. But it ossifies and decays over time, suggesting that even in a good society individuals may pursue power and fear the opinions of their neighbours. Utopia cannot transform human nature: the will to dominate is as 'central to human beings as the impulse to mutual aid is' (168). At the same time, Shevek and his friends create counter-tendencies, new ways to re-invigorate anarchist society. The 'close' of the novel is open-ended, stopping just before Shevek's landing on his return to Anarres. So Le Guin does not tell her readers whether he will be greeted with open arms, with violence or with some other change-making response. Neither static nor rigid, Anarres is constantly evolving.

Individuals also change. For instance, Shevek is transformed by significant life episodes, such as his enduring partnership with Takver and his fraught working relationship with Sabul, who accrues power and privileges as leader of the physics syndicate. Contrasts with other characters emphasize Shevek's changes and transformations. His critically astute friend Bedap fails to find a fulfilling direction to life; and Tirin, an imaginative playwright, cannot move beyond his first play. Unlike perfect – and insipid – characters who live in a structurally well-organized utopia and who simply choose or live within the confines of those structures, and unlike visitors to utopia who are converted to a belief in the utopia, for Shevek life is a process of change.

Change occurs because individuals make decisions and undertake initiatives that alter their lives and the lives of others. A perfected utopia, a utopia without change, or a utopia characterized (like *Looking Backward* or *A Modern Utopia*) by a rational structure within which people live – these types of utopias cannot encompass human actions that change the society; they can at most allow choices that do not disturb the utopia's order. In *The Dispossessed* Le Guin explores important dimensions of human freedom beyond the standard sense of freedom as choice.

On Anarres individuals do have freedom as choice. But they can also question existing social principles and practices, and act contrary to them, by individual or group initiative. In the face of Anarres's decay, Shevek and his friends decide to form a 'Syndicate of Initiative', which publishes material refused by existing syndicates and eventually undertakes other initiatives, such as communicating with Urras and advocating for Shevek to go to Urras. These initiatives involve 'the power of moral choice – the power of change, the essential function of life' (333) and can transform the basic principles and practices of society.

Arguing before the PDC, an anarchist coordinating system for all the syndicates, Shevek asserts that it is the 'right of the Odonian individual to initiate action harmless to others' (357), whatever that action might be – even if it is the novel action of travelling to Urras and returning, and even if some PDC members advocate Anarres's continuing isolation from Urras. But after the debate, Shevek decides to act on his own initiative by travelling to Urras. In a free society each person, alone or with others, acts on his or her own initiative. Individuals must themselves generate the circumstances in which they live. And individual freedom and initiative in turn undermine fixed structures and linearity.

In a world of change, neither nature nor logic provides stability. Takver loves the organic cycles in the fish she studies, but human beings are not fish, for 'whom the present is eternal' (187). Humans remember the past and can act to try to bring about a future. Humans also cannot rely on nature as a standard, a criterion, or basis for action: Shevek, feeling tremors, knows the 'earth itself was uncertain, unreliable' (314), a thought with particular resonance as we write this chapter, only months after the earthquake and tsunamis that devastated Japan. Nor can logic, interpretation, reason or constitutions provide stability: the intense argument at the PDC about Shevek's journeying to Urras and back indicates that reason provides a plurality of possible answers. In the face of nature's restlessness and reason's indeterminacy, 'the enduring, the reliable, is a promise made by the human mind' (314).

A promise intervenes in the cycles and movements of life, creating a new path to follow. A promise originates in freedom and is a self-imposed limitation on freedom: 'I promise' is to undertake that there are some things I shall do, and others I shall refrain from doing. Individuals themselves freely limit their freedom by committing to specific actions, and thus make possible the establishment of trust, union and community.

An individual can make a personal promise, as Shevek does when he promises himself that 'he would never act again but by his own free choice' (8). A couple can undertake mutual promises to create a small community of trust and commitment, as do Shevek and Takver. Larger groups are also built on promises and flourish with trust. The syndicates are built on the promise that everyone will be treated equally and fairly, and that no one will usurp administrative work into political power – a promise certainly broken by Sabul with the physics syndicate. Anarres was started by Odonians who committed to live together in an Odonian fashion on their new planet, and whose revolutionary song, sung by the protestors on Urras during Shevek's stay, refers hopefully to 'the promise kept' (299).

Promises are commitments made about the future by individuals speaking and acting in the present, whose commitments carry weight because of their past reliability. Building on their pasts, individuals create their futures by the act of promising. Those who live only in the present – such as hedonistic pleasure-seekers, or those who know only denial (378) – live within a recurring, unchanging cycle, or (in a different metaphor) the locked room of a present without past or future: 'Outside the locked room is the landscape of time, in which the spirit may, with luck and courage, construct the fragile, makeshift, improbable roads and cities of fidelity: a landscape inhabitable by human beings' (335).

In that fragile landscape shaped by promises, individuals freely engage in new undertakings. They make journeys. They set out with a project, a direction, a wish to work towards some different condition or state. But that aim is constantly revised as new constraints or possibilities arise and as intermediate directions are attained or change. For Le Guin, there is 'no end' or goal: 'There was process; process was all' (334). Moreover, the 'separation of means and ends' is 'false', as all means are ends (296, 334). So for Le Guin journeying is a process, an interplay in which means and ends are intermixed, interchangeable and continually changing.

In the process of the journey, travellers are transformed by their aims and activities, and their activities transform the landscape through which they travel. But the meanings of the changes do not become clear until the travellers return home; an action requires completion in order for it to be intelligible. (Indeed, because lives are made up of multiple journeys, any action's completion is but temporary, and its meanings subject to change in the light of future journeys.)

The journey to establish a rationalist or Euclidean utopia is a journey into a static and structured future with a set goal, a journey that leaves home and the past behind. For Le Guin, 'true journey is return', a return home to a new present transformed in unpredictable ways by the journey. The return home can prompt an awareness of what might be called 'the living present', an on-going, continuous present binding past experiences to present aims and directions for the future. In this living present, Tao-like, the present stretches through past and future, sameness includes change, and living involves activity without striving and motion with stillness. Grasping the wholeness of the living present requires not talk or reason but 'hand's touch. I touch the wholeness, I hold it' (190).

So Le Guin invites us, her readers, to explore dimensions of the living present. A train engineer takes journeys of fifteen days and then goes 'home' (310–11) to his partner of eighteen years, because for him the same partner means the most novelty and variety. After a breakdown from working too intensely and narrowly on physics with Sabul, a recovering Shevek meets Takver again, and they promise to bond with each other. The narrator observes:

> It was now clear to Shevek ... that his wretched years in this city [with Sabul] had all been part of his present great happiness, because they had led up to it, prepared him for it. Everything that had happened to him was part of what was happening to him now. (183)

He has returned home from his journeys and can now see their meaning as he looks backwards, and finds himself able to inhabit a living present with Takver. By means of their enduring love for one another they create a small community of trust that is rooted in the past and open to a shared future. In this living present of activity without striving, Shevek and Takver become central to the social life of their friends simply by being themselves (188–9), and in Shevek's work in physics he creates a theoretical structure 'that seemed nothing of his own but a knowledge working through him' (187).

'True journey is return' also because the return to a changed home inhabited by other, changed travellers is an invitation to future journeys that respond to the changes in self, home and others. Euclidean utopias assume an end to journeying when the utopia is attained. But Odonians have no 'expectation of ever stopping' (334) and every expectation of doing what they do best (333); so Shevek journeys to Urras and returns to Anarres.

As individuals journey and return so too do societies. As one commentator on the novel has observed, 'Shevek's individual journey out (away from home and to a foreign planet) is part of a homeward journey for his society (toward claiming the past, in the interest of continuing to build a future)'.[6] Anarres has been – and continues to be – a future of Urras. The existence of Anarres is a constant reminder that Urras can be different (295), and the renewed activities of revolutionaries hold out hope that Urras, a paradise in some ways and a hell in others, can change. Similarly, Shevek hopes that direct and meaningful engagement with the continuing reality of oppression and injustice on Urras will remind the Anarresti of why they must be eternally vigilant in testing, protecting and renewing their anarchism.

The promise of Anarres is that its revolution can be 'a permanent one, an on-going process' (176). *The Dispossessed* ends just as Shevek is returning home to an uncertain welcome on Anarres. With him is Ketho, an inhabitant of another planet, who is beginning his own journey. He is travelling to Anarres on his own initiative to study anarchy in action, to experience for himself its distinctive way of life, and ultimately to return home with 'an idea, a promise, a risk' (385) of social renewal.

The true journey is thus a creative venture into the unknown, linking past, present and future in an open circle. The utopian element in *The Dispossessed* is not so much Anarres as a society but Anarres as an open-ended promise, a 'potential permanent source of renewal of thought and perception',[7] which ensures that the past never assumes a final shape and the future never shuts its doors.

Stepping back from the text of *The Dispossessed* to return to the question of its significance in the context of the utopian tradition as a whole, we conclude that Le Guin's utopia differs from so many previous literary utopias by refusing to separate sharply past, present and future; is and ought; means and ends. Whereas the dominant rationalist utopia is a reaction of reason and will against and away from the here and now and the fetters of the past, *The Dispossessed* is an achieved example of a grounded utopia rooted in a rich landscape of time and place. It depicts utopian aspirations not as a star in the heavens or a fixed point on the horizon towards which we sail, but as an ever-present home to which we are continually returning.

Conclusion

Lyman Tower Sargent

In everyone's life there will be times when one is hopeful that one's personal life or the world in which we live is getting better or will get better. There will also be times of despair and times of resignation. In the hopeful times everything is just a bit brighter; we are aware of possibilities of personal and social betterment that elude us at other times, and those possibilities seem to be within reach. These moments have a history in that some people have chosen to write down the possibilities they see in those moments, and when the texts are primarily about social hope, we can call them utopian moments.

Such moments are immensely important because both individuals and societies need hope, need the sense that things do not have to be the way that they are, that things can be better. There are consistent elements in what we hope for, such as a full stomach, decent clothing and housing, and personal security, but beyond these elements what is included depends on time and place.

This book is about the social dreams or the utopian moments of a set of writers from Western Europe and the United States with seven British authors, seven French authors, two from the United States, and one each from Germany, Italy and Spain. The authors range from Thomas More who coined the word 'utopia' in 1516 to Ursula K. Le Guin, who, although the text chosen is from 1974, is still publishing utopias in the second decade of the twenty-first century. All the works highlighted are positive utopias presenting distinctly better places, although some could have used Le Guin's subtitle, *An Ambiguous Utopia*, and *The Isles of Pines* is more ambiguous than most of the utopias of its time period. Although all are important works within utopian literature and many are important in the history of political thought or intellectual or literary history, few are read today except by scholars and university students required to do so on their courses. This is unfortunate because they all have important, albeit very different, messages for their readers.

One is struck, but not really surprised, by just how different the better societies presented in these texts are. All utopias are written within multiple contexts, including the personal, the national, the cultural and the intellectual, and most are directed at debates that were current at the time they were written, and all those contexts are important for thoroughly understanding the utopias. Thus, the title of this collection, *Utopian Moments*, implies that each work was produced at a particular moment in time.

Given the specificity, therefore, can something be said about utopianism? To what extent are these works, individually and collectively, contributions to something bigger? That is what I attempt here. In 1961, the Dutch sociologist F.L. Polak published his *Images of the Future* in which he argued that utopias or 'positive images of the future', as he called them, are essential for the continuation of civilization. In 1969, R. Buckminster Fuller published a book entitled *Utopia or Oblivion: The Prospects for Humanity* and in 2005 the University of Porto published a book entitled *Utopia Matters* and in 2012 will publish a book entitled *Dystopia Matters*. Fuller and Polak were making strong statements about the importance of utopias and *Utopia Matters* included a number of short essays by a variety of scholars (myself included) saying why they think utopias are important.

At the same time, and particularly throughout much of the twentieth century, there have been consistent dire warnings about the dangers of utopia. While much of the anti-utopian literature was directed at the utopia of communism, which became a dystopia in practice, there have been similar attacks on the utopia of the free market as also producing a dystopia in practice. The twentieth century has been called the dystopian century and so far the twenty-first century seems to be following in its footsteps. But, even though the dystopia has been the dominant form in the literature, and there are only two twentieth-century positive utopias discussed in the book (Wells and Le Guin), positive utopias were published throughout the century and continue to be published in the twenty-first. Thus, an insistence on the importance of a positive view of utopianism and recognition of that view continues in both public debate and literature.

Why should something as seemingly harmless as imagining a better society be so threatening? Part of the answer can be seen in the distinction that Karl Mannheim drew between ideology and utopia. Simply put, Mannheim said that ideology is a system of beliefs that keeps those in power from seeing the weakness of their position and utopia is a system of beliefs held by those out of power that allows them to see themselves as overturning the existing order. For Mannheim, both ideology and utopia falsify the real positions, and he also says: 'The representatives of a given order will label as utopian all conceptions of existence which *from their point of view* can in principle never be realized. According to this usage, the contemporary connotation of the term 'utopian' is predominantly that of an idea which is in principle unrealizable.'[1]

Although there are exceptions, it is hard to see most utopias, including most of those discussed in this book, as threatening anybody. One partial exception is Edward Bellamy's *Looking Backward*, which produced movements in many countries with the goal of implementing Bellamy's ideas, or at least parts of them, and a number of the other authors were perceived by those in power to be threats, even though in most cases they probably were not. Still, specific examples aside, the whole idea of imagining a significantly better society is regularly thought of as bad because *significantly better* means different, probably different in major ways, and that frightens many people, both in and out of power.

One problem that leads people to see utopias as threatening when they are not is misunderstanding what utopias do. This misunderstanding, which I expect is at times not a misunderstanding but a deliberate misrepresentation, is to contend that utopias present pictures of societies that their authors believe to be perfect. Very, very few do, and none of the authors included in this book, who are exemplars of the mainstream of utopian writing, thought of their creations as representing perfection. The word 'perfect' implies fixed, permanent and unending and that contradicts our understanding of how people behave. But most utopias are like the one in H.G. Wells's *Men Like Gods* (1923), in which Wells says that the protagonist:

> had always thought of Utopia as a tranquillity with everything settled for good. Even to-day it seemed tranquil under that level haze, but he knew that this quiet was the steadiness of a mill race, which seems almost motionless in its quiet onrush until a bubble or a fleck of foam or some stick or leaf shoots along and reveals its velocity.[2]

For many the issue is just the changes, slow or rapid, that Wells refers to. A significantly better society will be a significantly different society, and many people, including those expected to benefit from the changes, worry about their position in an unknown situation. The familiar, even a familiar in which one is not very secure, can be more comfortable than the unknown. And, of course, those who are secure in the present are even more likely to be nervous about the unknown. But for others, and obviously that includes those writing utopias, the possibility of improvement, bettering lives, is what counts.

One way to consider the larger question of utopianism is to return to the specificity of the texts in their contexts and to see if, given their radical differences, there are commonalities. The first thing that any reader of a utopia is likely to notice is that the author is addressing problems in the period in which they are living. But, although there are differences in degree, the central problem of all utopias is that there are people living miserable lives through no fault of their own; and thus the fundamental utopia of adequate food, clothing, housing and personal security. The first question for the utopia writer is what causes the human misery and how to overcome it. Obviously, the causes will be seen differently by different people, as will the means of bringing about change. And a solution that seems utopian at one time or to one author may appear dystopian at another time or to another author.

When someone chooses to write a utopia a question that must be faced is whether to change institutions in the hope that better institutions will produce better people or change people who will then create the institutions that are right for them. The second choice leads anti-utopians to say 'you can't change human nature'. Perhaps for that reason, the second approach is rarely chosen except where religious conversion is the mechanism of change, and it is not the approach taken by any of the authors discussed in this book. Of course the choice is not as stark as I have put it here; the relationship between institutions and people is essentially dialectical with any change in one producing changes in the other.

But, given that one has chosen to change institutions, where does one start? The two most common answers are law and education, with law the most common choice from More's *Utopia* through the eighteenth century, and most of the works discussed here are based on law. At the same time, it is striking that a standard refrain found in utopias, including More's *Utopia*, is that there will be no lawyers. This relates to another standard refrain, that the laws should be few, simple and easy to understand, which means that there should be no need for lawyers to argue about how to interpret them.

While some reform utopias only change a few laws, the more common approach is widespread or wholesale change, often through a new constitution. The first written constitutions were in the American colonies, with The Fundamental Orders of Connecticut adopted in 1639 most commonly described as the first. It and many of the constitutions adopted by other American colonies and then in the United States from the Articles of Confederation, which was in use from 1771 but not ratified until 1781, the Constitution of 1789 and the first amendments to it known as the Bill of Rights (ratified 1791), can be read as parallel to the constitutions found in explicitly utopian texts like Thomas Northmore's *Memoirs of Planetes, Or a Sketch of the Laws and Manners of Makar* (1795) in that they are designed not just to codify procedure but to change behaviour. And it is interesting that there are late twentieth and early twenty-first century US utopias that propose revising or replacing the US Constitution in order to change both procedures and behaviour.

All law that is not simply procedural is a statement about what is acceptable behaviour and what is unacceptable. In the Anglo-American tradition, the emphasis is on what is unacceptable with the assumption that what is not prohibited is permitted. An alternative approach of specifying what is acceptable with the understanding that what is not permitted is prohibited is at least implied in some, mostly religious, utopias.

However, law is about something, so it is not just the fact that law is used to produce a better society that is important. The content of the law is crucial, and the content is embedded in the culture of the times so that a work that presents a clear improvement for its time will appear considerably less positive at another time. For example, More's *Utopia* and Bacon's *New Atlantis* are hierarchical, paternalistic and patriarchal while providing a better life for their inhabitants than was available to all but a few at the time. And More's *Utopia*, for all its inegalitarianism, is, in fact, quite egalitarian on some dimensions.

One thing that characterizes most law-based utopias, and reinforces my point that perfection is not the goal, is that even in utopia some people will break the law. As a result, there are procedures in place for determining that a law has actually been broken and punishments for those who are determined to have done so. Most utopias are designed to reduce law-breaking, but they recognize that some will still be broken, and in the early utopias punishment is harsh but generally less harsh than the actuality of the time when death was the punishment for many crimes.

Over time utopian punishment became less harsh and more educative and law-breaking is often treated as a curable illness, although in the twentieth-century USSR we saw how that approach can be perverted. In his *Erewhon; Or, Over the Range* (1872), Samuel Butler satirized the whole process by depicting a society in which criminals are treated by 'Straighteners' and illness is severely punished.

As suggested by the evolution of punishment in law-based utopias, education became more and more important as the basis for utopias. Robert Owen made this argument very strongly, writing: '*Any general character, from the best to the worst, from the most ignorant to the most enlightened, may be given to any community, even to the world at large, by the application of proper means; which means are to a great extent at the command and under the control of those who have influence in the affairs of men.*'[3] Furthermore, he said that children 'can be trained to *acquire any language, sentiments, belief, or any bodily habits and manners, not contrary to human nature*'.[4]

Utopians were at the forefront of the expansion of education. In the New Harmony community established by Robert Owen in the United States, education was intended to be for both males and females and to begin with kindergarten and extend through university. These plans were not fulfilled, but people who came from Europe to join the community stayed in the United States and helped establish a number of U.S. public universities and Owen's son, Robert Dale Owen, was elected to the U.S. Senate and wrote the legislation that established the Smithsonian Institution.

There are three issues that face utopias based on education: who to teach; what to teach; and how to teach. These issues can be combined, such as different classes and genders being taught different subjects depending on what is considered appropriate to their position in life. In the earliest utopias the lower classes and women were simply excluded.

A fourth issue was added in the nineteenth century: who pays. This was included because it began to be proposed that education needed to reach more people and that to do so required public funding. Initially even public funding provided education for a limited number of people; the idea of mass public education came later as an educated population was seen to be an essential condition for modern societies.

Although its importance waxed and waned and varies from country to country, utopia emerged as a literary genre embedded in religion, and, although it is much less important elsewhere in the West, religion continues to be central to much US utopianism. Most religious utopias are concerned with changing people, either through mass religious conversion or, more commonly, although the cause varies, through people coming to actually practice the precepts of Christianity. As a result, good people then create good institutions. Of course, both institutions and people change in all utopias, it is simply that in all but the religious utopias, institutions change first.

While there are simple, even simplistic utopias, the best ones, and most of those discussed here, recognize the complexity of human relations and are themselves complex works. In a number of instances, most notably in the case of More's *Utopia*, there are serious disagreements, after 500 years, over how to read them. While few of the other texts discussed here produce quite the same level of disagreement, none of them is simple, and that is one of the reasons they should still be read. They provide messages not just for their own time and place but ones that are relevant for our time and place. They still say it is important to hope that the conditions in which we live can be improved and, while the specific proposals may be dated, each work suggests that a better life is possible and provides ideas about how to bring about such a better life.

Suggestions for Further Reading

Given the very substantial quantity of writing on utopian literature, this list is necessarily highly selective. For each work covered in this volume we have tried, wherever possible, to include the most readily available reliable text (usually but not always in English), a full-scale scholarly edition and up to two works which help to contextualize the principal text and scholarly discussion of it.

General works on utopian thought

Roland Schaer, Gregory Claeys and Lyman Tower Sargent (eds), *Utopia: The Search for the Ideal Society in the Western World* (New York/Oxford: New York Library and Oxford University Press, 2002).

Gregory Claeys (ed.), *The Cambridge Companion to Utopian Literature* (Cambridge: Cambridge University Press, 2010).

Lyman Tower Sargent, *Utopianism: A Very Short Introduction* (Oxford: Oxford University Press, 2010).

Gregory Claeys, *Searching for Utopia: The History of an Idea* (London: Thames & Hudson, 2011).

More's *Utopia*

George M. Logan and Robert M. Adams (eds), *More: Utopia* (Cambridge: Cambridge University Press, revised edition, 2002).

George M. Logan, Robert M. Adams and Clarence H. Miller (eds), *More: Utopia* (Cambridge: Cambridge University Press, 1995) [Latin and English texts].

George M. Logan (ed.), *The Cambridge Companion to Thomas More* (Cambridge: Cambridge University Press, 2011).

J.H. Hexter, *More's 'Utopia': The Biography of an Idea* (Westport: Greenwood Press, 1976) [originally published 1952].

[Note that convenient versions of the texts of More's *Utopia*, Bacon's *New Atlantis* and Neville's *Isle of Pines* are to be found in Susan Bruce (ed.), *Three Early Modern Utopias* (Oxford: Oxford University Press, 1999).]

Antangil

Glenn Negley and J. Max Patrick, *The Quest for Utopia: An Anthology of Imaginary Societies* (Garden City: Anchor Books Doubleday & Company, Inc. 1962), pp. 300–6.

Bruna Consarelli, 'Histoire du grand et admirable Royaume d'Antangil', in *Dictionary of Literary Utopias*, edited by V. Fortunati and R. Trousson (Paris: Honoré Champion, 2000), pp. 283–4.

Frank Lestringant, 'Huguenots en Utopie, ou Le genre utopique et la Réforme (XVIe-XVIIIe siècle)', *Bulletin de l'histoire du Protestantisme français* (avril-juin 2000), 281–92.

Denis D. Grélé, 'Travail et justice au royaume d'Antangil (1616)', *Proceeding of the Western Society for French Studies*, 31 (2003).

Andreae's *Christianopolis*

Edward H. Thompson (trans. and ed.), *J. V. Andreae: Christianopolis* (Dordrecht: Kluwer Academic Publishers, 1999).

Campanella's *The City of the Sun*

Daniel J. Donno (trans. and ed.), *Tommaso Campanella: The City of the Sun* (Berkeley: University of California Press, 1982).

John M. Headley, *Tommaso Campanella and the Transformation of the World* (Princeton, NJ: Princeton University Press, 1997).

Germana Ernst, *Tommaso Campanella: The Book and the Body of Nature*, translated by David L. Marshall (Dordrecht: Springer, 2010).

Bacon's *New Atlantis*

Susan Bruce (ed.), *Three Early Modern Utopias* (Oxford: Oxford University Press, 1999).

Brian Vickers (ed.), *Francis Bacon: The Major Works* (Oxford: Oxford University Press, 2008).

Bronwen Price (ed.), *Francis Bacon's New Atlantis: New Interdisciplinary Essays* (Manchester: Manchester University Press, 2002).

Julie R. Solomon, 'To Know, To Fly, To Conjure': Situating Baconian Science at the Juncture of Early Modern Modes of Reading', *Renaissance Quarterly*, 44:3 (Autumn 1991), 513–58.

Markku Peltonen (ed.), *The Cambridge Companion to Francis Bacon* (Cambridge: Cambridge University Press, 1996).

Winstanley's *Law of Freedom*

Christopher Hill (ed.), *Winstanley: The Law of Freedom and Other Writings* (Cambridge: Cambridge University Press, [1973] 2006).

Thomas N. Corns, Ann Hughes and David Loewenstein (eds), *The Complete Works of Gerrard Winstanley*, 2 volumes (Oxford: Oxford University Press, 2009).

John Gurney, *Brave Community: The Digger Movement in the English Revolution* (Manchester: Manchester University Press, 2007).

Harrington's *Oceana*

J.G.A. Pocock (ed.), *Harrington: The Commonwealth of Oceana and A System of Politics* (Cambridge: Cambridge University Press, 1992).

J.G.A. Pocock (ed.) *The Political Works of James Harrington* (Cambridge: Cambridge University Press, 1977).

Neville's *Isle of Pines*

Susan Bruce (ed.), *Three Early Modern Utopias* (Oxford: Oxford University Press, 1999).

Peter Stillman, Gaby Mahlberg and Nat Hardy (eds), 'The Isle of Pines Special Issue', *Utopian Studies*, 17:1 (2006), 21–51.

Gaby Mahlberg, *Henry Neville and English Republican Culture in the Seventeenth Century: Dreaming of Another Game* (Manchester: Manchester University Press, 2009).

Jonathan Scott, *When the Waves Ruled Britannia: Geography and Political Identities, 1500–1800* (Cambridge: Cambridge University Press, 2011).

Veiras's *Sevarambia*

J. C. Laursen and C. Masroori (eds), *Denis Veiras: The History of the Sevarambians* (Albany: State University of New York Press, 2006).

J. C. Laursen, 'Denis Veiras's Utopia: Forward Looking Science Fiction, Backward Looking Politics', in *L'umanesimo scientifico dal Rinascimento all' Illuminismo*, edited by L. Bianchi and G. Paganini (Naples: Liguori, 2010), pp. 255–67.

Morelly's *Code de la Nature*

Albert Fried and Ronald Sanders (eds), *Socialist Thought: A Documentary History* (New York: Columbia University Press, 1964).

Nicolas Wagner, *Morelly, le méconnu des Lumières* (Paris: Klincksieck, 1978).

Sinapia

Miguel Avilés Fernández, *Sinapia: Una utopía Española del Siglo de las Luces* (Madrid: Editorial Nacional, 1976).

Stelio Cro, *Descripción de la Sinapia, Península en la Tierra Austral: A Classical Utopia of Spain* (Hamilton: Mac Master University, 1975).

Condorcet

Antoine-Nicolas de Condorcet, *Sketch for a Historical Picture of the Human Mind*, translated by J. Barraclough (Westport, Conn.: Hyperion Press, 1979).

Keith Michael Baker, *Condorcet: From Natural Philosophy to Social Mathematics* (Chicago and London: University of Chicago Press, 1975).

David Williams, *Condorcet and Modernity* (Cambridge: Cambridge University Press, 2004).

Charles Fourier's Utopianism

Charles Fourier, *The Theory of the Four Movements*, edited by Gareth Stedman Jones and Ian Patterson (Cambridge: Cambridge University Press, 1996).

Jonathan Beecher and Richard Bienvenu (eds), *The Utopian Vision of Charles Fourier: Selected Texts on Work, Love and Passionate Attraction* (Boston: Beacon Press, 1972).

Jonathan Beecher, *Charles Fourier: The Visionary and his World* (Berkeley and Los Angeles: University of California Press, 1986).

Jonathan Beecher, 'Parody and Liberation in the "New Amorous World" of Charles Fourier', *History Workshop*, 20 (Autumn 1985), 125–133.

Robert Owen

Gregory Claeys (ed.), *Selected Works of Robert Owen*, 4 vols. (London: Pickering and Chatto, 1993).

Gregory Claeys, *Citizens and Saints: Politics and Anti-Politics in Early British Socialism* (Cambridge: Cambridge University Press, 1989).

Gregory Claeys, *Machinery, Money and the Millennium: From Moral Economy to Socialism* (Princeton, NJ: Princeton University Press, 1987).

Saint-Simon's Utopianism

Frank E. Manuel, *The New World of Henri Saint-Simon* (Cambridge, Mass.: Harvard University Press, 1956).

Neil McWilliam, *Dreams of Happiness: Social Art and the French Left 1830–1850*, (Princeton, NJ: Princeton University Press, 1993).

Paul Bénichou, *Le Temps de prophètes: Doctrines de l'âge romantique* (Paris: Editions Gallimard, 1977).

Ettiene Cabet's *Icaria*

Étienne Cabet, *Travels in Icaria*, translated by Leslie J. Roberts, with an introduction by Robert Sutton (Syracuse, NY: Syracuse University Press, 2003). [English translation of Part One only.]

Étienne Cabet, *Voyage en Icarie* (Paris: Bureau du populaire, 1845). [Facsimile edition by Elibrion, 2005.]

Christopher H. Johnson, *Utopian Communism in France: Cabet and the Icarians, 1839–1851* (Ithaca, NY: Cornell University Press, 1974).

Jacques Rancière, *La nuit des prolétaires: Archives du rêve ouvrier* (Paris: Hachette, 2005).

Edward Bellamy

Edward Bellamy, *Looking Backward 2000–1887,* edited by Matthew Beaumont (Oxford: Oxford World's Classics, Oxford University Press, 2007).

Daphne Patai (ed), *Looking Backward, 1998–1888: Essays on Edward Bellamy* (Amherst, Mass.: University of Massachusetts Press, 1988).

H.G. Wells

H.G. Wells, *A Modern Utopia*, edited by Krishan Kumar (London: Dent, 1994).

Justin E.A. Busch, *The Utopian Vision of H. G. Wells* (Jefferson, NC/London: McFarland, 2009).

Patrick Parrinder, *Shadows of the Future: H. G. Wells, Science Fiction and Prophecy* (Liverpool: Liverpool University Press, 1995).

John S. Partington, *Building Cosmopolis: The Political Thought of H. G. Wells* (Aldershot: Ashgate, 2003).

Le Guin's *The Dispossessed*

Ursula K. Le Guin, *The Dispossessed: An Ambiguous Utopia* (New York: Perennial Classics, HarperCollins, 2003; or London: Millennium, Victor Gollancz, 1999).

Tony Burns, *Political Theory, Science Fiction, and Utopian Literature: Ursula K. Le Guin and The Dispossessed* (Lanham, Md.: Lexington Books, 2008).

Laurence Davis and Peter G. Stillman (eds), *The New Utopian Politics of Ursula K. Le Guin's The Dispossessed* (Lanham, Md.: Lexington Books, 2005).

Notes

Introduction

1 According to James Harrington, 'Here lieth the whole difficulty: such things as, try them never so often, they cannot make hang together, they will yet have to be practicable', while the imagined solution, however good, was dismissed as impractical. His answer was that his reader should imaginatively experience a different and better order through the medium of narrative fiction. See J.G.A. Pocock, *The Political Works of James Harrington* (Cambridge: Cambridge University Press, 1977), pp. 662–3

Chapter 1 Systemic Remedies for Systemic Ills: The Political Thought of More's *Utopia*

1 George M. Logan and Robert M. Adams (eds), *Thomas More: Utopia* (Cambridge: Cambridge University Press, 2002), p. 38. Page references to this edition will be given in parentheses throughout the text of this essay. For the Latin original of the present passage, see George M. Logan, Robert M. Adams and Clarence H. Miller (eds), *Utopia: Latin Text and English Translation* (Cambridge: Cambridge University Press, 1995), pp. 102–4

2 R.A.B. Mynors (trans.) and Peter G. Bietenholz (annotations), '*The Correspondence of Erasmus*', Vol. 7, in *Collected Works of Erasmus* (Toronto/Buffalo/London: University of Toronto Press, 1987), p. 24

3 See J.H. Hexter's *More's 'Utopia': The Biography of an Idea* (Princeton, NJ: Princeton University Press, 1952); reprinted with an Epilogue (New York: Harper Torchbooks, 1965), pp. 15–30, and 'The Composition of *Utopia*', in his section of the introduction to Edward Surtz and J.H. Hexter (eds), *Utopia*, Vol. 4 of *The Complete Works of St. Thomas More (CW)* (New Haven/London: Yale University Press, 1965), pp. xv–xxiii

4 Elizabeth Frances Rogers (ed.), *St. Thomas More: Selected Letters* (New Haven/London: Yale University Press, 1961), pp. 73, 76

5 Terence Cave (ed.), *Thomas More's 'Utopia' in Early Modern Europe: Paratexts and Contexts* (Manchester/New York: Manchester University Press, 2008), p. 6

6 Anne Lake Prescott, 'Afterlives', in *The Cambridge Companion to Thomas More (CCTM)*, George M. Logan (ed.) (Cambridge: Cambridge University Press, 2011), p. 275. The same thing happened on the European continent: Cave, *Thomas More's 'Utopia'*, p. 5

7 Hexter, *More's 'Utopia'*, p. 28; see also CW 4: xxvii–xli

8 *The Life of Thomas More* (London: Chatto & Windus, 1998), p. 46; cited by Elizabeth McCutcheon, 'More's rhetoric', CCTM, p. 46

9 See my essay: '*Utopia* and Deliberative Rhetoric', *Moreana*, 31 (1994), no. 118–19, pp. 103–20

10 See the entry for him in the *Oxford Dictionary of National Biography*

11 Richard S. Sylvester and Davis P. Harding (eds), *Two Early Tudor Lives* (New Haven/London: Yale University Press, 1962), p. 198

12 'Thomas More as humanist', *CCTM*, p. 30. And see Stephen Greenblatt, 'At the Table of the Great: More's Self-Fashioning and Self-Cancellation', in his *Renaissance Self-Fashioning: From More to Shakespeare* (Chicago/London: University of Chicago Press, 1980; reprinted with a new Preface, 2005), pp. 11–73, esp. 27–37

13 On this point, see *CCTM*, p. 55 and n. 27; p. 158 and n. 37

14 Later in the sixteenth century, Raphael Holinshed's *Chronicles* recorded that 72,000 thieves and vagabonds were hanged in the reign of Henry VIII alone (*Holinshed's Chronicles [of] England, Scotland, and Ireland*, 6 vols (1807; reprinted New York: AMS Press, 1965), 1:314)

15 *More's 'Utopia'*, p. 64; *CW* 4:ci. See also Russell Ames, *Citizen Thomas More and His Utopia* (Princeton, NJ: Princeton University Press, 1949), p. 176; Robert P. Adams, *The Better Part of Valor: More, Erasmus, Colet, and Vives, on Humanism, War, and Peace, 1496–1535* (Washington: University of Washington Press, 1962), pp. 125–6

16 In the *Republic*, only the ruling class – the Guardians – is communized, but in his last political work, the *Laws*, Plato declares that the best commonwealth would be communistic across the board. The metaphor of the statesman-physician is also employed – in a way that is in fact closer to More's use of it than is Plato's – in another Greek work that had an impact on *Utopia*, Plutarch's idealized biography of Lycurgus, the legendary lawgiver of Sparta. See 'Lycurgus' V.2

17 See *CU*, pp. xviii–xxvi. The clearest indication of More's debt to Plato and Aristotle, and to ancient Greek political theory and practice in general, is found in the many striking resemblances between Utopia and classical Greek city-states both real and ideal (the latter in Plato's and Aristotle's treatments of the ideal commonwealth and in the idealized Sparta of Plutarch's 'Lycurgus'). In religion, the Utopians lack Christian revelation (until knowledge of it is brought to them by Hythloday and his companions), and their religious principles are limited to those that, according to Thomas Aquinas, can be derived from unassisted reason (see *CU*, p. 66 and n. 65). That Utopia is not Christian means, of course, that it is not simply More's ideal commonwealth. Among many other things, it embodies his musings on the topic – much discussed by both scholastics and humanists – of the degree of compatibility between reason and revelation. For the best discussion of the general topic of *Utopia* and Greek political theory, see Eric Nelson, *The Greek Tradition in Republican Thought* (Cambridge: Cambridge University Press, 2004), pp. 19–48

18 See *CU*, pp. xxvi–xxviii, and, for more detail, my *The Meaning of More's 'Utopia'* (Princeton, NJ: Princeton University Press, 1983), pp. 218–53

Chapter 2 More's *Utopia*: Colonialists, Refugees and the Nature of Sufficiency

1 George M. Logan and Robert M. Adams (eds), *Thomas More: Utopia* (Cambridge: Cambridge University Press, 1989), pp. 55–6. Page references to this edition will be given in parentheses thoughout the text of this essay

2 Peter Kosminsky, 'The Promise', Channel 4

3 George M. Logan, *The Meaning of More's 'Utopia'* (Princeton, NJ: Princeton University Press, 1983), p. 223

4 Andrew Hadfield, *Literature, Travel and Colonial Writing in the English Renaissance 1545–1625* (Oxford: Clarendon Press, 1998), p. 11

5 Thomas Betteridge, *Borders and Travellers in Early Modern Europe* (Farnham: Ashgate, 2007), pp. 6–7

6 Jeffrey Knapp, *An Empire Nowhere: England, America and Literature from 'Utopia' to 'The Tempest'* (Berkeley: University of California Press, 1992), pp. 19–21

7 Louis Marin, *Utopics: The Semiological Play of Textual Spaces*, trans. Robert A. Vollrath (New York: Humanity Books, 1984), pp. 106–9

8 Knapp, *Empire Nowhere*, p. 31

9 The translator of this edition is Ralph Robinson; his translation is reprinted in Susan Bruce (ed), *Three Early Modern Utopias* (Oxford: Oxford University Press, 1999), p. 127

10 Richard Helgerson, *Forms of Nationhood: The Elizabethan Writing of England* (Chicago: Chicago University Press, 1992), pp. 12–13

11 I use 'Morus', following Stephen Greenblatt's *Renaissance Self-Fashioning* (Chicago: University of Chicago Press, 1980), to distinguish the More-within-the-text from the real-More-outside-it

12 See Patricia Fumerton, *Unsettled: The Culture of Mobility and the Working Poor in Early Modern England* (Chicago: University of Chicago Press, 2006)

13 Richard Halpern, *The Poetics of Primitive Accumulation: English Renaissance Culture and the Genealogy of Capital* (Ithaca: Cornell University Press, 1991), pp. 145–7

14 Christopher Kendrick, *Utopia, Carnival and Commonwealth in Renaissance England* (Toronto: University of Toronto Press, 2004), p. 66

15 Christopher Kendrick, *Utopia, Carnival and Commonwealth in Renaissance England* (Toronto: University of Toronto Press, 2004), p. 68

16 Halpern, *Poetics*, p. 165

Chapter 3 Goodbye to Utopia: Thomas More's Utopian Conclusion

1 George M. Logan and Robert M. Adams (eds), *Thomas More: Utopia* (Cambridge: Cambridge University Press, 1989), pp. 110–11. Page references to this edition will be given in parentheses throughout the text of this essay

2 See J.H. Hexter, 'The Composition of *Utopia*', in *The Complete Works of St. Thomas More*, vol. IV: Utopia, Edward Surtz and J.H. Hexter (eds) (New Haven and London: Yale University Press, 1965), especially pp. xx–xxii

3 On their 'imperialism', see Chapter 2 above

4 Compare Aristotle, *Politics* (II. i–v)

5 On these themes see J.C. Davis, 'Thomas More's *Utopia*: Sources, Legacy and Interpretation', in *The Cambridge Companion to Utopian Literature*, Gregory Claeys (ed.) (Cambridge: Cambridge University Press, 2010), pp. 28–50

6 The printing in Basel of the March 1518 edition was held up for this letter

7 Act 5: 1–11

8 For other vindications of utopian practice as more akin to proper Christian conduct, see pp. 109, 127, 130

9 For the virtue of plain speaking, see pp. 5, 36, 37

10 For the theatre as a key theme in *Utopia*, see Davis, 'Thomas More's *Utopia*'

11 John 20: 24–9

Chapter 4 So Close, So Far: The Puzzle of Antangil

1 *Histoire du grand et admirable royaume d'Antangil. Incogneu jusques à présent à tous Historiens et Cosmographes: composé de six vingts Provinces très belles*

et très-fertiles. Avec la description d'icelui, & de sa police nompareille, tant civile que militaire. De l'instruction de la jeunesse. Et de la religion. Le tout compris en cinq livres. Par I.D.M.G.T. A Saumur: par Thomas Portau, 1616, pp. 124–5. [An Account of the Great and Wonderful Kingdom of Antangil Unknown until the Present Time to All Historians and Cosmographers: Composed of Twenty-Six Highly Beautiful and very Fertile Provinces. With a Description of them and of their Unparalleled Polity, both Civil and Military. Also, an Account of the Education of their Youth, and their Religion]. Translations are from this text and are hereafter cited by page numbers in the text. For the translation of the title and an English abstract of *Antangil*, see: Glenn Negley and J. Max Patrick, *The Quest for Utopia: An Anthology of Imaginary Societies* (Garden City: Anchor Books Doubleday & Company, Inc, 1962), pp. 300–6

2   The identification of the author, indicated with the initials IDMGT, has sparked a lively debate and led to various hypotheses. Frédéric Lachèvre supports the thesis of a French officer of noble origin; Nicolas van Wijngaarden says that this is Joachim du Moulin, a Protestant minister in Saumur, while according to Alexandre Cioranescu, he could be Jean de Moncy, a schoolteacher in the small Dutch town of Tiel. See: F. Lachèvre, 'La première utopie du XVIIᵉ siècle : Le Royaume d'Antangil', appendice à *Les successeurs de Cyrano de Bergerac* (Paris: Honoré Champion, 1922), pp. 261–9 and 'Une utopie protestante : Histoire du grand et admirable Royaume d'Antangil', in *Glanes bibliographiques*, vol. II (Paris: L. Giraud-Badin, 1929), pp. 196–7; N. van Wijngaarden, *Les odyssées philosophiques en France entre 1616 et 1789* (Genève-Paris: Slatkine Reprints, 1982; réimpression de l'édition d'Haarlem, 1932); A. Cioranescu, 'Le Royaume d'Antangil et son auteur', *Studi francesi*, XXVIII (1963), pp. 17–25

3   On political and social aspects in particular, see: Bruna Consarelli: '*Libero pensiero' e Utopia nel 'Grand Siecle'* (Pesaro: Flaminia editrice, 1990) and 'Histoire du grand et admirable Royaume d'Antangil', in *Dictionary of Literary Utopias*, V. Fortunati and R. Trousson (eds) (Paris: Honoré Champion, 2000), pp. 283–4

4   Consarelli, '*Libero pensiero' e Utopia nel 'Grand Siecle'*, p. 13

5   On religion, see: Frank Lestringant, 'Huguenots en Utopie, ou Le genre utopique et la Réforme (XVIᵉ-XVIIIᵉ siècle)', *Bulletin de l'histoire du Protestantisme français* (avril-juin 2000), pp. 281–92

6   Geographical and cartographic aspects are studied in: Olivier Leplatre, 'Déplier l'utopie (Histoire du grand et admirable Royaume d'Antangil, 1616)', *Teximage*, n°2: Cartes et plans (été 2008), pp. 1–30

7   'Arts and sciences are acquired only through books and practice; yet, to succeed, one needs to be taught by good teachers. Being aware of this, the wise architects who founded this state wanted to introduce, among their most attractive decrees, a rule that the children of the nobility and of the richest members of the society with a good natural disposition, be trained freely in all civil and military disciplines, an academy or facility being built for such purpose ... in an airy, elevated and open location'

8   'Considering that a republic in which only men are learned and wise cannot be perfect: the Senate ordered that the girls be educated by the parishes in the same way as the boys'

9   M. Magendie, *La politesse mondaine et les théories de l'honnêteté en France au XVIIᵉ siècle, de 1600 à 1660,* I (Genève: Slatkine Reprint, 1993 ; réimpression de l'édition de Paris, 1925), p. 56–7

10 Van Wijngaarden, *Les odyssées philosophiques en France entre 1616 et 1789*, p. 35, notes that the author probably has in mind the Protestant academies of a different cultural tenor

11 Henri Desroche, 'L'origine utopique', *Esprit* (octobre 1974), pp. 337–66

Chapter 5 Microcosm, Macrocosm and 'Practical Science' in Andreae's *Christianopolis*

1 J.V. Andreae, *Christianopolis*, intro and trans. Edward H. Thompson (Dordrecht: Kluwer, 1999), pp. 236–7. Page numbers to this edition will be given in parentheses throughout the text of this essay

2 Donald Dickson, *The Tessera of Antilia* (Leiden: Brill, 1998), ch. 2 and 3

3 Claus Bernet 'Johann Valentin Andreaes *Christianopolis* as Himmlisches Jerusalem', *Zeitschrift für Württembergische Landesgeschichte* (2007), pp. 147–82

4 Elizabeth Hansot, *Perfection and Progress: Two Modes of Utopian Thought* (Cambridge, Mass.: MIT Press, 1974), p. 84, n. 14

5 J.V. Andreae, *Christianae societatis imago* (Strasbourg, 1619)

6 J.V. Andreae, *Mythologiae Christianae, sive Virtutum & vitiorum vitae humanae imaginum* (Strasbourg: Zetzner, 1619), Book 1, Manipulus I, ch. 32

7 John W. Montgomery, *Cross and Crucible*, vol. I (The Hague: Nijhoff, 1973), pp. 91–6

8 J.V. Andreae, *Collectaneorum mathematicorum decades XI* (Tübingen: J.A. Cellius, 1614), Plates 31– 3

9 Andreae, *Christianopolis*, ch. 49

10 Hartlib Papers 31/1/56B (Beale to Hartlib, 15 September 1657)

11 Andreae, *Collectaneorum*, Plate 36

12 J.V. Andreae, *Turris Babel, sive Judiciorum de Fraternitate Rosaceae Crucis Chaos* (Strasbourg: Zetzner, 1619), ch. 5

13 Andreae, *Mythologiae* Book 1, Manipulus I, ch. 32

14 J.V. Andreae, *Verae Unionis in Christo Jesu Specimen*, (n.p., 1628), introduction

15 Andreae, *Christianae Societatis imago*, p.3

Chapter 6 Tommaso Campanella, *The City of the Sun* and the Protective Celestial Bodies

1 The translation into English of this essay originally written in Italian has been possible due to the funds of the academic project *El Tiempo de los Derechos*, Programa Consolider-Ingenio 2010, CSD 2008-00007

2 Tomasso Campanella, *The City of the Sun: A Poetical Dialogue*, trans., introduction and notes Daniel J. Donno (Berkeley: University of California Press, 1982), p. 86. Page references to this edition will be given in parentheses throughout the text of this essay

3 Tomasso Campanella, 'Astrologicorum libri VII in quibus Astrologia omni superstitione Arabum et Iudaeorum eliminata physiologice tractatur', in *Opera latina Francofurti impressa annis 1617–1630*, a cura di L. Firpo, (Torino: Bottega d'Erasmo, 1975), Vol. 2, VI, 4, 1, pp. 1305–6

4 Claudio Tolomeo, *Le previsioni astrologiche* (*Tetrabiblos*), a cura di S. Feraboli (Milan: Mondadori 1998), p. 15

5   Tolomeo, *Le previsioni astrologiche (Tetrabiblos)*, p. 31

6   Tolomeo, *Le previsioni astrologiche (Tetrabiblos)*, p. 83

7   Thomas More, *Utopia*, eds George M. Logan and Robert M. Adams (Cambridge: Cambridge University Press, 1999), p. 67. Thomas More makes a distintion between astronomy and astrology, raising the first to the dignity of a science (which allows one to profitably comprehend the signs of nature) and confining the second to the role of vain superstition

8   Tomasso Campanella, 'Come evitare il fato astrale', in *Opuscoli astrologici*, a cura di G. Ernst (Milan: Rizzoli, 2003), p. 65

9   Tomasso Campanella, *Il senso delle cose e la magia*, a cura di A. Bruers (Bari: Laterza, 1925), p. 315

10 '[T]he human mind is far superior and beyond the heavens. Therefore, the heavens only exert influence on the mind of man by accident. Whilst it may alter the body and the vegetative soul and the senses, over the human intellect, it has an indirect influence, as stated by St. Thomas regarding its operations on the body and senses' (Tomasso Campanella, 'Disputa sulle bolle dei ss. Pontefici Sisto V e Urbano VIII contro gli astrologi', in *Opuscoli astrologici*, p. 193)

Chapter 7 'A Dark Light': Spectacle and Secrecy in Francis Bacon's *New Atlantis*

1   Francis Bacon, 'New Atlantis', in Susan Bruce (ed.), *Three Early Modern Utopias* (Oxford: Oxford University Press, 1999), p. 177. Page references to this edition will be given in parentheses throughout the text of this essay

2   For *New Atlantis*'s use of the travel narrative genre, see Paul Salzman, 'Narrative contexts for Bacon's *New Atlantis*', in Bronwen Price (ed.), *Francis Bacon's New Atlantis* (Manchester: Manchester University Press, 2002), pp. 30–8

3   See, for example, Brian Vickers, *Francis Bacon* (Harlow: Longman, 1978), pp. 28–9

4   See, for example, David C. Innes, 'Bacon's *New Atlantis*: The Christian Hope and the Modern Hope', *Interpretation*, 22:1 (1994), pp. 3–37

5   'Bacon's Use of Theatrical Imagery', in William A. Sessions (ed.), *Francis Bacon's Legacy of Texts* (New York: AMS Press, 1990), pp. 171–213

6   Bruce, *Three Early Modern Utopias*, p. 235, fn. 165. Bacon often uses the spelling 'Salomon' for Solomon in other works

7   Sidney Warhaft (ed.), *Francis Bacon: A Selection of His Works* (Indianapolis: Bobbs-Merrill, 1965), p. 314

8   Warhaft, *Francis Bacon*, p. 337

9   Warhaft, *Francis Bacon*, pp. 300–1

10 'Ethics and Politics in the *New Atlantis*', in Price (ed.), *Francis Bacon's New Atlantis*, p. 62

11 See Bronwen Price, 'Introduction', in Price (ed.), *Francis Bacon's New Atlantis*, pp. 10–11

12 Warhaft, *Francis Bacon*, p. 323

13 'Advancement', in Brian Vickers (ed.), *Francis Bacon: A Critical Edition of the Major Works* (Oxford: Oxford University Press, 1996), pp. 147–8. See, for example, 'The Great Instauration', in Warhaft (ed.), *Francis Bacon*, pp. 314–15

14 John E. Leary, *Francis Bacon and the Politics of Science* (Ames: Iowa State University Press, 1994), p. 258

15 Vickers (ed.), *Critical Edition*, p. 390

16 See Price, 'Introduction', pp. 12–13, for further detail about this feature

17 'Introduction', in Bruce (ed.), *Three Early Modern Utopias*, p. xxxv
18 See Julie Robin Solomon, '"To Know, To Fly, To Conjure": Situating Baconian Science at the Juncture of Early Modern Modes of Reading', *Renaissance Quarterly*, 44:3 (1991), pp. 522–8, 553–5
19 Vickers (ed.), *Critical Edition*, p. 439

Chapter 8 Gerrard Winstanley's *The Law Of Freedom*: Context and Continuity

1 Gerrard Winstanley, *The Law of Freedom in a Platform: Or, True Magistracy Restored* (1652): prefatory address to Oliver Cromwell
2 *The Complete Works of Gerrard Winstanley*, 2 vols, eds Thomas N. Corns, Ann Hughes and David Lowenstein (Oxford: Oxford University Press, 2009), vol. 1, pp. 101–471. Volume and page references to this edition will be given in parentheses throughout the text of this essay
3 The activities of the Diggers are explored in John Gurney, *Brave Community: The Digger Movement in the English Revolution* (Manchester: Manchester University Press, 2007), pp. 121–209
4 J.C. Davis, *Utopia and the Ideal Society* (Cambridge: Cambridge University Press, 1981), pp. 170–1, 182, 190
5 Gurney, *Brave Community*, pp. 98–104, 126, 176–9
6 Gurney, *Brave Community*, p. 102
7 Davis, *Utopia*, pp. 182, 190–202
8 Hugh Peter, *Good Work for a Good Magistrate: Or, A Short Cut to Great Quiet* (1651)
9 Blair Worden, *The Rump Parliament, 1648–1653* (Cambridge: Cambridge University Press, 1974), pp. 272, 274–5, 279
10 D.T., *Certain Queries* (1651); Edmund Leach, *The Down-fall of the Unjust Lawyers* (1652); John Shepheard, *Certaine Proposals for Regulating the Law* (1652); Samuel Duncon, *Severall Propositions of Publick Concernment* (1652); S.D., *Certaine Assayes Propounded* (1652); Henry Robinson, *Certain Considerations in Order to a More Speedy, Cheap and Equall Distribution of Justice Throughout the Nation* (1652). Cf. Nicholas Culpeper, *An Ephemeris for the Year 1652* (1651); Charles George Cock, *English-Law* (1651)
11 Gurney, *Brave Community*, p. 214
12 Peter, *Good Work*, pp. 27–8
13 Peter, *Good Work*, pp. 27–57
14 Peter, *Good Work*, pp. 18–23, 57
15 Peter, *Good Work*, pp. 19, 20, 22, 27, 51, 54, 62, 64–72, 78–82, 89–109
16 *Works*, 2, pp. 282, 333, 369; Peter, *Good Work*, p. 35; Robinson, *Certain Considerations*, epistle dedicatory
17 *Works*, 2, pp. 332, 368, 369; Shepheard, *Certaine Proposals*, pp. 1–2; Peter, *Good Work*, p. 33. Cf. John Rogers, *Sagrir* (1653), pp. 31, 51, 55, 59–60
18 *Works*, 2, pp. 321, 322–3, 324, 325, 328, 329, 378; Peter, *Good Work*, pp. 24, 25, 29; Duncon, *Severall Propositions*, pp. 4–6. Cf. D.T., *Certain Queries*, p. 17; Robinson, *Certaine Considerations*, p. 4
19 Isaac Penington junior, *The Fundamental Right, Safety and Liberty of the People* (1651); *Mercurius Politicus*, 69 (25 Sept.–2 Oct. 1651), 91 (26 Feb.–3 March 1652), 109 (1–8 July 1652)
20 Winstanley, unlike Nedham, did not take from Penington the latter's clear distinction between executive and legislative powers

21 Isaac Penington junior, *A Word for the Common Weale* (1650), pp. 8–9;
    Penington, *Fundamental Right*, prefatory address. Cf. *Works*, 2, pp. 305, 331,
    332, 340, 368–9

22 Penington, *Word for the Common Weale*, pp. 8–9, 16, 17. Cf. *Works*, 2, pp. 331,
    333–40

23 Ibid., pp. 294–5; Penington, *Fundamental Right*, prefatory address. Cf. *Mercurius
    Politicus*, 69

24 Gurney, *Brave Community*, pp. 159–60, 163, 179–80, 181–4

25 *A Declaration of the Commoners of England, to his Excellency The Lord General
    Cromwell* (1652); *Articles of High Treason* (1652); *A New Way to Pay Old
    Debts: Or, The Law and Freedom of the People Established* (1652); *Faithful
    Scout*, 56 (6–13 Feb.), 439; 58 (20–27 Feb.), 454–5; *French Intelligencer* (4–11
    Feb.), 87; (11–18 Feb. 1652), 90

26 Gurney, *Brave Community*, p. 216

27 *The Levellers New Remonstrance or Declaration* (1649), pp. 1–3, 6; *The King of
    Scots Declaration* (1649), pp. 4–5; *Englands Moderate Messenger* (12–19 June
    1649), 58–60; *Works*, 2, p. 55, n.1

28 *Faithful Scout*, 66 (16–23 April, 1652), 518–19; Gurney, *Brave Community*, p. 216.

29 Davis, *Utopia*, pp. 181–3

30 Cf. ibid., p. 180

Chapter 9 *'De Te Fabula Narratur'*: *Oceana* and James Harrington's Narrative Constitutionalism

1 J.G.A. Pocock (ed.), *Harrington: The Commonwealth of Oceana and a System
   of Politics* (Cambridge: Cambridge University Press, 1992), p. 1. (Page references
   to this edition will be given in parentheses throughout the rest of the text of this
   essay.) This epigraph, which appears on the title page of the first printings of
   Oceana, is taken from Horace, *Satires*, I, pp. i, 68–70 and may be translated as:
   'Tantalus, thirsting forever, keeps straining to taste the retreating waters forever
   eluding his lips. Why do you laugh? Change the names and the story is told about
   you.' I have here adapted the translation of H. Rushton Fairclough (trans. and ed.),
   Horace: Satires, Epistles and Ars Poetica (London: Heinemann, 1955), pp. 9–10

2 J.G.A. Pocock, *The Machiavellian Moment: Florentine Republican Thought and
   the Atlantic Republican Tradition* (Princeton, NJ: Princeton University Press, 1975)

3 See J.C. Davis, 'The Prose Romance of the 1650s as a context for *Oceana*',
   forthcoming

4 There is a more detailed discussion of this in J.C. Davis, '"*De te Fabula narratur*":
   Narrative Constitutionalism and the Kinetics of James Harrington's *Oceana*',
   forthcoming

5 See Blair Worden, '*Oceana*: Origins and Aftermath', in *Republicanism, Liberty
   and Commercial Society 1649–1776*, David Wootton (ed.) (Stanford: Stanford
   University Press, 1994), pp. 120–4; Blair Worden, *Literature and Politics in
   Cromwellian England: John Milton, Andrew Marvell, Marchamont Nedham*
   (Oxford: Oxford University Press, 2007), pp. 109–10

6 David Norbrook, *Writing the English Republic: Poetry, Rhetoric and Politics
   1627–1660* (Cambridge: Cambridge University Press, 1999), pp. 189–91

7 Blair Worden, 'Oliver Cromwell and the sin of Achan', in *History, Society and
   the Churches*, Derek Beales and Geoffrey Best (eds) (Cambridge: Cambridge
   University Press, 1985), pp. 125–45

8   For a full description of *Oceana* see J.C. Davis, *Utopia and the Ideal Society* (Cambridge: Cambridge University Press, 1981), ch. 8

9   For example, by John Milton, Marchamont Nedham and Henry Stubbe. See Davis, 'Prose Romance'

Chapter 10   An Island with Potential: Henry Neville's *The Isle Of Pines*

1   Henry Neville, *The Isle of Pines, or, A late Discovery of a Fourth Island near Terra Australis, Incognita by Henry Cornelius Van Sloetten* (London, 1668), p. 3. Page references to this edition will be given in parentheses throughout the text of this essay. See also Gaby Mahlberg, 'The Critical Reception of *The Isle of Pines*', *Utopian Studies*, 17:1 (2006), pp. 133–42. Gaby Mahlberg, *Henry Neville and English Republican Culture in the Seventeenth Century: Dreaming of Another Game* (Manchester: Manchester University Press, 2009)

2   Jonathan Scott, *When the Waves Ruled Britannia: Geography and Political Identities, 1500–1800* (Cambridge: Cambridge University Press, 2011)

3   Although the date on the pamphlet is 27 June, the Stationer's Register has 4 July. The 'Letter' was published as *A New and further Discovery of The Isle of Pines in A Letter from Cornelius Van Sloetten a Dutch-man ... to a Friend of his in London* (London, 1668)

4   J.C. Davis, *Utopia and the Ideal Society: A Study of English Utopian Writing 1516–1700* (Cambridge: Cambridge University Press, 1981), pp. 24–6. The core text is sometimes published on its own. Cf. Philip Henderson (ed.), *Shorter Novels: Seventeenth Century* (London: Everyman, 1930), pp. 225–35

5   Thomas Paine, *Common Sense* in Thomas Paine, *Rights of Man, Common Sense and Other Political Writings*, ed Mark Philp (Oxford: Oxford World's Classics, 1995) p. 5.

6   James Harrington, 'The Commonwealth of Oceana', in *The Commonwealth of Oceana and A System of Politics*, ed. J.G.A. Pocock (Cambridge: Cambridge University Press, 1992), p. 35

7   Slingsby Bethel, *The Present Interest of England Stated* (London, 1671), f. A2v, p. 5

8   Harrington, 'Oceana', p. 75

9   William Petty, *A Treatise of Taxes & Contributions* (London, 1662), p. 5; John Graunt, *Natural and Political Observations Made upon the Bills of Mortality* (London, 1662); William Petty, *Political Arithmetick* (London, 1690), p. 23; John Locke, *Two Treatises of Government*, II, ed. Peter Laslett (Cambridge: Cambridge University Press, 1988), ch. v

10   Steve Pincus, *1688: The First Modern Revolution* (New Haven and London: Yale University Press, 2009), pp. 366–99

11   Adam R. Beach, 'A Profound Pessimism about the Empire: *The Isle of Pines*, English Degeneracy and Dutch Supremacy', *The Eighteenth Century*, 41:1 (2000), pp. 21–36

Chapter 11   The Persian Moment in Denis Veiras's *History of the Sevarambians*

1   Denis Veiras, *The History of the Sevarambians*, eds J.C. Laursen and C. Masroori (Albany: State University of New York Press, 2006), p. 203. Page references to this edition will be given in parentheses throughout the text of this essay

2 For a brief biography of the author and more information about the text, see the introduction to Veiras, *The History of the Sevarambians*, pp. vii–xxvii

3 Veiras, *The History of the Sevarambians*, p. 90; cf. p. 66

4 Thomas More, *Utopia*, ed. David Wootton (Indianapolis: Hackett, 1999), pp. 70–3

5 Herodotus, *The Histories*, trans. A. de Sélincourt, revised by John Marincola (London: Penguin, 2003), p. 61

6 Strabo, *The Geography of Strabo*, Book 15, ch. 3, p. 13

7 For example, Plutarch, *Lives of the Noble Grecians and Romans* and Quintus Curtius, *The Life of Alexander*

8 'We revere Mithra (heavenly light) ruler of all countries, whom Ahura Mazda has created full of luster' (*Khordeh Avesta: Zoroastrian Prayer Book, with Prayers in Roman Script and Translation in English*, trans. T.R. Sethna (n.p., n.p.: 1975), p. 45 (also see pp. 19 and 41))

9 'We revere the shining sun, eternal brilliant and emitting strong (light). We revere Mithra (heavenly light)' (*Khordeh Avesta*, trans. Sethna, 45)

10 See C. Masroori, 'Cyrus II and the Political Utility of Religious Toleration', in J.C. Laursen (ed.), *Religious Toleration: 'The Variety of Rites' from Cyrus to Defoe* (New York: St. Martin's Press, 1999), pp. 13–36

11 Justin, *The First Apology*, ch. 66

12 Archelaus, *Acts of the Disputation with the Heresiarch Manes*, Act 36

13 See Wilhelm Schmitt-Biggemann, *Philosophia perennis: Historical Outlines of Western Spirituality* (Dordrecht: Springer, 2004), p. 33

14 See Schmitt-Biggemann, *Philosophia perennis*, p. 172, and Michael Stausberg, *Faszination Zarathushtra* (Berlin: De Gruyter, 1998), pp. 93–261

15 See Stausberg, *Faszination Zarathushtra*, pp. 621 ff., 638–641

16 Cited in Nora K. Firby, *European Travelers and Their Perceptions of Zoroastrians in the 17th and 18th Centuries* (Berlin: Reimer Verlag, 1988), p. 25

17 Cited in David Blow, *Persia Through Writers' Eyes* (London: Eland, 2007), pp. 115–16

18 Jean Chardin, *Le couronnement de Soleimaan, troisiéme Roy de Perse de cette nomme* (Paris, 1671), cited from *The Coronation of Solyman, The Third of That Name*, appended to *The Travels of Sir John Chardin into Persia, and the East Indies* (London, 1689), p. 98

19 Edward Herbert, *Pagan Religion: A Translation of De religione gentilium*, trans. J.A. Butler (Binghampton: Medieval and Renaissance Texts, 1996), pp. 82–97

20 J. A. Butler, trans., 'Introduction' to Herbert, *Pagan Religion*, p. 38

21 Butler, 'Introduction', p. 15

22 Butler, 'Introduction', p. 19

23 Henry More, *An Antidote Against Atheism*, second edition (London, 1655), pp. 240–4

24 Jonathan Israel, *Radical Enlightenment: Philosophy and the Making of Modernity 1650–1750* (Oxford: Oxford University Press, 2001), pp. 591–2, 597

Chapter 12 Nature and Utopia in Morelly's *Code De La Nature*

1 Etienne-Gabriel Morelly, *Code de la Nature* (Par-Tout: Chez le Vrai Sage, 1755), pp. 29–30 and 78–80

2 On Morelly, see Edouard Dolléans, *Notice in Morelly Code de la Nature* (Paris: Geuthner, 1910); Nicolas Wagner, *Morelly, le méconnu des Lumières* (Paris: Klincksieck, 1978); Guy Antonetti, 'Morelly. L'homme et sa famille', *Revue*

d'histoire littéraire de la France (May–June 1983), pp. 390–402; Guy Antonetti, 'Morelly. L'écrivain et ses protecteurs', *Revue d'histoire littéraire de la France* (Jan.–Feb. 1984), pp. 19–52

3 Morelly, *La Basiliade, ou les naufrages des isles flottantes* (Messine: Société de Libraires, 1753). Concerning a comprehensive analysis of the text, see Claudio De Boni, 'La Basiliade nello sviluppo dell'opera di Morelly', *Morus – Utopia e Renascimento*, 1 (2004), pp. 89–102

4 Morelly, *Essai sur l'esprit humain, ou Principes naturels de l'éducation* (Paris: Delespine, 1743); Morelly, *Essai sur le coeur humain, ou Principes naturels de l'éducation* (Paris: Delespine, 1745)

5 Morelly, *Essai sur l'esprit humain*, p. 3

6 Friedrich Engels, *L'evoluzione del socialismo dall'utopia alla scienza* (Roma: Editori Riuniti, 1971), p. 70

7 A. Lichtenberger, *Le socialisme au XVIIIᵉ siècle* (Paris: Alcan, 1895), p. 114

Chapter 13 *Sinapia*, A Political Journey to the Antipodes of Spain

1 Anónimo, *Descripción de la Sinapia, Península en la Tierra Austral* [no date]. References to *Sinapia* contain two page numbers divided by a forward slash. The first refers to Miguel Avilés' edition of *Sinapia* (*Sinapia. Una utopía Española del Siglo de las Luces* (Madrid: Editorial Nacional, 1976); the second one to the paragraph of the facsimile edition included in Stelio Cro, *Descripción de la Sinapia, Península en la Tierra Austral. A Classical Utopia of Spain* (Hamilton: Mac Master University, 1975)

2 See Susan Bruce's chapter in this book. Examples like this can be found throughout the text of Sinapia

3 José Santos Puerto, 'La Sinapia: luces para buscar la utopía de la ilustración', *Bulletin Hispanique*, 103:2 (2001), pp. 481–510. Curiously, another Spanish Enlightenment author, José de Cadalso, close to Pedro Pablo Abarca de Bolea, count of Aranda, who also was President of the Council of Castille in 1766–1773, wrote a book, now lost, entitled *Observaciones de un oficial holandés en el nuevamente descubierto Reino de Feliztá* [Observations of a Dutch officer in the new discovered Kingdom of Happiness] in which it is elaborated as a system of government (Russell P. Sebold, 'Introducción', in José de Cadalso, *Cartas Marruecas/Noches lúgrubes*, Russell P. Sebold (ed.) (Madrid: Cátedra, 2008), p. 25)

4 See George M. Logan's chapter in this book

5 See J. C. Davis and John Gurney's chapters in this book

6 Barbara Goodwin, 'Economic and social innovation in Utopia', in *Utopias*, P. Alexander and R. Gill (eds), (London: Duckworth, 1984), p. 82

7 The project was set in motion in July 1767 once the *Fuero de población* (which until 1835 regulated the social, economic and political life of the founded settlements) was passed (Pedro Ruiz Torres, *Reformismo e Ilustración* (Madrid: Marcial Pons, 2010), p. 419)

8 'We made no inquiries, however, about monsters, which are the routine of travellers' tales. Scyllas, ravenous Celaenos, and man-eating Lestrygonians and that sort of monstruosity you can hardly avoid, but to find governments wisely established and sensibly ruled is not so easy' (Thomas More, *Utopia*, eds George M. Logan and Robert M. Adams (Cambridge: Cambridge University Press, 1999), p. 12)

9 Raymond Trousson, *Historia de la Literatura Utópica. Viajes a Países Inexistentes*, trans. C. Manzano (Barcelona: Península, 1995), p. 43

10 Sebold, 'Introducción', p. 39
11 Sebold, 'Introducción', p. 41
12 Miriam Eliav-Feldon, *Realistic Utopias* (Oxford: Clarendon Press, 1982), p. 2
13 Abel Janzszoon Tasman (1603–59) who appears in the republic of Sinapia – 'I do not know how some notes that Abel Tasman had written of his journey came to my hands' (69/1) – was a sailor working for the Netherlands East India Company. Moreover, the animal life and flora described belong to the American continent, not to the Australasian one (Cro, *Descripción de la Sinapia*, p. 75, n. 23)
14 Darko Suvin, 'Defining the literary genre of Utopia: Some Historical Semantics, Some Geneology, a Proposal and a Plea', *Studies in the Literary Genre*, 6:2 (1973), p. 126
15 Tom Moylan, *Demand the Impossible: Science Fiction and Utopian Imagination*, (London: Methuen, 1986), p. 39
16 Moylan, *Science Fiction*, p. 40
17 Tom Moylan, *Scraps of the Untainted Sky* (Oxford: Westview, 2000), p. 43; Darko Suvin, 'On the poetics of the science fiction genre', *College English*, 34:3 (1972), p. 374
18 See Cyrus Masroori and John Christian Laursen's chapter in this book
19 J.C. Davis, 'Science and Utopia: The History of a Dilemma', in *Nineteen Eighty-Four: Science between Utopia and Dystopia*, E. Mendelshon and H. Nowotny (eds) (Dordrecht: Reidel, 1984), pp. 21–48
20 Miguel A. Ramiro Avilés, 'Law based Utopia', in *The Philosophy of Utopia*, B. Goodwin (ed.) (London: Frank Cass, 2001), pp. 221–48; *Utopía y Derecho: El sistema jurídico en las sociedades ideales* (Madrid: Marcial Pons, 2002), pp. 305–60
21 Charles de Secondat, Baron de Montesquieu, *The Spirit of the Laws*, trans Thomas Nugent (Ontario: Batoche Books, 2001) p. 180.
22 Eliav-Feldon, *Realistic Utopias*, p. 9
23 Ruiz Torres, *Reformismo e Ilustración*, p. 435
24 See Sebold, 'Introducción', p. 50

Chapter 14 Condorcet's Utopianism: Faith in Science and Reason

1 Marie Jean Antoine Nicolas Caritat, marquis de Condorcet, *Esquisse d'un tableau historique des progrès de l'esprit humain* [written in 1793; first published in 1795], in *Oeuvres de Condorcet*, publiées par A. Condorcet O'Connor et M.F. Arago (Paris: Firmin Didot, 1847), t. 6, pp. 11–276. Translation by K. Steven Vincent from the text. The pages translated are pp. 236–7, 244–5 and 250–1, drawn from the chapter 'Tenth Stage: Of the Future Progress of the Human Mind'
2 Frank E. Manuel, *The Prophets of Paris* (Cambridge, Mass.: Harvard University Press, 1962), p. 65
3 Condorcet, *Discours prononcé dans l'Académie Française* (le jeudi 21 février 1782), in *Oeuvres de Condorcet*, publiées par A. Condorcet O'Connor et M.F. Arago (Paris: Firmin Didot, 1847–9), t. 1, p. 395
4 See Keith Michael Baker, *Condorcet: From Natural Philosophy to Social Mathematics* (Chicago and London: University of Chicago Press, 1975)
5 David Williams, *Condorcet and Modernity* (Cambridge: Cambridge University Press, 2004), p. 109
6 See the articles in *Condorcet: Homme des Lumières et de la Révolution*, texts réunis par Anne-Marie Chouillet et Pierre Crepel (Fontenay/Saint-Cloud: ENS

Editions, 1997); and Baker's article 'Condorcet', in *A Critical Dictionary of the French Revolution*, F. Furet and M. Ozouf (eds) (Cambridge, Mass.: Harvard University Press, 1989), pp. 204–12. For an analysis that stresses Condorcet's appreciation of the diversity of opinion and the importance of civilized conflict, see Emma Rothschild, *Economic Sentiments: Adam Smith, Condorcet, and the Enlightenment* (Cambridge, Mass.: Harvard University Press, 2001), esp. pp. 157–217

7 Condorcet, *Esquisse d'un tableau historique des progrès de l'esprit humain*, t. 6, p. 13

8 Condorcet, *Esquisse d'un tableau historique des progrès de l'esprit humain*, p. 237

9 Quoted by Paul Cheney, *Revolutionary Commerce: Globalization and the French Monarchy* (Cambridge, Mass.: Harvard University Press, 2010), p. 147. Cheney contrasts this 'scientism' of the Physiocrats with the comparative historical approach of other economic thinkers of the era, strongly influenced by Montesquieu

10 Cheney, *Revolutionary Commerce*, p. 235. Bronislaw Baczko has analysed this passage and the connection in Condorcet's thought between scientific prediction and history. See Baczko's *Utopian Lights: The Evolution of the Idea of Social Progress*, trans. J.L. Greenberg (New York: Paragon House, 1989), pp. 144–57

11 Bronislaw Baczko, 'Le tournant culturel de l'an III', in *1795 Pour une République sans Révolution*, sous la direction de Roger Dupuy and Marcel Morabito (Rennes: Presses Universitaires de Rennes, 1996), pp. 17–37

12 Condorcet, 'Fragment de justification', *Oeuvres de Condorcet*, t. 1, (juillet 1793), p. 574

13 For the reference to 'association', see the *Communist Manifesto* in Karl Marx, *Selected Writings*, ed. David McLellan (Oxford: Oxford University Press, 1997), p. 238; for the statement about labour and its relation to 'the true realm of freedom', see *Capital*, vol. 3, in Marx, *Selected Writings*, pp. 496–7

14 Stuart Hampshire, 'Introduction' for Antoine-Nicolas de Condorcet, *Sketch for a Historical Picture of the Human Mind*, trans. J. Barraclough (Westport, Conn.: Hyperion Press, 1979), p. xii

15 It comes as no surprise that Condorcet believed that 'the modern form of knowledge' would emphasize the study of the sciences as 'the most certain means of developing the intellectual faculties, learning to reason correctly, [and] analyzing ideas well'. These quotes from Condorcet's *Rapport sur l'organisation générale de l'instruction publique* (1792); cited by Josiane Boulad-Ayoub, '*Le moyen le plus sûr ... ou les parti-pris de Condorcet, Président du premier comité révoluionnaire d'instruction publique*', in *Condorcet: Homme des Lumières et de la Révolution*, pp. 109–19; these quotes, pp. 109–10. In one of his last writings, Condorcet outlined an ambitious plan for the creation of an organization devoted to the direction and coordination of science – it was to be independent of politics, and would be a key element for human progress. See 'Fragment sur l'Atlantide, ou efforts combinés de l'espèce humaine pour le progrès des sciences', *Oeuvres de Condorcet*, t. 6, pp. 597–660

16 Baker, *Condorcet: From Natural Philosophy to Social Mathematics*, p. 57

17 Condorcet, *Esquisse d'un tableau historique des progrès de l'esprit humain*, this phrase, p. 92

18 Condorcet, *Esquisse d'un tableau historique des progrès de l'esprit humain*, p. 595

Chapter 15 Women's Rights and Women's Liberation in Charles Fourier's Early Writings

1   Charles Fourier, *Théorie des quatre mouvements et des destinées générales*, in *Oeuvres complètes de Charles Fourier* [OC], 12 vols (Paris: Anthropos, 1966–8), pp. 130–3

2   Charles Fourier, 'Le Sphinx sans Oedipe, ou l'énigme des quatre mouvements', *La Phalange*, IX (1849), p. 197; and Brunot-Labbe, bookseller, to Fourier, 14 January 1809, Archives Nationales 10AS 25 (2)

3   For a more detailed discussion of the 'riddle' of *Quatre mouvements* and Fourier's response to the failure of his book see Jonathan Beecher, *Charles Fourier: The Visionary and his World* (Berkeley: University of California Press, 1986), pp. 116–39

4   *Bulletin de Lyon*, 11 Frimaire, Year XII (3 December 1803): PM I: OC 10:52–3

5   OC 1:7

6   Gareth Stedman Jones, 'Introduction' to Charles Fourier, *The Theory of the Four Movements* (Cambridge: Cambridge University Press, 1996), pp. viii–ix

7   OC 1:130

8   OC 1:150

9   Michèle Riot-Sarcey, *La Démocratie à l'épreuve des femmes: Trois figures critiques du pouvoir, 1830–1848* (Paris: Albin Michel, 1994), pp. 81–3, 111–15, 160–1, 183–4, 220; and Claire Goldberg Moses and Leslie Wahl Rabine, *Feminism, Socialism, and French Romanticism* (Bloomington: Indiana University Press, 1993), pp. 37–9, 62–3, 75–6, 207

10 This point emerges clearly in the chapter on Fourier in Marguérite Thibert's still valuable *Le Féminisme dans le socialisme français de 1830 à 1850* (Paris: Marcel Giard, 1926), pp. 99–121. See also Claire Goldberg Moses, *French Feminism in the Nineteenth century* (Albany: State University of New York Press, 1984), pp. 90–8

11 OC 1:132–3. Fourier's italics

12 OC 1:89

13 OC 12:622. Manuscript dating from around 1806

14 OC 1:117–30, 133–44

15 Henri Brun to Fourier, 9 May 1808, Archives Nationales 10AS 25 (3bis)

16 On *Le Nouveau monde amoureux* see Beecher, *Charles Fourier*, pp. 297–317

17 OC 7:439–45

18 Thanks to the heroic editorial work of Simone Debout-Oleskiewcz, *Le Nouveau monde amoureux* appeared as volume VII of *Oeuvres complètes de Charles Fourier* published by the Editions Anthropos in 1967

19 Long ago Marguérite Thibert posed the crucial questions with regard to Clarisse Vigoureux (1789– 1865), one of Fourier's very first disciples and a woman known for her '*grande pureté de moeurs*'. How could she reconcile Fourier's amoralism and his unlimited sexual curiosity with her own natural modesty and prudishness? And how could she be seized by a 'religious' enthusiasm in reading *Quatre mouvements*? The answer, it seems, is that Clarisse Vigoureux believed sincerely that if women were completely free to follow their natural instincts, they would spontaneously follow a law of modesty and fidelity. Thibert, *Le Féminisme*, p. 132. This, of course, was far from Fourier's view

Chapter 16 A Tale of Two Cities: Robert Owen and the Search for Utopia, 1815–17

1   Robert Owen, 'Address Delivered to the Inhabitants of New Lanark' (1816), in *Selected Works of Robert Owen*, 4 vols, vol. 1, Gregory Claeys (ed.) (London: Pickering and Chatto, 1993), p. 134

2   The 'religion of charity' is discussed in 'Peace on Earth – Good Will towards Men! Development of the Plan for the Relief of the Poor and the Emancipation of Mankind' in *Selected Works*, vol. 1 (1817), p. 4

3   The word had been invented by Coleridge to denote a society equally governed by all its members. Owen had actually met Coleridge in the mid-1790s, but this does not appear to have been amongst the topics they discussed (Owen, 'The Life of Robert Owen', *Selected Works*, vol. 4, p. 88)

4   Owen, 'The Life of Robert Owen', p. 283, which describes Spence as the 'advocate of an equal division of land' – nothing like Owen's own plan, in short

5   Their relations are discussed in Geoffrey Carnall, *Robert Southey and His Age* (London: Clarendon Press, 1960), pp. 153–5

6   The tract is reprinted in *Restoration and Augustan British Utopias*, ed. G. Claeys (Syracuse, NY: Syracuse University Press, 2000), pp. 188–205

7   Frank Podmore, *Robert Owen: A Biography* (London: George Allen & Unwin, 1923), p. 233

8   Sargant stresses that Owen 'was become a fanatic' in 1817 in order to explain his assumption of a prophet-like role (*Robert Owen and His Social Philosophy*, 1860, p. 123). He also explains Owen's adoption of socialism in terms of a desire to 'extend to the world at large, the benefits he had undoubtedly conferred on the people of New Lanark' (p. xix)

9   For the wider context of these efforts, see Gareth Stedman Jones, 'Religion and the Origins of Socialism', in Ira Katznelson and Gareth Stedman Jones (eds), *Religion and the Political Imagination* (Cambridge: Cambridge University Press, 2011), pp. 171–89

10 *Selected Works of Robert Owen*, vol. 1, p. 130. See in particular, W.H. Oliver, 'Owen in 1817: the Millennialist Moment', in Sidney Pollard and John Salt (eds), *Robert Owen: Prophet of the Poor* (London: Macmillan, 1971), pp. 166–87, which stresses that Owen's strategy in 1817 was 'to persuade the influential to adopt his scheme for poor relief'. See also Robert A. Davis, 'Robert Owen and Religion', in Noel Thompson and Chris Williams (eds), *Robert Owen and His Legacy* (Cardiff: University of Wales Press, 2011), pp. 91–112

11 For example, Arthur John Booth, *Robert Owen, The Founder of Socialism in England* (1869), p. 67: 'The movement dates from 1817'. Podmore takes Owen's description of his 'Plan' on 12 March 1817 as the starting-point for 'the beginning of modern socialism' (*Robert Owen*, pp. 217, 227). Morton takes the Report to the Committee for the Relief of the Manufacturing Poor (1817) as 'the first statement of Owen's famous Plan' (A.L. Morton, *The Life and Ideas of Robert Owen* (London: Lawrence & Wishart, 1962), p. 29)

12 Owen, *Selected Works*, vol. 1, p. 112

13 William Hazlitt, *Political Essays, With Sketches of Public Characters* (1819), pp. 97–104

14 *New Letters of Robert Southey*, Kenneth Curry (ed.), 2 vols, vol. 2 (New York/ London: Columbia University Press, 1966), p. 141

15 *The Life and Correspondence of Robert Southey*, 6 vols, vol. 4., Charles Cuthbert Southey (ed.) (London: Longman, Brown, Green and Longmans, 1849), pp. 195–6, 204

16 Mark Storey, *Robert Southey: A Life* (Oxford: Oxford University Press, 1997),
    p. 276; Robert Southey, *Journal of a Tour in Scotland in 1819* (John Murray,
    1929), pp. 263–4. But elsewhere Southey admitted that 'I myself have a much
    stronger inclination to believe him right in the opinion, that to a community
    of lands we must come at last, than I should choose to avow' (Robert Southey,
    Selections from the Letters of Robert Southey, 4 vols, vol. 3, ed. John Wood
    Warter (London: Longman, Green, Brown, Longmans & Roberts, 1856), p. 45,
    letter of September 1816)
17 *The Life and Correspondence of Robert Southey*, vol. 4, p. 384. This was also
    William Wilberforce's main objection to Owen (*The Life of William Wilberforce*,
    5 vols, vol. 5 (London: John Murray, 1844), p. 46)
18 Robert Southey, *Sir Thomas More; Or, Colloquies on the Progress and Prospects
    of Society*, 2 vols, vol. 1 (1829), pp. 132–47
19 The classic account of the original scheme is James Robertson McGillivray,
    The Pantisocracy Scheme and Its Immediate Background (Toronto: University of
    Toronto Press, 1931)
20 See Owen, 'The New Religion' and 'Second Lecture on the New Religion',
    Selected Works, vol. 2, pp. 167–201
21 Owen, *Selected Works*, vol. 1, p. 167
22 Podmore, *Owen*, p. 237
23 Owen, *Selected Works*, vol. 4, p. 185
24 Podmore, *Owen*, pp. 228–9

Chapter 17 How to Change the World: Claude-Henri de Rouvroy, comte de Saint-Simon

1 Claude-Henri de Rouvroy, Comte de Saint-Simon [hereafter Claude-Henri de
   Saint-Simon], 'L'Artiste, le savant et l'industriel. Dialogue', in *Opinions littéraires,
   philosophiques et industrielles* (Paris, 1825), pp. 335–7. Page references to this
   edition will be given in parentheses throughout the text of this essay
2 For discussion of the *Dialogue*'s authorship, see Neil McWilliam, *Dreams of
   Happiness: Social Art and the French Left 1830–1850* (Princeton, NJ: Princeton
   University Press, 1993), p. 45, n. 38
3 See Martin S. Staum, *Cabanis: Enlightenment and Medical Philosophy in the
   French Revolution* (Princeton, NJ: Princeton University Press, 1980), pp. 207–43
4 Claude-Henri de Saint-Simon, *Du système industriel* (Paris, 1821), p. xix
5 The use of the term *avant-garde* in this passage has attracted a good deal
   of comment; see *Dreams of Happiness*, p. 46, n. 40 for a critique of these
   interpretations
6 The Artist: 'None of us, gentlemen, is happy with his position. Well! It is within
   our power to change it; to succeed, we have only to a give a new direction to our
   labours, and change the nature of the relations that exist between us' (*Dreams of
   Happiness*, p. 332)
7 Claiming that the change they wish to bring about represents a 'moral
   insurrection', the artist argues that all three are sincere in their respect for royalty
   and will provide more effective support than is offered by the crown's current
   alliance with the aristocracy and catholic church. This qualification may simply be
   dictated by prudence in the restrictive atmosphere prevailing under Charles X
8 See, for example, Anne Vincent-Buffault, *Histoire des larmes: XVIIIe-XIXe siècles*
   (Paris: Payot, 2001)

9   See Mona Ozouf, *Festivals and the French Revolution* (Cambridge, Mass.: Harvard University Press, 1988)
10 The second proposal echoes the announcement at the beginning of the publication: 'We will shortly publish, in a second volume, the *Suite de nos opinions*. This work will be the forerunner of a Journal that we propose to publish for the development and application of our doctrine'
11 Théodore Jouffroy, *Mélanges philosophiques* (Paris, 1833), pp. 20–1. The article first appeared in the liberal *Le Globe* on 24 May 1825, which, coincidentally, was five days after Saint-Simon's death
12 See Serge Zenkine, 'L'Utopie religieuse des Saint-Simoniens: le sémiotique et le sacré', in *Etudes saint-simoniennes,* Philippe Régnier (ed.) (Lyon: Presses Universitaires de Lyon, 2002), pp. 33–60
13 See Philippe Régnier (ed.), *Le Livre nouveau des Saint-Simoniens* (Tusson: Du Lérot, 1991); Neil McWilliam, *Dreams of Happiness*, pp. 78–84
14 Prosper Enfantin, 'Enseignements', 3 December 1831, in *Oeuvres complètes de Saint-Simon et d'Enfantin,* vol. 14 (Paris, 1868), p. 115

Chapter 18 The Utopian Organization of Work in Icaria

1   See *Voyage en Icarie*, 60/51. Page references to *Voyage en Icarie* will be given in parentheses throughout the text of this essay. References to Cabet's novel contain two page numbers divided by a forward slash. The first refers to Étienne Cabet, *Voyage en Icarie*, 3rd edition (Paris: Bureau de Populaire, 1845); the second refers to the English translation (of Part One only), Étienne Cabet, *Travels in Icaria*, trans. Leslie J. Roberts, intro. Robert Sutton (Syracuse, NY: Syracuse University Press, 2003)
2   Christopher H. Johnson, *Utopian Communism in France: Cabet and the Icarians, 1839–1851* (Ithaca, NY: Cornell University Press, 1974), p. 37
3   Cabet knew Buonarroti, lodged in London with the Jacobin socialist Berrier-Fontaigne, and his unpublished manuscripts confirm his interest in the 'Conjuration des Égaux' (see items 75–80 of the Étienne Cabet papers held in the International Institute of Social History (IISG) in Amsterdam). For scepticism about Owen's influence, see Jules Prudhommeaux, *Icarie et son Fondateur Étienne Cabet* (Paris: Edouard Cornely, 1907), p. 137f
4   Johnson, *Utopian Communism*, p. 185
5   Cabet's *Vrai Christianisme suivant Jésus Christ* (1846) was proscribed by Pope Pius IX in 1848
6   The 600 francs required to join the émigrés was equivalent to the annual wage of an unskilled labourer
7   On Cabet's American communitarianism, see Robert P. Sutton, *Les Icariens: The Utopian Dream in Europe and America* (Urbana, IL: University of Illinois Press, 1994), chapters 4–7; Diana M. Garno, *Citoyennes and Icaria* (Lanham, MD: University Press of America, 2005), chapters 3–12; and Jacques Rancière, *The Nights of Labor: The Workers' Dream in Nineteenth-Century France* (Philadelphia: Temple University Press, 1989), chapter 12
8   Piotrowski completely ignores its literary form owing to its 'sociological' irrelevance. See Sylvester A. Piotrowski, *Étienne Cabet and the Voyage en Icarie* (Washington DC: The Catholic University of America, 1935), p. 73 n. 27
9   See Cabet, *Icarie*, ch. 33
10 See Cabet, 'Preface to Second Edition', *Icarie,* pp. iv/lix

11   On gender in Icaria and Icarian communities in America, see Leslie J. Roberts, 'Étienne Cabet and his Voyage en Icarie, 1840', *Utopian Studies*, 2/1-2 (1991), pp. 76–94; and Garno, *Citoyennes and Icaria*

Chapter 19   The Horror of Strangeness: Edward Bellamy's *Looking Backward*

1   Edward Bellamy, *Looking Backward 2000–1887*, ed. Matthew Beaumont (Oxford: Oxford World Classics, 2007), ch. 8. Page references to this edition will be given in parentheses throughout the text of this essay
2   Henry Demarest Lloyd, *Wealth against Commonwealth* (New York: Harper, 1894), p. 528
3   A. Morris, *Looking Ahead! A Tale of Adventure (Not by the Author of 'Looking Backward')*, revised edition (London: Henry, 1892), p. 38
4   Krishan Kumar, *Utopia and Anti-Utopia in Modern Times* (Oxford: Blackwell, 1987), p. 135
5   William Morris, '"Looking Backward"', in *Political Writings: Contributions to Justice and Commonweal, 1883–1890*, Nicholas Salmon (ed.) (Bristol: Thoemmes Press, 1994), p. 420
6   Krishan Kumar, *Utopia and Anti-Utopia in Modern Times* (Oxford: Blackwell, 1987), p. 151
7   Edward Bellamy, 'Why I Wrote "Looking Backward"', in *Edward Bellamy Speaks Again! Articles, Public Addresses, Letters* (Kansas City: Peerage Press, 1937), p. 202
8   Kumar, *Utopia and Anti-Utopia*, p. 151
9   Edward Bellamy, *Miss Ludington's Sister* (London: Reeves, 1893), pp. 96, 98
10 Fredric Jameson, *Archaeologies of the Future: The Desire Called Utopia and Other Science Fictions* (London: Verso, 2005), p. 227
11 Edward Bellamy, 'The Blindman's World', in *Apparitions of Things to Come: Edward Bellamy's Tales of Mystery and Imagination*, Franklin Rosemont (ed.) (Chicago: Charles H. Kerr, 1990), p. 45
12 Tom H. Towers, 'The Insomnia of Julian West', *American Literature*, 47 (1975), pp. 56, 53
13 Edward Bellamy, *Talks on Nationalism* (Chicago: Peerage Press, 1938), pp. 98–9
14 Edward Bellamy, 'A Midnight Drama', in *Apparitions of Things to Come*, p. 102
15 Edward Bellamy, 'The Old Folks' Party', in *Apparitions of Things to Come*, p. 54
16 Bellamy, 'The Old Folks' Party', p. 62
17 Jameson, *Archaeologies of the Future*, p. 339

Chapter 20   'The Incompatibility I Could Not Resolve': Ambivalence in H.G. Wells's *A Modern Utopia*

1   H.G. Wells, *A Modern Utopia*, ed. Krishan Kumar (London: Dent, 1994), p. 5. Page references to this edition will be given in parentheses throughout the text of this essay
2   On the open quality of Wells's utopian thinking see Justin E. A. Busch, *The Utopian Vision of H. G. Wells* (Jefferson, NC/London: McFarland, 2009); on his scientific outlook see Roslynn D. Haynes, *H. G. Wells: Discoverer of the Future. The Influence of Science on His Thought* (London/Basingstoke: Macmillan, 1980). Harvey N. Quamen, 'Unnatural Interbreeding: H. G. Wells's *A Modern Utopia* as Species and Genre', *Victorian Literature and Culture*, 33 (2005), pp. 67–84, here: 77, characterizes *A Modern Utopia* as a thought experiment

3   Consequently, Wells's text has been characterized as a 'meta-utopia'; cf. Patrick
    Parrinder, *Shadows of the Future: H. G. Wells, Science Fiction and Prophecy*
    (Liverpool: Liverpool University Press, 1995), p. 96 ff., and June Deery,
    'H. G. Wells's *A Modern Utopia* as a Work in Progress', in Donald M Hassler and
    Clyde Wilcox.(eds), *Political Science Fiction* (Columbia, SC: University of South
    Carolina Press, 1997), pp. 26–42, here: 27 f

4   This point is also stressed by Deery, 'H. G. Wells: *A Modern Utopia*', p. 36 f., and
    Quamen, 'Unnatural Interbreeding', 74 f

5   On the (post-)modernist aspects in Wells's writings cf. Sylvia Hardy,
    'H. G. Wells the Poststructuralist', in *H. G. Wells's Fin-de-Siècle: Twenty-First
    Century Reflections on the Early H. G. Wells. Selections from the Wellsian*, John
    Partington (ed.) (Frankfurt a.M.: Lang, 2007), pp. 113–25

6   Wells's essay 'Scepticism of the Instrument' was first published in 1903; it is
    included in Kumar's edition of 1994, which has been used for this essay

7   Busch, *The Utopian Vision*, p. 96

8   A 'new aristocracy' had already been called for by Thomas Carlyle. The idea was
    further developed by the followers of Friedrich Nietzsche, by the members of the
    Fabian Society and many others

9   On *Anticipations* cf. John S. Partington, *Building Cosmopolis: The Political
    Thought of H. G. Wells* (Aldershot: Ashgate, 2003), p. 51 ff

10 See, for instance, Bruno Schultze, 'Herbert G. Wells: A Modern Utopia (1905)',
    in *Die Utopie in der angloamerikanischen Literatur: Interpretationen*, Hartmut
    Heuermann and Bernd-Peter Lange (eds), (Düsseldorf: Bagel, 1984), p. 161–75

11 Ernst Bloch, *Das Prinzip Hoffnung* (Frankfurt a.M.: Suhrkamp, 1959)

Chapter 21   Utopian Journeying: Ursula K. Le Guin's *The Dispossessed*

1   Ursula K. Le Guin, *The Dispossessed: An Ambiguous Utopia* (New York: Eos
    HarperCollins, 2001 (1974)), p. 386. Page references to this edition will be given
    in parentheses throughout the text of this essay. For those using a different edition
    of *The Dispossessed*, see the detailed table comparing the paginations of English-
    language texts in Laurence Davis and Peter G. Stillman (eds), *The New Utopian
    Politics of Ursula K. Le Guin's* The Dispossessed (Lanham, Md.: Lexington
    Books, 2005), pp. vii–viii

2   See on this point Antonis Liakos, 'Utopian and Historical Thinking: Interplays
    and Transferences', *Historein*, 7 (2007), p. 28

3   Ursula K. Le Guin, 'A Non-Euclidean View of California as a Cold Place to Be'
    (1982), in *Dancing at the Edge of the World: Thoughts on Words, Women, Places*
    (New York: Grove Press, 1989), p. 81

4   Le Guin, 'Non-Euclidean View', p. 98

5   For further discussion of 'grounded' utopias, see Laurence Davis, 'History,
    Politics, and Utopia: Towards a Synthesis of Social Theory and Practice', *Journal
    of Contemporary Thought*, 31 (Summer 2010), pp. 79– 94; reprinted in Patricia
    Vieira and Michael Marder (eds) *Existential Utopia: New Perspectives on
    Utopian Thought* (London and New York: Continuum Press, forthcoming 2012)

6   Jennifer Rodgers, 'Fulfillment as a Function of Time, or the Ambiguous Process of
    Utopia', in *New Utopian Politics*, pp. 181–2

7   Ursula K. Le Guin, 'A Response, by Ansible, from Tau Ceti', in *New Utopian
    Politics*, p. 306

Conclusion

1   Karl Mannheim, *Ideology and Utopia: An Introduction to the Sociology of Knowledge*, trans. Louis Wirth and Edward Shils (New York: Harcourt, Brace & Co., 1936), pp. 176–7. Original emphasis

2   H.G. Wells, *Men Like Gods* (London: Cassell, 1923), p. 158

3   Robert Owen, *A New View of Society: Or, Essays on the Principle of the Formation of the Human Character, and the Application of the Principle to Practice*, by One of His Majesty's Justices of the Peace for the County of Lanark [pseud.]. In *Selected Works of Robert Owen, Volume 1 Early Writings*, ed. Gregory Claeys (London: William Pickering, 1993), p. 33. Original emphasis

4   Owen, *A New View of Society*, p. 34. Original emphasis

Index